James Baldwin
and the 1980s

James Baldwin and the 1980s

Witnessing the Reagan Era

JOSEPH VOGEL

UNIVERSITY OF
ILLINOIS PRESS
Urbana, Chicago, and Springfield

Publication of this book was supported by funding from the
    Merrimack College School of Liberal Arts and English
    Department.

Library of Congress Cataloging-in-Publication Data
Names: Vogel, Joseph, 1981– author.
Title: James Baldwin and the 1980s : witnessing the Reagan era /
    Joseph Vogel.
Description: Urbana : University of Illinois Press, 2018. | Includes
    bibliographical references and index.
Identifiers: LCCN 2017041044| ISBN 9780252041747 (hardcover :
    acid-free paper) | ISBN 9780252083365 (pbk. : acid-free paper)
Subjects: LCSH: Baldwin, James, 1924–1987—Criticism and
    interpretation. | Literature and society—United States—
    History—20th century. | American literature—African
    American authors—History and criticism. | African
    Americans—Intellectual life—20th century. | Nineteen
    eighties.
Classification: LCC PS3552.A45 Z93 2018 | DDC 818/.5409—dc23
LC record available at https://lccn.loc.gov/2017041044

E-book ISBN 978-0-252-05041-1

[The writer's] responsibility, which is also his joy and his strength and his life, is to defeat all labels and complicate all battles by insisting on the human riddle, to bear witness, as long as breath is in him, to that mighty, unnamable, transfiguring force which lives in the soul of man, and to aspire to do his work so well that when the breath has left him, the people—*all people!*—who search in the rubble for a sign or a witness will be able to find him there.

—James Baldwin, "Why I Stopped Hating Shakespeare," 1964

There will be different things written in the future, coming out of a different past, and creating another reality.

—James Baldwin, "Looking towards the Eighties," 1979

Contents

Acknowledgments

I am grateful to Merrimack College for its generous support, including a Faculty Development Grant and subvention, which assisted in the completion and publication of this book. I want to thank my colleagues at Merrimack, especially Marie Plasse, Steven Scherwatzky, Ellen McWhorter, Emma Duffy-Comparone, and Sean Condon, for their friendship, encouragement, and belief in this project during its various stages. Thank you also to my colleagues and mentors at the University of Rochester, particularly Jeffrey Tucker, for feedback and suggestions in the early stages of researching and writing about James Baldwin. In addition, I want to thank the staff at the Houghton Library at Harvard University for their assistance and generosity. Viewing Baldwin's unpublished play, *The Welcome Table*, and related notes was one of the highlights of my research on the author. I express sincere gratitude as well to the people at the Harold F. Johnson Library at Hampshire College, and in particular Anne Macon, for allowing me access to archives and photos of Baldwin from his tenure there in the early 1980s.

Thank you to the academic journals that featured my work on Baldwin and allowed for its republication in this book. Chapter 2 is a revised and expanded version of "Freaks in the Reagan Era: James Baldwin, the New Pop Cinema, and the American Ideal of Manhood," which was first published in the *Journal of Popular Culture* 48, no. 3 (June 2015). That article received the Russell B. Nye Award for Best Article Published in the *Journal of Popular*

Culture in 2016. It is reproduced with permission from Wiley Periodicals, Inc. A slightly modified version of Chapter 4, titled "'To Crush the Serpent': James Baldwin, the Religious Right, and the Moral Minority," first appeared in the *James Baldwin Review* 2, no. 1 (November 2016). It is reproduced with permission from Manchester University Press.

I owe an enormous debt of gratitude to a number of James Baldwin scholars who were willing to look at early drafts, offer suggestions, and point me in helpful directions. In particular, I would like to thank Ed Pavlic, Douglas Field, D. Quentin Miller, Magdalena Zaborowska, and Justin A. Joyce. I am also very grateful to the anonymous readers of this manuscript who offered invaluable insights and feedback.

I would like to thank my family—Tiffany, Sofi, and Jude—for giving me the time, space, and support to write. And finally, thank you to James Baldwin, for the inspiration.

James Baldwin
and the 1980s

Introduction

Unless a writer is extremely old when he
dies, in which case he has probably become a
neglected institution, his death must always
seem untimely. This is because a real writer is
always shifting and changing and searching.

—James Baldwin, "Eight Men," 1961

What do James Baldwin and the 1980s have to do with each other?

Baldwin is seldom associated with the post–civil rights era, let alone the 1980s. His most canonized works—*Go Tell It on the Mountain* (1953), *Notes of a Native Son* (1955), *Giovanni's Room* (1956), "Sonny's Blues" (1957), *Another Country* (1962), and *The Fire Next Time* (1963)—all emerge from the postwar and civil rights eras. The apex of his career is often symbolized by his appearance on the cover of *Time* magazine on May 17, 1963, just months before the March on Washington. It perhaps foreshadowed his reception going forward, however, that Baldwin was excluded from speaking at the event, most likely because of his sexual orientation.[1]

Over the next couple of decades, Baldwin's reputation declined precipitously. Various explanations were given. Some ascribed it to a falling out with the white literary establishment, who believed Baldwin sacrificed his literary promise for political and moral commitments. Others felt it had something to do with Baldwin's insecure role with black America. According to Hilton Als, "When Baldwin became the official voice of black America, he immediately compromised his voice as a writer, sacrificing his gifts in order to gain acceptance from the Black Power movement."[2] Yet others argued just the opposite: Baldwin lost his place, they claimed, precisely because he could not be easily categorized, because he refused to identify with the essentialist logic of identity politics and any of its associated movements. Notes Lynn Orilla Scott: "Baldwin's work has presented problems to readers from almost every perspective—liberal, black nationalist, feminist, and homosexual—and to some extent each of these constituencies in their inability to accommodate Baldwin's complexity has helped to marginalize him."[3] Still others believed his diminishment resulted from becoming too angry and bitter. Baldwin, they said, refused to acknowledge the great progress America had made since the 1950s. This evaluation began appearing frequently in reviews of his work in the late 1960s and 1970s; by the 1980s it was the default script. As the *New York Times'* Michael Anderson wrote in a 1998 review of Baldwin's collected essays: "Little wonder he lost his audience: America did what Baldwin could not—it moved forward."[4]

James Baldwin and the 1980s challenges the logic of such assessments. Against the conventional narrative of Baldwin's "decline," a fresh look at his late work reveals a still-razor-sharp, provocative writer who, with the benefit of hindsight, holds up as one of the most prescient observers of the post–civil rights landscape. Indeed, while Baldwin is most often associated with earlier historical moments (Michael Anderson authoritatively claims his "significance ended in 1964"), he remained prolific in his final decade, publishing his most ambitious novel in 1979 (*Just Above My Head*), several noteworthy essays and articles (including landmark pieces such as "The Cross of Redemption," "Notes on the House of Bondage," "Freaks and the American Ideal of Manhood," and "To Crush the Serpent"), a collection of poems in 1984 (*Jimmy's Blues*), a major nonfiction book in 1985 (*The Evidence of Things Not Seen*), and arguably his best play (the as-yet-unpublished *The Welcome Table*).[5] In addition, he gave numerous illuminating interviews and speeches, narrated a documentary (*I Heard It through the Grapevine*), and even collaborated on a spoken-word music album with jazz musician and composer David Linx (*A Lover's Question*).

What emerges from this substantial body of work? In contrast to the notion that Baldwin no longer had his finger on the pulse of America, Baldwin proves remarkably engaged with the cultural milieu of a new generation, commenting on everything from the culture wars to the New South, the deterioration of inner cities to the disproportionate incarceration of black youth, the Reagan Revolution to the Religious Right, gender-bending in pop culture to the AIDS crisis. In response to these historical changes, Baldwin's work took on intriguing new features. Among the most noteworthy aspects of his late work is what I characterize as a "cultural turn": an increased emphasis, that is, on the social and psychological consequences of mass media and popular culture. Baldwin was always interested in the relationship between literature, culture, and representation. But little of his early work is engaged in a sustained way with popular culture.

Yet by the post–civil rights era—and certainly by the 1980s—the cultural landscape had shifted, and Baldwin's work reflects this. Young people were much more likely to be influenced by hip hop, MTV, or the latest sequel of *Star Wars* than a novel or poem. In his essay "What Is This Black in Black Popular Culture?" cultural theorist Stuart Hall describes postmodernism as "modernism in the streets . . . a shifting of the terrain of culture toward the popular."[6] The traditional view of "culture" as an elite, civilizing force—as Matthew Arnold famously conceived it, "the best which had been thought and said in the world"—came under intense scrutiny in the 1980s in what came to be referred to as the "canon wars."[7] The question at the center of the canon wars was what should be studied and taught. On campuses throughout America, the traditional answer to that question—esteemed white men operating in the so-called "high arts"—was no longer a given. Increasingly, professors began to make room in the curriculum for authors of color, women, and "lower" forms of art, including film and popular music.

University of Chicago philosopher Allan Bloom's book *The Closing of the American Mind*, which offered a passionate defense of the Western canon against outsiders, minorities, and "low art," hit such a cultural nerve it became an unexpected bestseller in 1987. For Bloom, popular culture threatened to destroy civilization with its anarchic values, ephemerality, and undirected passions. "As long as they have the Walkman on," wrote Bloom, "[young people] cannot hear what the great tradition has to say. And, after its prolonged use, when they take it off, they find they are deaf."[8] For Bloom, that is, the idea of taking popular culture seriously was not only absurd, but also dangerous.

In his early essays, perhaps most notably "Stranger in the Village," Baldwin grappled with the meaning of the Western tradition to *him*: a black man from a poor home in Harlem. He knew he could not simply dismiss it. There were certain authors he deeply admired—among them, Henry James,

Honoré de Balzac, and Fyodor Dostoevsky—and many more he found ways to learn from, appropriate, and use with his own intention. Yet as a "kind of bastard of the West," he was compelled to be on guard and highly skeptical of all esteemed cultural production and cultural gatekeepers.[9] In his work, he tended to quote from "low" black art forms like spirituals, blues, and gospel songs much more frequently than Milton, Shakespeare, or Hemingway. Thus, while many of Baldwin's contemporaries clung to notions of a revered canon or tradition dominated by white men, Baldwin did not buy in. "That concept," he stated, "I assure you, has had its day."[10]

For Baldwin, popular culture was not inherently better than the "high arts." In certain ways, it could be worse (see, for example, his scathing critiques of Hollywood). But it *was* often closer to the people. Its sources tended to be more diverse, its outcomes less predictable. "The mass culture," explained Baldwin, "can only reflect our chaos: and perhaps we had better remember that this chaos contains life—and a great transforming energy."[11] While critics like Bloom believed mass culture anesthetized the masses, then, Baldwin saw it as a site of struggle and possibility. It could not simply be dismissed. This was particularly important for Americans in the Reagan era. In the 1980s, as Stuart Hall notes, the United States emerged as the world's dominant superpower and its "center of global cultural production and circulation."[12] Never before was American pop culture as globally pervasive. It was the dawn of neoliberalism and the height, some argue, of the "monoculture"—a pre-internet era of blockbusters, megastars, and cultural crazes.

American hegemony, however, was not absolute, nor was it a monolith. Hall notes the subversive possibilities inherent in postmodern popular culture, particularly in black popular culture. "This emergence," he writes, "is both a displacement and a hegemonic shift in the *definition* of culture—a movement from high culture to American mainstream popular culture and its mass-cultural, image-mediated, technological forms."[13] Ironically, in spite of, or perhaps partially in response to, concerns about a mass-produced monoculture, the 1980s was a crucial decade for the "cultural politics of difference, of the struggles around difference, of the production of new identities, of the appearance of new subjects on the political and cultural stage."[14] Popular culture thus became an important stage whereon different images, narratives, and representations were produced and contested.

Such concepts aligned closely with Baldwin's views on popular art and entertainment and the role it played in shaping culture, or, as Hall put it, "shifting dispositions of power."[15] Baldwin was fascinated with how America's myths and fantasies informed one's reality and identity. The idea of Baldwin as a cultural critic rather than a traditional literary figure is perhaps less foreign than associating him with the 1980s, particularly given his now-prominent standing in both the Black Lives Matter movement and the LGBTQ community. As early as the McCarthy era, Baldwin was responding to specific cultural events and transformations, as well as the ways in which art mediated or spoke to such developments.[16] In a 1959 essay, "Mass Culture and the Creative Artist," he wrote prophetically that we were "in the middle of an immense metamorphosis here, a metamorphosis which will, it is devoutly to be hoped, rob us of our myths and give us our history."[17]

Yet Baldwin's own metamorphosis—or cultural turn—really took place at precisely the moment Michael Anderson, among many others, pinpoint as the beginning of his decline: the mid-1960s. Increasingly, Baldwin felt compelled to respond to the pressing, volatile, media-saturated events around him—often using forms besides the traditional literary essay, novel, or short story. In 1964, he teamed up with childhood friend and renowned photographer Richard Avedon on his first published multimedia project: a collection of striking images and accompanying text, titled *Nothing Personal*.[18] The *New York Times* described it as a "non-book": "Manufactured in Switzerland by a special process, boxed and unpaginated, set between snow-white covers with sterling silver titles, and measuring eleven by fourteen inches in size, this tome consists of enormous photographs by Richard Avedon and alternating commentary by James Baldwin, the text set in huge type with about an inch of space between each of the lines."[19] The *Times* ultimately dismissed the project as an extravagant luxury item. Yet it represents an important departure for Baldwin, made all the more remarkable by the author's brilliant media and cultural criticism in its pages. "I used to distract myself, some mornings before I got out of bed, by pressing the television remote control gadget from one channel to another," he writes in the book's introduction.

This may be the only way to watch TV: I certainly saw some remarkable sights. Blondes and brunettes and, possibly, redheads—my screen was colorless—washing their hair, relentlessly smiling, teeth gleaming like the grillwork of automobiles, breasts firmly, chillingly encased—packaged, as it were—and brilliantly uplifted, forever, all sagging corrected, forever, all middle age bulge—*middle age bulge!*—defeated, eyes as sensuous and mysterious as jelly beans, lips covered with cellophane, hair sprayed to the consistency of aluminum, girdles forbidden to slide up, stockings defeated in their subversive tendencies to slide down, to turn crooked, to snag, to run, to tear, hands prevented from aging by incredibly soft detergents, fingernails forbidden to break by superbly smooth enamels, teeth forbidden to decay by mysterious chemical formulas, all conceivable body odor, under no matter what contingency, prevented for twenty-four hours of every day, forever and forever and forever, children's bones knit strong by the foresight of vast bakeries, tobacco robbed of any harmful effects by the addition of mint, the removal of nicotine, the presence of filters and the length of the cigarette, tires which cannot betray you, automobiles which will make you feel proud, doors which cannot slam on those precious fingers or fingernails, diagrams illustrating—proving—how swiftly impertinent pain can be driven away, square-jawed youngsters dancing, other square-jawed youngsters, armed with guitars, or backed by bands, howling; all of this—and so much more!—punctuated by the roar of great automobiles, overtaking gangsters, the spatter of tommy-guns mowing them down, the rise of the organ as the Heroine braces herself to Tell All, the moving smile of the housewife who has just won a fortune in metal and crockery; news—*news? from where?*—dropping into this sea with the alertness and irrelevancy of pebbles, sex wearing an aspect so implacably dispiriting that even masturbation (by no means mutual) seems one of the possibilities that vanished in Eden, and murder one's last, best hope—sex of an appalling coyness, often in the form of a prophylactic cigarette being extended by the virile male toward the aluminum and cellophane girl. They happily blow smoke into each other's face, jelly beans, brilliant with desire, grillwork gleaming; perhaps—poor, betrayed exiles—they are trying to discover if, behind all that grillwork, all those barriers, either of them has a tongue. Subsequently, in the longer and less explicit commercials in which these images are encased, the male certainly doesn't seem to have a tongue—perhaps one may say that the cat's got it; father knows best, these days, only in politics, which is the only place we ever find him, and where he proves to be—*alas!*—absolutely indistinguishable from the American boy. He doesn't even seem much closer to the grave—which fact, in the case of most of our most influential politicians, fills a great many people, all over the world, with despair.[20]

I quote this passage at length to highlight its penetrating description of the psychological and social effects of television—the same year as Marshal McLuhan's groundbreaking *Understanding Media: The Extensions of Man* (1964) and a decade before Raymond Williams's influential book, *Television: Technology and Cultural Form* (1974). What Baldwin is describing in this passage is *flow*: the process by which networks sustain an audience's attention by seamlessly moving from one program to another. Williams calls it "the defining characteristic of broadcasting, simultaneously as a technology and as a cultural form."[21] For McLuhan, the flow of this new medium was, in fact, the *message*. For Baldwin, however, no medium was inherently better or worse than what preceded it: content still mattered most. It was the images and ideas and stories that shaped our understanding of identity and the world around us.

It was this conviction, indeed, that led to Baldwin's participation in a movie on the life of Malcolm X in the late 1960s. Cinema, he had long recognized, was a powerful medium in which the way we understood the world was relayed. But merely critiquing it was not enough; the medium must also be used by African Americans (and other minorities) to tell their stories. As Brian Norman writes, Baldwin believed that "inclusion of Black history into Hollywood forms could *transform* its 'charge' and could, in fact, imbue Hollywood with political relevance. . . . Baldwin, that is, did not automatically conflate the appeal and growth of visual culture with the loss of progressive politics and counter-cultures that had successfully used the printed word in pamphlets and newspapers as vehicles for disseminating systemic critiques."[22]

Baldwin began working on the Malcolm X script with author Alex Haley in 1968, with the intention of turning the icon's autobiography into a play. Soon after, producer Marvin Worth bought the rights for Columbia Pictures. It had always been Baldwin's dream to work in film, yet he was understandably wary of how Hollywood would tell the story. Baldwin nonetheless accepted the invitation to continue working on his script for Columbia. It didn't take long, however, before conflicts emerged. Creative differences began over who would play Malcolm—Baldwin preferred Billie Dee Williams (with whom he had formed a close friendship at the time), while Columbia wanted Sidney Poitier, James Earl Jones, or a "darkened up" Charlton Heston.[23] Columbia also became dissatisfied with Baldwin's script. As biographer David Leeming writes, "Columbia wanted a tempered

story, a sanitized Malcolm, but Baldwin was determined not to let the studio interfere with his work."[24] Baldwin did not want something safe and
contained—a film that simply reassured American audiences of historical
closure and progress (thus his working title, *One Day, When I Was Lost*).[25]
Columbia ultimately decided to bring in another scriptwriter, Arnold Pearl,
to help with the project since Baldwin had never written for the screen. Still
determined to "witness" for Malcolm, Baldwin accepted Pearl's assistance
but became increasingly exasperated with Hollywood's attempts to alter
his script.

In the midst of working on the film came another major blow: the assassination of Martin Luther King Jr. Baldwin had seen King just weeks
earlier. In April 1968 he left Hollywood for Atlanta to attend the funeral,
feeling a mixture of despair and rage. He now felt more responsible than
ever to tell Malcolm's story—and by extension the story of black America.
Yet when he returned, the rift between Baldwin and producer Marvin Worth
grew bigger. Overwhelmed by accumulated frustration, stress, and his own
personal troubles, Baldwin overdosed on sleeping pills and had to be rushed
to the hospital. Soon after, he relinquished his position as screenwriter on
the project.

All told, Baldwin spent more than two years on the script.[26] In a 1969
New York Times article titled "The Price May Be Too High," he writes of the
complicated role of black artists in a white-dominated industry, concluding
that "refus[ing] to play this particular ball game" may in fact be the most
noble choice.[27] Ironically, Baldwin had explored these very issues in his
1968 novel, *Tell Me How Long the Train's Been Gone*, a first-person account
of a famous black actor, Leo Proudhammer, grappling with the trappings
of success and fame. The difficult role of black popular artists in America
would become one of Baldwin's central themes in the ensuing years.

As disillusioned as Baldwin felt, however, he could not let go of his preoccupation with film and questions of representation in popular culture more
broadly. In the mid-1970s, he began working on *The Devil Finds Work* (1976),
a slim but incisive book that blended autobiography and film criticism. "I am
fascinated," he writes on the opening page, "by the movement on, and off,
the screen, that movement which is something like the heaving and swell-
ing of the sea . . . and which is also something like the light which moves
on, and especially beneath, the water."[28] In the pages that follow, Baldwin
details his discoveries, shocks, identifications, confusions, pleasures, and

disappointments as he watches movies, from *Great Expectations* to *The Birth of a Nation*, from *Guess Who's Coming to Dinner* to *The Exorcist*.

Cinema, Baldwin makes abundantly clear, played a crucial role in his life, perhaps just as important as literature—indeed, in Baldwin's narrative the two are often intertwined. As a young boy in Harlem, going to the movies was an escape—from poverty, despair, his father, and, ultimately, religion. Yet it also became a way to understand the world and his relation to it. Of his introductory moviegoing experience, he writes: "My first conscious calculation as to how to go about defeating the world's intentions for me and mine began on that Saturday afternoon in what we called *the movies*, but which was actually my first entrance into the cinema of my mind."[29]

For Baldwin, Hollywood was a producer of unquestionably pervasive racism, sexism, and homophobia; its heroes were overwhelmingly straight white men and glamorous white women; but it was also a space in which the spectator, regardless of identity, possessed agency and could negotiate the meanings of the images and stories on the screen. Watching a film, for Baldwin, was not a passive viewing, but an active confrontation. Resistance, of course, was not easy for the average audience member, since the very goal of most Hollywood films was to render invisible their construction, their choices. As Baldwin puts it, "It is said that the camera cannot lie, but rarely do we allow it to do anything else, since the camera sees what you point it at: the camera sees what you want it to see. The language of the camera is the language of our dreams."[30] The magic of a Hollywood film, that is, was to create a fantasy that felt real—at least in the brief moment it flashed inside a darkened theater and pleasure-stimulated brain—that corroborated what we wanted to believe.

At the time of its publication in 1976, reviews of *The Devil* were mixed.[31] The *New York Times* dismissed it as cynical and unoriginal. "*The Devil Finds Work* is disappointing," writes Orde Coombs, "because the author must repeat, from a distance, what he has been telling us for a long time, and what he knows we know that he knows."[32] Other critics were confused by his "long literary silence."[33] When would he get back to writing novels and short stories like his literary contemporaries? What was significant about *The Devil*, however, was precisely this shift from literature to cultural studies. It showed that he now took a popular medium like film seriously enough to dedicate an entire book to it. It also highlights his role as someone who has moved from the margins of society into the belly of the beast. As biographer David Leeming writes: "The voice speaking in the pages of *The Devil Finds Work* is that of a celebrity/elder statesman who dares to carry his work as a witness into the heart of popular culture."[34]

Baldwin goes deeper into this territory in his next book, *Just Above My Head*, which I explore in greater depth in chapter 1. Black music had been a pervasive theme throughout Baldwin's work, both fiction and nonfiction. But *Just Above My Head* was not only about black music; it was about black *popular* music, an important distinction. The main character, Arthur Montana, is not an unknown singer on the streets, or in a church, or at a smoke-filled club; he is a celebrity. He is known throughout America and the world. Fame and the complicated position of the black artist in relation to his country are some of the central concerns of the novel. *Just Above My Head* is Baldwin's ultimate statement on the triumph and tragedy of black popular music, arguably America's most influential artistic innovation.

Over the course of his career, then, Baldwin became increasingly attuned to, and engaged with, popular culture. In his interviews, essays, and books, he alludes constantly to popular movies and songs, musicians and actors, from John Wayne to Sidney Poitier, Miles Davis to Diana Ross, Gary Cooper to Bette Davis. He attempted collaborations with Charlie Chaplin, Marlon Brando, and Elia Kazan. He reviewed the bestselling-book-turned-television-series sensation, *Roots* (1977) and riffed on the poetic genius of Stevie Wonder. He wrote for popular newspapers and magazines like the *New York Times*, the *Nation*, and *Playboy*. He gave interviews to *TV Guide* and *Essence*. He wrote about televangelism, infotainment, and the new faces on MTV. Recalls David Linx: "He was always young—I remember sitting with him waiting for the new Michael Jackson video to be shown on TV and he was really excited."[35] That passion and vitality comes through in his work. Far from being stagnant or intransigent, "the writer refuses to stay still," as Douglas Field observes; even in his final decade, he "moves around," he adapts and evolves, as he witnesses and illuminates a rapidly changing society.[36]

Forging a New Language

As the 1980s dawned, Baldwin felt reinvigorated. This was due in part to the fact that he had had time to process, and at least partially recover, from the shock and disillusionment of the late 1960s.[37] The 1970s were a difficult decade for Baldwin personally and professionally. Once held in high esteem by blacks and whites alike, his public reception had changed dramatically. In his bestselling book *Soul on Ice* (1968) Eldridge Cleaver infamously denounced Baldwin for "bending over and touching [his] toes for the white man."[38] When Cleaver made the inflammatory comments, Baldwin refused to publicly engage, many believed for fear of further fallout. In a 1984 interview, however, Baldwin reflected on the painful experience: "My real difficulty with Cleaver, sadly, was visited on me by the kids who were following him, while he was calling me a faggot and the rest of it. I would come to a town to speak, Cleveland, let's say, and he would've been standing on the very same stage a couple of days earlier. I had to try to undo the damage I considered he was doing."[39] Cleaver was perhaps the most prominent, but by no means the only, example of the backlash to Baldwin within the black community. "A new generation, so it seemed, was determined to define itself by everything Baldwin was not," observes Henry Louis Gates. "By the late '60s Baldwin-bashing was almost a rite of initiation."[40] Meanwhile, white authors such as Norman Mailer, who was once close to Baldwin, dismissed him as "too charming a writer to be a major . . . even the best of his paragraphs are sprayed with perfume."[41]

Biographer David Leeming notes that by the 1970s Baldwin felt "estranged" from both white and black intellectuals. Many whites, Baldwin believed, had retreated to safety and given up the fight, while for many blacks "the discussion on race had heat, but not much light."[42] Asked about the reasons for this estrangement in one of his final interviews with Quincy Troupe, Baldwin responded bluntly: "Well, because I was right. That's a strange way to put it. I *was* right. I was right about what was happening in the country. What was about to happen to all of us really, one way or another. And the choices people would have to make. And watching people make them and denying them at the same time. I began to feel more and more homeless."[43] He seemed to feel most comfortable with nonliterary artists, many of whom came to visit him at his Saint-Paul-de-Vence home. While Baldwin was initially skeptical of the women's liberation movement, he also admired the rising generation of black female writers, including Maya Angelou, Gayl Jones, Nikki Giovanni, Audre Lorde, Alice Walker, and Toni Morrison. "What they have to say is somewhat terrifying, but true," he acknowledged in a 1986 speech at the National Press Club. "[They] are excavating us all from a very dangerous myth."[44]

As a new decade began, Baldwin believed he was on the cusp of something new: a more precise exploration of identity and culture that incorporated not only race, class, and nationality, but also gender and sexuality—a concept subsequently elaborated by black feminists as "intersectionality."[45] "I'm in the process of experimenting," explained Baldwin. "I say a new language. I might say a new morality, which, in my terms, comes to the same thing. And that's on all levels—the level of color, the level of identity, the level of sexual identity, what love means, especially in a consumer society, for example. Everything is in question, according to me."[46]

Baldwin's work was also acutely attuned to the sociocultural zeitgeist in America. This may have had something to do with the fact that Baldwin spent a great deal of time in the United States during these years. While he was still based in France, he acknowledged that he felt a strong pull to return "home" in the 1980s as he had during the civil rights era. With Medgar, Malcolm, and Martin gone, he saw himself as the "last witness" of his generation.[47] On a more practical level, his prolonged residencies in the United States in his final decade were due to his new role working with young people in American classrooms. In 1978, Ernest Champion, professor of ethnic studies at Bowling Green State University, invited Baldwin to teach at the university. Baldwin accepted. It was his first official affiliation with an academic institution in his life; his residency from 1979 to 1981 also became his longest stay in the United States since working on the Malcolm X script in Hollywood in the late 1960s. Asked why he accepted the invitation from Bowling Green, a less prestigious university in rural Ohio, Baldwin responded bluntly: "Nobody had asked me before."[48]

The experience proved invigorating for the author. On the first day of class, he recalls, a white student asked bluntly, "Why does the white hate the nigger?" "I was caught off guard," Baldwin confessed. "I simply had not had the courage to open the subject right away. I underestimated the children, and I am afraid that most of the middle-aged do. The subject, I confess, frightened me, and it would never have occurred to me to throw it at them so nakedly. No doubt, since I am not totally abject, I would have found a way to discuss what we refer to as interracial tension. What my students made me realize (and I consider myself eternally in their debt) was that the notion of interracial tension hides a multitude of delusions and is, in sum, a cowardly academic formulation."[49] Baldwin goes on to explain how, before long, the students hardly needed him. "They were talking of their desire to know one another . . . each was trying to enter into the experience of the other."[50]

Inspired by his experience at Bowling Green, Baldwin spent a great deal of his remaining years working with and thinking about young people. In the late 1970s, he lectured at several other universities, including Wayne State University in Detroit and Hunter College in New York City. In early 1979 he conducted a month-long lecture series at the University of California Berkeley. In 1983 he was invited to be a visiting professor of literature at the five-college consortium of liberal-arts colleges in western Massachusetts: Amherst, Hampshire, Mount Holyoke, Smith College, and UMass Amherst. For the next three years—from 1983 to 1986—Baldwin lived primarily in Pelham, Massachusetts, and taught a wide variety of courses in alternating semesters, mostly at Hampshire College and UMass Amherst. He saw the charge of his late years as working with young people. "I would like to use the time that's left," he said, "to change the world, to teach children or to convey to the people who have children that everything that lives is holy."[51]

In addition to his time on college campuses, Baldwin traveled extensively through different parts of the United States. The 1982 documentary *I Heard It through the Grapevine* follows the author from Washington, D.C., to Jacksonville, to Selma, to Atlanta, to New York City, as it assesses the conflicted legacy of the civil rights movement. Directed by Dick Fontaine and Pat Hartley, the film was not the triumphant story America liked to tell itself; rather, it allowed Baldwin to "witness" to the complex and sometimes disheartening realities of the post–civil rights landscape. Baldwin's trip to Atlanta also became the impetus for his most comprehensive appraisal of the so-called "New South": *The Evidence of Things Not Seen*. Baldwin returned to Atlanta several times from 1980 to 1983. His first account appeared in *Playboy* in 1981 and was later expanded and published as his final major book in 1985 (both texts are considered in greater depth in chapter 5).

Baldwin's presence in the classrooms and on the streets of America in the late 1970s and early 1980s, then, had a profound impact on his thinking and his work. He witnessed what he saw and heard and felt—even if it conflicted with the era's dominant narrative. While the Reagan era is often characterized as a decade of renewed patriotism, optimism, and economic prosperity, Baldwin rightfully saw the picture as more complex, particularly for African Americans. Certainly, there had been inroads. The 1980s saw the rise of numerous prominent black female writers, from public intellectuals like bell hooks and Michelle Wallace to novelists like Alice Walker (whose novel *The Color Purple* won the Pulitzer Prize and National Book Award in 1983) and Toni Morrison (whose novel *Beloved* garnered the Pulitzer Prize and National Book Award in 1988). The 1980s also saw the rise of African American scholars, perhaps most notably Henry Louis Gates Jr., who produced groundbreaking work and paved new paths for African American studies in higher education (a character based on Henry Louis Gates appears in Baldwin's unpublished play, *The Welcome Table*). In politics, more black mayors and executives, state senators and other elected officials assumed positions of power and leadership than ever before (including Ron Brown's 1989 election as chairman of the Democratic National Committee and General Colin Powell's promotion to chairman of the Joint Chiefs of Staff). The 1980s also saw Jesse Jackson make the first viable, nationwide campaigns by an African American for president of the United States (in 1984 and 1988), which Baldwin spoke about at length in a 1984 forum at UMass Amherst.

In popular culture, meanwhile, "crossover" pop icons like Michael Jackson, Prince, Lionel Richie, Whitney Houston, and Janet Jackson changed racialized programming on radio and television, while hip hop emerged as the most important musical movement since rock and roll. *The Cosby Show* changed the color of television, ranking No. 1 in the Nielsen ratings for five consecutive seasons, from 1985 to 1990; Eddie Murphy emerged as one of America's highest-paid actors; Spike Lee became one of its hottest young directors; Oprah Winfrey began her revolution of daytime television; and athletes like Magic Johnson and Michael Jordan became global icons. Over the course of the decade, the black middle class and upper class more than doubled and integrated into all facets of American life, from college campuses to the media to politics. By 1989, one in seven black families made over $50,000 annually (more than 1 million people).[52] African American publications such as *Ebony* and *Jet* documented and celebrated these "success stories" of upward mobility in popular culture, business, and media. White media likewise praised those who "overcame" or "crossed over" as proof that race was no longer an inhibiting factor in the Reagan era. Anyone could achieve the American Dream if he or she worked hard enough.

There was a darker underbelly to this narrative, however. The 1980s also saw the gutting of urban communities, the unraveling of civil rights legislation, the defunding of government programs, the epidemics of crack and

AIDS, extreme inner-city poverty, and mass incarceration. Ronald Reagan, always the optimist, rarely acknowledged these realities in his speeches. In 1980 he kicked off his campaign for the presidency with a speech in Philadelphia, Mississippi, the same city where three civil rights workers were infamously lynched in 1964. He made no mention of the tragedy but did reinforce his belief in the importance of state's rights. The Reagan campaign's "New Southern Strategy," orchestrated by Lee Atwater, became masterful at obliquely appealing to white prejudice through racial codes to antagonize minorities and reduce the role of government.[53] Reagan himself came across as affable and strong—leading to two landslide electoral victories—but the Reagan worldview was unambiguously Manichean, from its aggressive Cold War foreign policies to its equally aggressive policing of America's social and cultural "values." His speeches frequently cast aspersion on the poor, particularly the ethnic poor. "What I really found unspeakable about the man," acknowledged Baldwin, who had first observed Reagan as governor of California, "was his contempt, his brutal contempt, for the poor."[54] Whether intended or not, Reagan's infamous denunciation of "welfare queens" stigmatized poor black single mothers as moochers of the welfare system, while black men became the face of crack addiction and inner-city crime.

In response to these perceived threats, Reagan dramatically reduced government spending in urban areas, and dramatically increased policing, leading to an unprecedented spike in the incarceration of black men, which more than doubled over the course of the decade, mostly due to drug-related crimes.[55] The crack epidemic, in particular, hit impoverished black neighborhoods with a vengeance. Far from solving the problem, Reagan's "War on Drugs" simply saw an increase in profiling and arrests. According to studies, while drug use among blacks and whites was similar, blacks were *ten times* as likely to be arrested.[56] The net effect of these and other factors for black urban communities was devastating. By the end of the 1980s, nearly 50 percent of black children were living below the poverty line. "The great, vast, shining Republic knows nothing about them and cares nothing about them," wrote Baldwin, "recognizes their existence only in times of stress, as during a military adventure, say, or an election year, or when their dangerous situation erupts into what the Republic generally calls a 'riot.'"[57]

Drawing from a report on race and class in the 1980s from the Population Reference Bureau, the *Associated Press*'s Taynia Mann concluded: "Evidence points to two African-American communities: one of middle-class and af-fluent blacks who took advantage of the increased opportunities provided by the civil rights movement, the other of poor, largely urban blacks who remain socially and economically isolated from the American mainstream."[58] Yet for Baldwin, this neat division of the black community—an aspirational, postracial middle class and an unmotivated, isolated lower class—while neat and tidy, was incomplete. Most middle-class African Americans were not attempting to distance themselves from their race, but from misery, poverty, and despair. Most lower-class African Americans, meanwhile, had not simply passed on "increased opportunities"; they never had them to begin with—or if they had, they were lost when blue-collar factory jobs diminished by 42 percent from 1970 to 1987.[59]

Lower-class and middle-class African Americans alike operated in a sys-tem stacked against them. Regardless of racial and gender inroads, white men still dominated every apparatus of power, from Hollywood to gov-ernment to the news media to Wall Street. The success stories of African Americans were meaningful, but they hardly represented "overcoming" inequality. This was the "betrayal," Baldwin felt, in the aftermath of the civil rights movement. "Yes," he wrote, "we have lived through avalanches of tokens and concessions but white power remains white. And what it appears to surrender with one hand it obsessively clutches in the other."[60] Baldwin's concern in the age of "integration" was complacency: that while the evidence proved the nation still possessed catastrophically misguided perceptions about class, race, sexuality, and gender, it preferred to congratulate itself and pretend the struggle was over, the work was done. Those left behind were left behind because of their own failures. The struggle was now less about fighting discrimination than it was about convincing people that discrimination against minorities still existed. This, of course, depended in part on the stories and images, slogans and myths promulgated in popular culture.

Writing in this context, James Baldwin spoke of people of color "shat-tering, redefining and recreating history—making all things new—simply by declaring their presence, by delivering their testimony. The empire never intended that this testimony should be heard, but, if I hold my peace, *the very stones will cry out*."[61] Baldwin's prophetic urgency was often dismissed as hyperbole, yet he remained adamant about the crossroads the 1980s represented. "This is the charged, the dangerous, moment, when everything must be re-examined, must be made new," he wrote, "when nothing at all can be taken for granted. . . . We have come to the end of a language and are now about the business of forging a new one."[62]

We Are Our History

Much has changed, of course, since Baldwin wrote these words more than thirty-five years ago; and much remains the same—or at least very similar. Like the 1980s, the 2010s have been characterized by striking contradictions. It is an era of great progress and furious backlash, of Occupy Wall Street and the Tea Party, of Black Lives Matter and Make America Great Again, of the first African American president and the first president in the modern era to openly embrace white nationalism. James Baldwin would likely be the least surprised by the ascendance of Donald Trump. Trump, after all, not only rose to prominence in the 1980s; he was seen as the embodiment of its ethos. He possessed nearly all of the grotesque qualities Baldwin saw on the rise in the Reagan era, from his scapegoating of minorities to his unapologetic greed, to his promises to build walls and restore "law and order," to his exploitation of celebrity and manipulation of mass media. Yet his success reveals something much deeper about America. What has come to be identified as Trumpism is not merely about Trump but about a movement fueled by white rage and resentment. It is distinct from Reaganism in its lack of subtlety or code; Trumpism rejects "political correctness": it wears its bigotry and violence as a badge of honor. As Stanford University professor Tomás Jiménez put it to the *New York Times*, Trump has turned the "dog whistle into an air horn."[63] Reagan, for all his flaws, still believed in civil discourse, decorum, and personal decency. Trump is more the outgrowth of image-based celebrity culture and the far-right strains that emerged in the Reagan era—the seeds that birthed talk radio, Fox News, the Tea Party, and the religious right. His explicit attacks against Latinos, Muslims, African Americans, women, and the disabled, as well as the favor he garnered from the "alt-right" and Ku Klux Klan, would have been shocking even in the Reagan era. This was aptly illustrated by Trump's choice for attorney general, long-time Alabama senator Jeff Sessions, who was considered too racist to appoint to a federal judgeship in 1986. Not surprisingly, among people of color, Trump lost every state in America in the 2016 election; among whites, however, he won 58 percent to 37 percent.[64]

CNN commentator Van Jones described the election as a "whitelash" to the first black president, and more broadly to the changing demographics and social progress of the country.[65] Certainly it testifies to the fact that social progress is never inevitable.

Baldwin repeatedly emphasized that "history is not the past. It is the present. We carry our history with us. We are our history."[66] This sentiment was echoed by President Barack Obama, following the George Zimmerman verdict in 2013, when, in a rare moment of racial candor, he not only acknowledged that if he had a son, he would look like Trayvon Martin, but recognized that the incident was part of "a history that doesn't go away."[67] Yet if history doesn't go away, neither should the voices of those who slice through its glossy veneer, who unwrap its safe packaging, who interrogate its distant authority; voices that push us always to dig deep and reexamine—voices, that is, like James Baldwin's.

In our fraught present moment, Baldwin's work remains both vital and urgent. Part of the challenge for Baldwin studies, however, is to find spaces where his work can be read and studied. In an April 24, 2014, article, the *New York Times* noted that Baldwin was "fading" in American classrooms, offering as explanation Baldwin's complexity, as well as his provocative explorations of race and sexuality.[68] Baldwin's name and books were excluded from the appendix of the Common Core State Standards, a set of learning goals adopted by more than forty states and the District of Columbia.[69] Baldwin is often similarly overlooked in higher-education courses. While his reputation is much stronger among scholars, general survey courses in American literature and African American literature still tend to exclude or marginalize his work. In my own undergraduate and graduate studies at three different institutions, I confronted his work in only one class: a graduate seminar in which we read his essay "Everybody's Protest Novel."

Part of what makes this exclusion so striking is how relevant and near-universally revered Baldwin now is among African American authors, scholars, and critics, as well as among socially conscious readers of all races. More than any other civil rights leader—including Martin Luther King Jr. and Malcolm X—Baldwin has been referenced in relation to the Black Lives Matter movement. His righteous indignation and prophetic warnings speak to the exasperated mood of the present; his words appear on signs at rallies, in speeches and blogs, and on social media sites like Twitter and Facebook. President Obama even quoted him at the dedication of the Smithsonian

National Museum of African American History and Culture in 2016. "In numerous palpable ways," writes Thomas Chatterton Williams, "he has come to occupy a more hallowed, almost sacrosanct, position [now] . . . than he ever enjoyed among the audiences of his day—eclipsing in the twenty-first century his closest mentors, competitors, and peers. Some of this is surely the result of our culture's general, unremitting tendency toward nostalgia for all things. But mostly it has to do with the man himself. Where his cosmopolitan, nonconformist interests and way of life rendered him suspect to many in his later years, he now appears prescient, too enlightened for his time."[70]

James Baldwin scholarship has similarly flourished. In 2014, a new open-access journal dedicated to the author launched (the *James Baldwin Review*), while the *African American Review* devoted an entire special issue to Baldwin. Meanwhile, major celebrations commemorated what would have been the author's ninetieth birthday in 2014, including "The Year of James Baldwin," a citywide series of events jointly hosted by the Harlem Stage, New York Live Arts, and Columbia University School of the Arts. In 2016, an international James Baldwin Conference was held in Paris, France, while Raoul Peck's documentary on Baldwin, *I Am Not Your Negro*, premiered to widespread acclaim, including an Oscar nomination.

➤ This renaissance in Baldwin studies began in earnest with the publication of the groundbreaking collection *James Baldwin Now* (1999), edited by Dwight A. McBride. In his astute introductory essay, McBride noted that in many ways we are just catching up to the author. "Given the advent of cultural studies in the academy—with its focus on interdisciplinarity or transdisciplinarity, critical theory, and an ever broadening notion of 'culture'—it seems more possible today than ever before to engage Baldwin in all of the complexity he represents to critical inquiry, considering the various roles he has occupied."[71] McBride's collection offered a fresh, dynamic approach to Baldwin that, for the first time, demonstrated Baldwin's relevance to contemporary academic concerns. A year later, D. Quentin Miller's collection, *Re-viewing James Baldwin: Things Not Seen* (2000), began looking at some of his less canonical work. "The time has come," Miller declared, "to reconsider some of Baldwin's lesser-known and later writings."[72] Two other important books emerged in the 2000s that focused on Baldwin's later work—Lynn Orilla Scott's close readings of the author's fiction from the late 1960s and 1970s, *James Baldwin's Later Fiction: Witness to the Journey*

(2002), and Magdalena J. Zaborowska's revealing *James Baldwin's Turkish Decade: Erotics of Exile* (2009).

Several other important books on Baldwin have appeared in just the last few years, including Cora Caplan and Bill Schwarz's collection, *James Baldwin: America and Beyond* (2011), D. Quentin Miller's *A Criminal Power: James Baldwin and the Law* (2012), Matt Brim's *James Baldwin and the Queer Imagination* (2014), Douglas Field's *All Those Strangers: The Art and Lives of James Baldwin* (2015), Ed Pavlic's *Who Can Afford to Improvise? James Baldwin and Black Music, the Lyric and the Listeners* (2015), and Michele Elam's edited collection, *The Cambridge Companion to James Baldwin* (2015).[73] Each of these books contributes insightful new pieces to the puzzle that is James Baldwin. A few even dedicate some space to his work in the 1980s, most notably Pavlic's historicized overview of Baldwin in the Reagan era in *Who Can Afford to Improvise?* There has also been a significant increase in attention devoted to his engagement with popular culture.[74]

Such recognition is well-deserved. While the roots of cultural studies are typically traced back to postwar Europe—to the Frankfurt School in Germany, the Birmingham School in the United Kingdom, or the structuralist and poststructuralist schools in France—Baldwin should be considered among its independent pioneers. His critique of Marxism and reductive leftist politics, his belief in the constitutive, active nature of culture, his scrutiny of power and ideology, his interest in and engagement with mass media and popular culture, his rejection of the high/low artistic hierarchy, his investment in issues of representation, and his emphasis on the intersectional and socially constructed nature of identity are all features now associated with the "official" cultural studies movement, its foundational texts, and its institutions. But Baldwin was blazing a parallel track and indeed was often ahead of the curve. While certainly less academic than prominent cultural theorists, Baldwin's ideas are often more accessible, nuanced, and daring. It is not uncommon to find ideas in his work that were later rearticulated (often in less intelligible prose) in critical race theory, gender studies, queer theory, and media studies. As Ta-Nehisi Coates puts it: "All of us are chasing Baldwin—even if we don't know it."[75]

In *James Baldwin and the 1980s*, I use five thematic entry points to demonstrate Baldwin's engagement with popular culture in the context of the Reagan era. I should clarify at the outset that this book is not intended to be a comprehensive overview of all the work Baldwin produced in the 1980s;

rather, I have chosen what I believe is a sampling of some of his best work from his final decade and, as important, work that directly engages with the cultural moment in which it was written.

I begin with *Just Above My Head* for three reasons: one, because it is James Baldwin's last major work of fiction; two, because that work of fiction is explicitly engaged with one of the most prominent issues in post–civil rights culture: the crossover dream; and three, because its publication date and setting offer both a helpful prologue and bridge to the 1980s. The year 1979, when *Just Above My Head* was published, was a threshold moment for America—indeed, Baldwin's book release coincided with Reagan announcing his candidacy for president of the United States. Like Reagan, Baldwin is invested in the myth of the American Dream, though, not surprisingly, the two come to very different conclusions about its meanings. Baldwin's vehicle for scrutinizing this dream is black popular music, which became one of the most popular (if not the most popular) and influential artistic forms of the twentieth century. While it was widely considered a "success story" in traditional American terms, Baldwin became increasingly concerned with how this story was mediated and understood. How have black popular artists been read, represented, and evaluated in American media and culture? What was the price of "crossing over," of playing to increasingly mass, cross-racial audiences, of working for white labels, of conforming to the demands of a white industry? Why was black success so often accompanied by tragedy? Chapter 1 explores why black music—and the black popular artist—was so important to Baldwin, and what his final novel suggests about its paradoxical power and vulnerabilities.

Chapter 2 transitions to the domain of television and film, drawing on Baldwin's brilliant 1985 essay, "Freaks and the American Ideal of Manhood," to examine how the Reagan-era ideal of masculinity was delineated and contested in popular culture. By the 1980s, Baldwin contends, Americans continued to cling to an ideal of masculinity "so paralytically infantile that it is virtually forbidden—as an unpatriotic act—that the American boy evolve into the complexity of manhood."[76] In "Freaks," Baldwin recognizes the rise of "androgyny" in popular culture as a significant alternative to the era's dominant representations of hypermasculine male heroes. The chapter situates Baldwin's essay in its historical moment, considering the rise of and backlash to androgynous black "crossover" artists such as Michael Jackson and Prince, and the challenges they posed to the decade's more traditional representations of American manhood (among them, Reagan, Rambo, and Bruce Springsteen).

Chapter 3 examines Baldwin's unpublished play, *The Welcome Table*, within the context of the AIDS epidemic. The play's reference to AIDS comes in act 1 in an extended dialogue between two of the play's main characters: Edith and Rob. While it is not referenced explicitly again, it serves as a significant backdrop to the events that follow. AIDS, that is, is not merely a trivial, passing reference in the text, but plays an important role as subtext and context. At its core, *The Welcome Table* is about intimacy and connection. In a climate of uncertainty, panic, ostracization, and tragedy, Baldwin's "welcome table" serves as a space in which people can have real conversations about their fears, desires, regrets, and dreams. Modeled after the elliptical drama of Russian playwright Anton Chekhov, *The Welcome Table* is intentionally ambiguous. As Baldwin put it: "Nothing is resolved in the play. The play is simply a question posed—to all of us— how are we going to live in this world?"[77] This chapter attempts to flesh out Baldwin's question by placing the play within the social and cultural context of the 1980s, specifically in the midst of the AIDS crisis. Since *The Welcome Table* remains unpublished and largely unavailable to the general public, the chapter also attempts to showcase a relatively unknown but significant work from Baldwin's final decade that should add new dimensions to our understanding of the author and the 1980s.

Chapter 4 turns to Baldwin's final major essay, "To Crush the Serpent" (1987), to examine the rise of the Religious Right and Baldwin's alternative vision of morality. Religion played a crucial role in Baldwin's work, going back to *Go Tell It on the Mountain*. In the 1980s, however, as Baldwin recognized, a major transformation had occurred in the sociopolitical functions of religion. His critique adapted accordingly, focusing on the ways in which religion (particularly evangelical Christianity) had morphed into a movement deeply enmeshed with mass media, conservative politics, and capitalism. Religion in the Reagan era was being leveraged, sold, advertised, and politicized in ways never before seen, from charismatic televangelists to Christian-themed amusement parks to megachurches. "The people who call themselves 'born again' today," wrote Baldwin, "have simply become members of the richest, most exclusive private club in the world, a club that the man from Galilee could not possibly hope—or wish—to enter."[78] The new movement was often characterized as the "Religious Right" or the

"Moral Majority" and was central to Reagan's political coalition as well as the broader culture wars. For Baldwin, this development had wide-ranging ramifications for society and the individual. In "To Crush the Serpent" he narrows in on the definitions and uses of the sinner or transgressor in the context of Reagan-era obsessions with the body and sexuality.

Finally, chapter 5 reads Baldwin's award-winning essay "Atlanta: The Evidence of Things Not Seen" and elaborated final nonfiction book, *The Evidence of Things Not Seen*, as a corrective to sensationalist media accounts of the Atlanta child murders and simplistic gloss-overs of the New South. Far from the optimistic, "colorblind" ethos of the 1980s, Baldwin insisted that the Terror in Atlanta was indicative of a country that had simply not progressed the way it claimed. Not only did the post–civil rights landscape remain largely segregated (physically and psychologically) and unequal in spite of legislative triumphs; black life remained widely expendable. Baldwin draws on the Atlanta child murders and subsequent trial and conviction of Wayne Williams to reveal a city (and country) "tyrannized" by the weight of history and unwilling to "pay the bill." This chapter argues that while *Evidence* is perhaps Baldwin's most neglected work (both upon publication and today), it offers one of the most penetrating examinations of the paradoxes, hypocrisies, and illusions of the Reagan era. It also presciently anticipates the "post-racial" violence that continued in the Obama era, from Trayvon Martin to Mike Brown, to Sandra Bland, to the Charleston Nine.

It is my hope, through these chapters, to introduce a James Baldwin at once familiar and fresh. The conventional wisdom, not only for Baldwin but also for most authors and artists, holds that age takes its toll, particularly in one's ability to recognize and tap into new cultural transformations. Yet for all the dismissals of his post–civil rights output, Baldwin defies this narrative. His late writing is acutely dialed into the debates, figures, stories, politics, and media of the time. His work, as he so often put it, was his witness.

Given what he saw, there was much to be bitter and angry about. "In some ways," Baldwin explained, "I've changed precisely because America has not. I've been forced to change in some ways. I had a certain expectation for my country years ago, which I know I don't have now."[79] Yet Baldwin ultimately believed in the possibility—if not the inevitability—of change. In a 1979 interview with *The Black Collegian*, he speaks of his hope for the next generation. "People are very critical and very despairing of the young.

But I can only say that in my own experience, and admittedly it's limited, and even admitting I'm in somewhat of a special situation, I must say that my experience in all these years on campus has given me a great deal of hope. Kids ask real questions, I begin to suspect that, in fact, the elders who are so despairing of the young are actually despairing of themselves."[80] *The Black Collegian* later follows up: "You are obviously hopeful about the eighties," to which Baldwin responds. "Yes, but that doesn't mean it's going to be easy. But I'm far from being in despair. We cannot afford despair."[81] Baldwin's hope depended on new representations: in film, on television, in magazines, music, literature, and culture. As he put it: "The world changes according to the way people see it, and if you alter, even but a millimeter, the way . . . people look at reality, then you can change it."[82]

1

The Price of the Beat

Black Popular Music and the Crossover Dream

> It is only in his music . . . that the Negro in America has been able to tell his story.
> —James Baldwin, "Many Thousands Gone," 1955

The year 1979—when James Baldwin's *Just Above My Head* hit bookstores—was technically one year before the 1980s began. Yet the Reagan revolution was already well underway. Having served as Governor of California from 1967 to 1975, Reagan made his first run for president in 1976. After a fiercely contested primary with Republican incumbent Gerald Ford, Reagan came just 117 delegates short of the nomination. Ford eventually lost to Democratic challenger Jimmy Carter in the general election.

Reagan officially announced his second candidacy for president of the United States on November 13, 1979, in New York City—the same season in which *Just Above My Head* was published. America was in a bleak mood. The 1970s had been a rough decade for the country, from Vietnam to Watergate, from spiking divorce rates to a steep decline in national morale. While Jimmy Carter promised to restore honesty and integrity to the office of president, his tenure provoked disappointment and anger from both the Left and the Right. Inflation and unemployment kept rising, while the energy crisis had the public in a panic. News stories showed labyrinthine lines at gas stations. Several major cities, including New York City, were forced to close gas stations due to overwhelming demand. Some politicians proposed gas rationing as a solution.

By the summer of 1979, President Jimmy Carter's approval rating was lower than Richard Nixon's at the height of Watergate. After huddling with advisors at Camp David, the beleaguered president delivered, on July 15, 1979, what would become perhaps his most famous speech. Often referred to as the "malaise speech," Carter spoke not only of the country's energy crisis but also of "a crisis of confidence." "It is a crisis," he asserted, "that strikes at the very heart and soul and spirit of our national will. We can see this crisis in the growing doubt about the meaning of our own lives and in the loss of a unity of purpose for our nation. The erosion of our confidence in the future is threatening to destroy the social and the political fabric of America."[1] Carter proceeded to speak bluntly about the emptiness of overconsumption and materialism, about apathy and despair, about "paralysis and stagnation and drift," about "wounds that have never been healed."[2] It was a remarkably honest and astute diagnosis, and initially the American public seemed to respond positively, as Carter's approval rating jumped 11 points.[3]

But in the months to come, as the Iran hostage crisis compounded perceptions of Carter's, and by extension America's, ineptitude, the speech came to be associated with accepted failure. Critics claimed Carter wallowed in negativity and weakness—that he accepted a diminished future for the United States and failed to provide clear solutions to the problems he identified. The speech, and circumstances, offered the perfect opening for the charismatic, always-optimistic Ronald Reagan. In his own campaign-announcement speech that fall, Reagan rejected leaders who "tell us we must learn to live with less, and teach our children that their lives will be less full and prosperous than ours have been; that the America of the coming years will be a place where—because of our past excesses—it will be impossible to dream and make those dreams come true. I don't believe that. And, I don't believe you do either."[4] Reagan's alternative vision was about possibility. He spoke of his own life growing up during the Great Depression, seeing his father lose his job and his dignity, but refusing to give up. Through hard work, faith, and ingenuity, his family made it. Reagan held himself up as the living embodiment of the American Dream: an ordinary boy from Illinois who made it to Hollywood, an ordinary actor who now aspired to the highest office in the land. If he could do it, anyone could.

If he could succeed, so could America. It was a persuasive story, one with deep roots in the American psyche.

This context is significant to understanding *Just Above My Head*, a novel profoundly interested in the efficacy of the American Dream. Not surprisingly, Baldwin's narrative complicates Reagan's myth—most obviously by recognizing its entanglement with race, gender, and sexuality. Yet it does so, ironically, by zooming in on a "success story": the success of an individual who pursues and achieves his dreams, and the success more broadly of black music in America. "You're going to see my life," declares the novel's protagonist, Arthur Montana, renowned gospel singer, in the opening pages. "I don't want to hide anything from you, brother."[5] This desire to be *seen* and understood is at the heart of James Baldwin's final novel. Yet it is tangled, ironically, by the protagonist's fame—the fact, that is, that so many people "know" him. Unlike musician characters in Baldwin's earlier works, Arthur Montana is not an obscure singer in the streets or church or club—or rather, he does not *remain* obscure. By the time of his death—which opens the novel—he is known throughout America and the world. From humble circumstances, he becomes a *star*, living and grappling with the "crossover" dream. For Baldwin, however, this dream, and the progress it seems to signify, is as complex as the individual who embodies it.

He would know. Baldwin, after all, bears many resemblances to his protagonist. In a 1984 interview with the *New York Times*, he mused:

> There is a decidedly grave danger of becoming a celebrity, of becoming a star, of becoming a personality. Again, I'm very well placed to know that. It's symptomatic of the society that doesn't have any real respect for the artist. You're either a success or a failure and there's nothing in between. And if you are a success, you run the risk that Norman [Mailer] has run and that I run, too, of becoming a kind of show business personality. Then the legend becomes far more important than the work. It's as though you're living in an echo chamber. You hear only your own voice. And, when you become a celebrity, that voice is magnified by multitudes and you begin to drown in this endless duplication of what looks like yourself. You have to be really very lucky, and very stubborn, not to let that happen to you.[6]

In the same interview, Baldwin compared being a celebrity to

> a garment I wear. But the celebrity never sees himself. I have some idea what I'm doing on that stage; above all, I have some idea what sustains me on

that stage. But the celebrity is not exactly Jimmy, though he comes out of
Jimmy and Jimmy nourishes that, too. I can see now, with hindsight, that
I would've had to become a celebrity in order to survive. A boy like me with
all his handicaps, real and fancied, could not have survived in obscurity. I
can say that it would have had to happen this way, though I could not see
it coming.[7]

Of course, as Baldwin's novel demonstrates, surviving in notoriety can
be just as challenging as surviving in obscurity—or at the very least, it
presents its own set of obstacles. Published at a crucial turning point for
black music, black America, and American culture more broadly, Baldwin's
novel offers a version of the American Dream that refuses to accept the
terms of popular discourse.

Baldwin himself was of course deeply influenced by music. It was perhaps the most valuable gift he took from his time in the church.[8] It was the
means by which he discovered his own voice as a writer in the mountains
of Switzerland. From the beginning to end of his career, his work is packed
with song lyrics, riffs on the effects of music, and allusions to musical artists. Among the many names that populate his work are Bessie Smith, Louis
Armstrong, Duke Ellington, Fats Waller, Ma Rainey, Billie Holiday, Ella
Fitzgerald, Nina Simone, Dinah Washington, Miles Davis, John Coltrane,
Charlie Parker, James Brown, Mahalia Jackson, Billy Preston, Ray Charles,
Frank Sinatra, Aretha Franklin, Luther Vandross, Otis Redding, Sam Cooke,
Marvin Gaye, Stevie Wonder, and Michael Jackson.

Several chapters and articles have deftly engaged with Baldwin and mu-
sic, including Josh Kun's "Life According to the Beat: James Baldwin, Bessie Smith, and the Perilous Sounds of Love," Warren Carson's "Manhood,
Musicality and Male Bonding," and D. Quentin Miller's "Using the Blues:
James Baldwin and Music." Perhaps the most comprehensive overview of
Baldwin's important relationship with black music is Ed Pavlic's 2015 book,
*Who Can Afford to Improvise? James Baldwin and Black Music, the Lyric and
the Listener*. In volume 2 of the *James Baldwin Review*, Pavlic also compiled
a playlist of songs that mattered to Baldwin and "offer his readers access
to deeper meanings in his work."[9] Scholarship focused specifically on *Just
Above My Head* has been rather thin but has begun to garner more attention
in recent years, including work by Craig Werner, Lynn Orilla Scott, Julie
Nash, D. Quentin Miller, Ed Pavlic, and Christopher Hobson. This chapter
attempts to add to this growing body of work by focusing specifically on

what *Just Above My Head* reveals about the complex mediation of black music and musicians in the late twentieth century as it emerged as one of the most influential forces in American culture. How have black popular artists been read, represented, and evaluated in American media and culture? What was the price of "crossing over," of playing to increasingly mass, cross-racial audiences, of working for white labels, of conforming to the demands of a white industry? Why was black success so often accompanied by tragedy? For Ronald Reagan, the American Dream was a simple story of persistence and bootstrap individualist achievement. For Baldwin, however, success, as traditionally understood, was elusive for many Americans; and for those who did "make it," it remained replete with obstacles. This chapter explores why the story of black music—and the black artist—were particularly important to Baldwin, and what his final novel reveals about the complexities of the "crossover dream."

Don't Stop 'til You Get Enough

In the late 1970s, black music was at an important crossroads. Long marginalized as "race music," it was on the cusp of leaping to unprecedented levels of mainstream success. While the music industry as a whole was struggling, black music was adapting, evolving, and innovating. The late 1970s marked the birth of hip hop and the beginning of a new pop renaissance that would transform the sound and look of the 1980s. According to estimates, black records accounted for more than 25 percent of the music industry's $4 billion in sales in 1978; by the mid-1980s that number had doubled.[10] Gloria Gaynor's anthem, "I Will Survive" and Sister Sledge's classic, "We Are Family" debuted in 1979; it was the year of Donna Summer's *Bad Girls*, Earth, Wind & Fire's *I Am*, and Prince's eponymous breakthrough album. Perhaps most prominently, it was the year of Michael Jackson's first solo album, *Off the Wall*. Produced by music legend Quincy Jones, *Off the Wall* quickly became the bestselling album to date by a black artist. Fueled by crossover hit singles, "Don't Stop 'til You Get Enough" and "Rock with You," the album sold an estimated 9 million copies in just two years. Eventually, it spawned four Top Ten hits, a record at that point for a solo artist on one album. Just as important, it set up Jackson's stratospheric rise in the 1980s.

Yet the album's reception provides a window into the struggles and paradoxes of black popular music in America, particularly in the late 1970s and early 1980s. Despite its commercial success, Jackson's album was slighted at the 1980 Grammy Awards, where it was passed over for all major awards, including Album of the Year, Record of the Year, and Song of the Year (white artists won in each of these categories). Like that of many black artists, Jackson's work was dismissed as frivolous dance music, was relegated to racialized categories like "R&B" or "disco." That same year, popular music's most visible magazine, *Rolling Stone*, refused to put Jackson on the cover despite his clear cultural significance. In a note to Jackson's manager, *Rolling Stone* editor Jann Wenner wrote that while the magazine was willing to consider the artist for an article, Jackson did not merit front-cover status.

This treatment spoke to broader racial biases in popular music. The infamous Disco Demolition Night at Comiskey Park in Chicago, when piles of disco albums were burned to the delight of an overwhelmingly white male crowd, also occurred in 1979. The event, charged with racial and homophobic epithets, nearly led to a riot. "Disco sucks" became a mantra for rockists in the early Reagan era, whose intense hatred for the genre seemed to cross far beyond aesthetic preferences. As Craig Werner writes, "The attacks on disco gave respectable voice to the ugliest kinds of unacknowledged racism, sexism, and homophobia."[11] In addition to public demonstrations, critics dismissed disco and other black-associated musical genres as formulaic, inauthentic, and shallow. White rock, by contrast, was described as authentic, serious, and important.

Such evaluations led directly to programming decisions on radio, and eventually to cable television channels such as MTV. In our tendency to think of race relations in America as a linear story of progress, we often forget that music became increasingly segregated over the course of the 1970s. As Nelson George notes, "The best year for crossover was 1970, when fifteen of the top black songs in America reached the top fifteen on the pop chart, and seven went to number one [including four by the Jackson 5]."[12] The best period for racial diversity on the charts to that point had been from 1967 to 1973, the height of Motown's influence. The years 1974 to 1982, however, saw a steep decline in black crossover hits on the charts and in airplay. FM radio in particular banished black music from the airwaves, favoring instead safe white rock bands that catered to their target demographics, groups like the Eagles, Journey, and REO Speedwagon. "In this environment," notes Steve Greenberg, "number one urban contemporary hits, such as Roger Troutman's 'Heard It through the Grapevine' or 'Burn

Rubber' by the Gap Band, failed to even crack the Top 40. Prince's '1999,' which would later emerge as a pop culture anthem, flopped at Top 40 radio even as it soared up the urban chart. A black superstar like Rick James could sell over 4 million albums while remaining unknown to most listeners of white-oriented radio."[13]

In the late 1970s and early 1980s, then, black music found itself in a familiar position: commercially popular and culturally influential, yet simultaneously marginalized and critically devalued. This indeed had been the story of black popular music throughout the twentieth century, going back to jazz, gospel, and the blues. There were ebbs and flows in its "mainstream" success and recognition; but the overarching story was plagued by marginalization, exploitation, appropriation, and misrepresentation (or no representation at all). James Baldwin spoke to such issues in his 1979 essay, "Of the Sorrow Songs: The Cross of Redemption." The essay uses white music historian James Lincoln Collier's book *The Making of Jazz* (1979) as an illustration of how the story of black music has been distorted and misunderstood. The history Collier presents, Baldwin writes, is as "precise as [it] is deluded."[14] He cites one passage as indicative of the book's fatal flaw: "There have been two authentic geniuses in jazz. One of them, of course, was Louis Armstrong, the much loved entertainer, striving for acceptance. The other was a sociopath named Charlie Parker who managed . . . to destroy his career—and finally himself."[15]

Against such a narrative—first, the absurd assertion that there are only two "authentic geniuses" in the history of jazz, and second, that they can both be neatly reduced to caricatures—Baldwin writes that he feels an "obligation to attempt to clarify the record."[16] He does not want future generations to believe this "comprehensive history," written by a man who seems to see and hear so little, where Baldwin sees, hears, and *feels* so much. Baldwin feels compelled, that is, not simply to offer a corrective of any one particular reductive black biography or history, but to reframe the story with an entirely different vocabulary. While the European author of *The Making of Jazz* may have conducted meticulous research, he misses its soul and its context—that is, the *true story*.

For Baldwin, the true story goes far deeper than historical minutiae, or notes or lyrics. It is about all that goes into a song—and about how prepared the listener is to hear those many valences of meaning. To understand Arthur Montana (and what and whom he represents), then, one must read between—or beneath, or *just above*—the lines; one must *feel* what cannot easily be captured in language, certainly not the reductive language of Collier's history. Baldwin's novel, then, acts as a kind of bridge between artist and audience, particularly those audiences less intimately familiar with where the music—and artist—comes from.

They Didn't Know Who You Were

Just Above My Head stretches over three generations, from the 1940s to the late 1970s. A substantial chunk of the narrative, however, takes place in the 1950s. What does it have to do then, one might ask, with the late-1970s context in which the novel was published, or with the Reagan era more broadly? As Baldwin frequently reminded, what's past is not only prologue; it is *present*. The 1980s did not suddenly appear fully formed out of a vacuum. The Reagan era was the accumulation of forces underway for decades—and profoundly connected to the 1950s in particular.

Numerous scholars have noted the connections between the 1950s and 1980s. In his book *Back to the Fifties: Nostalgia, Hollywood Film, and Popular Music of the Seventies and Eighties*, Michael Dwyer describes how 1950s nostalgia permeated the Reagan era, from films like *Back to the Future* and *Stand by Me* to the revival of rockabilly and doo wop, to the retro music videos of Michael Jackson and Madonna. Ronald Reagan himself not only embodied the 1950s through his clean-cut, masculine, screen-icon image, he frequently recalled it in speeches and commercials as a golden era of prosperity, wholesome family values, strength, and safety. Dwyer quotes a 1986 *Esquire* cover story in which the 1980s are defined by the cultural process of "replay, recycle, retrieve, reprocess, and rerun."[17]

For Baldwin, then, post–civil rights America can only be understood by understanding pre–civil rights America; they are connected, as are the myths that accompany them. Likewise, understanding Arthur Montana—and, by extension, the story of black music—can only be realized by digging back in time and tracing the story over decades. *Just Above My Head*, of course, provides a much different account of the 1950s than the nostalgic version Reagan conjured. Indeed, the express purpose of the novel, from its opening pages, is about offering an alternative history—that is, telling a different story of how we got here. The novel opens with reductive media obituaries of Arthur Montana, the Emperor of Soul, as "a nearly forgotten," "emotion filled . . . moaner and groaner."[18] Arthur was thirty-nine years old. "No one told how he died," says Hall Montana, Arthur's brother and manager (and Baldwin's narrator).[19] More significant to Baldwin, however, was that no one told how he lived.

To tell his brother's story, we return to the postwar era, before Arthur became a star. It is very different in this way than the stories told in the press. Arthur's story will not be simplified to appease expectations or conform to easy templates about success and failure, triumph and tragedy. Such templates, Baldwin suggests, fail to reveal the subject—and in fact may reveal far more about the subject position of the media/writer. In a 1968 speech, Baldwin spoke of how the Western world was "unable to comprehend the force of such a woman as Mahalia Jackson, who does not sound like anyone in Canterbury Cathedral, and unable to accept the depth of sorrow, out of which a Ray Charles comes."[20] In "The Uses of the Blues" he similarly writes of the "subterranean" world contained "in the tone and in the face of Ray Charles."[21] This is the world explored in *Just Above My Head*. It is a different kind of history, at once more personal and universal. "History," as Baldwin explained to *The Black Scholar* in 1973, "was someone you touched, you know, on Sunday mornings or in the barbershop. It's all around you. It's in the music, it's in the way you talk, it's in the way you cry, it's in the way you make love. Because you are denied your official history you are forced to excavate your real history."[22]

Through the intimate narration of his brother, then, we begin a deep dive into Arthur's past and in relation to the people who knew him best. In addition to his brother, Hall, this includes his lover, Jimmy, and his first love, Crunch. It also includes his parents, Paul and Florence, and his close friends and neighbors: Peanut, who is killed in Atlanta; Red, who becomes a junkie; and, most prominent, Julia, a child preacher who is in many ways blessed and cursed with a gift similar to Arthur's (Julia leaves the church at a young age, is molested by her stage-managing father, but manages to survive this history and write a new story for herself as an adult).

In interviews, Baldwin said that *Just Above My Head* was not "autobiographical" in the traditional sense; there were no "direct one-on-one relationships between my life and the lives of the people in that book."[23] Yet the stories of the traveling gospel quartet were clearly inspired by the real-life experiences of his brother, David, and other musician friends. Moreover, each of the characters, particularly the main characters—Arthur,

Hall, Jimmy, and Julia—contains traces of Baldwin. Indeed, Lynn Orilla
Scott argues convincingly that these four characters all represent different
dimensions of Baldwin and thus become a "form of self-representation
that does justice to the complexity of African American subjectivity."[24] The
character of Arthur Montana certainly contains many obvious parallels
with his author. Like Baldwin, he is an artist; he is famous; and he is gay.
Yet Arthur's story is relayed from the point of view of his brother, Hall,
another character with striking parallels to Baldwin. Hall is a witness, a
protector, and, as Julie Nash observes, a blues hero in his own right. While
he doesn't play music or sing like his brother, he hears and translates it. He
understands its meanings and histories.

The reader learns quickly from Hall's narrative that Arthur Montana's life
as a public figure was accompanied by controversy. In the opening pages,
Hall, acting as Arthur's manager and PR representative, desperately tries to
rescue his brother's reputation. "I've been so busy, covering up for Arthur,
strong-arming the press, flying over half the goddamn globe," he writes.[25]
But for most people, Arthur laments, including the millions who bought
and listened to his records, they will never understand Arthur, the human
being. He is simply an image, a brand, a spectacle. The celebrity artist, as
object of the public's desire, is "treated with an unbelievable brutality, a
brutality made all the more hideous by presenting itself as love."[26] But "what
is lacking in every fantasy," observes Hall, "is that sweat of love which is
called *respect*."[27]

Among the main reasons for the controversy swirling around Arthur,
the reader learns, is the fact that he is gay. "I once heard myself shouting
at some asshole white producer," Hall recalls, "who was giving me some
mealy-mouthed crap about my brother's private life being a problem."[28]
Hall, like Baldwin, believes one's sexuality is a private matter. It is up to
the individual, not society, to decide how public they should be about such
matters. This point is driven home in multiple scenes in the novel. Earlier
in his career, Arthur's manager, Webster, directly confronts him and then-
lover Crunch about their relationship. "What's going on between you two?"[29]
When Crunch evades the question, Webster says he has heard rumors that
Crunch and Arthur are "lovebirds."[30] Crunch again avoids being pinned
down, saying simply that "boys will be boys."[31] But Webster is persistent in
his interrogation. As Ed Pavlic notes, "true to his name, [he is] fixated on
definitions and categories."[32] After Crunch resists being outed on Webster's

terms several times, Webster makes a confession and a threat after Crunch challenges him with "You don't know what we doing, but you might want to do it too": "Why not?" Crunch says. "Or—I can always make you change rooms."[33] Crunch, however, throws the threats right back. "You ain't going to make no changes, you slimy mother-fucker . . . I'll beat your brains out if you try."[34] He continues: "Anyway, you *can't* do what we do, brother. You can't sing."[35]

Crunch's assertion—you can't sing—suggests more than the manager's inability to carry a note, of course. Singing, in this context, is ultimately a way of living, a way of loving. Later in the novel, Hall describes his brother's relationship with Jimmy as a kind of song. "I have rarely heard, or seen, a freedom like that, when they played and sang together," he says. "It had something to do with their youth, of course, it had something to do with the way they looked, it had something to do with their vows, with their relation to each other: but it was more, much more than that. It was a wonder, a marvel—a mystery: I call it holy."[36] The song, then, for Arthur and Jimmy, is a kind of "sacrament."[37]

Part of the great tragedy of the black artist, however, is that the sacred and intimate nature of his or her song is often distorted. Hall recalls a day, toward the end of Arthur's career, when his brother cries out, weeping, "*Look! what they done to my song!*"[38] The distortion of the song is inextricably connected to the distortion of the singer. This, Hall tells us, is precisely what happened to Arthur. As his fame grew, "lots of people tried to gang-rape him in indescribable ways—oh, yes, believe me, it's cold out there—and Arthur began to sink beneath the double weight of the judgment without and the judgment within."[39] His final lover, Jimmy, elaborates on this judgment and its corrosive effects: "Now, sometimes, when I try to talk about Arthur, I feel like a freak. And, for whatever it's worth, I guess I *am* a freak. But, dig it, baby, when I held your brother in my arms, when he had his arms around me, I didn't feel like a freak then. Even when people started talking about us, the way they did, you remember, I really did not give a shit. I was only hurt because Arthur was hurt."[40] The pain and confusion, however, deepened for Jimmy after Arthur's death. He confesses: "It's only since he left us, and I've been so alone and so unhappy, that all the other *moral* shit, what the world calls moral, started fucking with my mind. Like, why are you like this instead of like that? Well, how the fuck am I supposed to know? I know this: the question wouldn't even come up if I wasn't so alone, and so scared, wouldn't come up, I mean, in my own mind. I'm scared, and I'd like to be safe, and nobody likes being despised. I can't break faith with Arthur, I can't ride and hide away somewhere, and treat my love, and let the world treat my lover, like shit."[41]

Jimmy concludes that it is the world that "doesn't have any morality."[42] Arthur's death—and life—can only be understood within this context. "Arthur got hurt, trapped, lost somewhere in there," Jimmy tells us. "All Arthur wanted was for the people who had *made* the music, from God-knows-who, to Satchmo, Mr. Jelly-Lord, Bessie, Mahalia, Miles, Ray, Trane, his *daddy*, and *you*, too! mother-fucker, *you*! It was only when he got scared about what *they might think of what he'd done to their song—our* song—that he really started to be uptight about our love."[43] These are crucial revelations. Arthur wanted to honor the tradition and heritage from which he came. He recognized that he was part of a larger, collective "song." But he also had his own individual song. "I've got to live the life I sing about in my song," he says, which Hall interprets as meaning "he could not afford to live a lie."[44] His brother Hall encourages him to "go the way his blood beats" but recognizes the enormous external pressure as Arthur becomes more famous.[45] Sexuality, of course, has haunted the careers of a number of well-known black artists, from Bessie Smith to Little Richie to Michael Jackson. For Baldwin, Arthur becomes a vessel for these queer singers and the crushing weight imposed on them by the prying, normative gaze of society.

How will such artists be remembered? This becomes Hall's—and by extension, Baldwin's—purpose in the pages of *Just Above My Head*: to witness for the black popular artist, particularly the black popular queer artist, who has been so disparaged and distorted by the media and public. Relaying the true story, or history, to the rising generation is especially important for Baldwin, as demonstrated in one of the novel's early passages, in which Hall has a brief moment alone with his son, Tony, discussing Arthur's identity:

> "What was my uncle—Arthur—like? [he asks]
> "Well—why do you ask? *You* knew him."
> "Come on. I was a baby. What did I know?"
> "Well—what are you asking?"
> "A lot of the kids at school—they talk about him."
> "What do they say?"
> "They say—he was a faggot."[46]

Hall seems caught off guard. He is not quite prepared to explain the plexity of his brother to his son directly. He talks around the issue, h but his son is persistent. He wants to know. Yes, Hall confirms, Arthu with men. He loved Jimmy, in particular, very deeply. "I'm proud of my brother, your uncle, and I'll be proud of him until the day I die. You should be, too. Whatever the fuck your uncle was, and he was a whole lot of things, he was nobody's faggot."[47] Arthur refuses to allow his brother to be defined by a slur and, in fact, prods his son: "Didn't me and your mother raise you right? didn't I—we—tell you, a long time ago, not to believe in labels?"[48] Tony affirms that they did, but that he "just wanted you to tell me."[49] He wanted, that is, something to validate his own impression of Arthur and to counteract the bigotry and slander he hears about his uncle at school.

That bigotry, ultimately, comes from both black and white; it also comes from within the church, as it did to real-life figures like Ray Charles and Sam Cooke (and Baldwin). "I remember," says Hall, "how those people treated Arthur when he branched out from gospel."[50] It is hard not to read into such statements Baldwin's own rejection from the church as he attempted to become more honest about his identity and tackle forbidden territory in his work. Yet the family, for Baldwin, offers a kind of fortress of unconditional love. In Arthur's case, his brother is perhaps his greatest public "witness." But his mother, too, has not forsaken him. She, like Arthur, "feels that the people in the church, when they turned against him, became directly responsible for his death."[51] After her son's death, she leaves the city and attends a small, private church in New Orleans, "away from all the spiteful people whose tongues so lacerated her boy."[52] Here, alone, "she can sing to herself, without fear of being mocked, and find strength and solace in the song that says, *They didn't know who you were.*"[53]

A Love Song

Such intimate glimpses allow us to see and understand more of Arthur and what he meant to the people around him. Yet even this portrait, Baldwin is quick to qualify, is incomplete. "No one knows very much about the life of another," writes Hall.[54] Throughout his narration, Hall zooms in on his brother from different angles, at different times, in different emotional states. As he explains: "I put a certain kind of picture together—in time—out of the fragments Arthur let me see, or couldn't hide, or what I divined."[55]

Yet even as his brother, one of a handful of people who knows him better than anyone, Arthur repeatedly acknowledges that what he sees or reveals of his brother is not the whole picture. There are limitations. "I wasn't in his skin, or in his beds, or in his voice," acknowledges Hall.[56] In another passage, he describes following Arthur's eyes, "which happens when you care about someone," but quickly concedes that while he can speculate on Arthur's thoughts, "I'm not Arthur, my eyes are not his eyes."[57] One's younger brother, he says, "begins his life (you think) within the sturdy gates of one's imagination. He is what you think he is."[58] Gradually, this begins to change: "Love forces, at last, this humility: you cannot love if you cannot *be* loved, you cannot see if you cannot be seen."[59]

In numerous moments throughout the novel, love allows revelations to occur. Hall sees Arthur (and other characters) in new ways. Toward the end of book 1, the brothers get drunk together at a bar where everyone knows Arthur, and suddenly Hall notices something different. "It was the first time I ever watched my brother in a world which was his, not mine. . . . That joy and wonder and terror and pride surged and danced in me that night, making my life new, making my brother new."[60] A similar recognition occurs between brothers in "Sonny's Blues." Such revelations continue to unfold throughout the novel, as Hall watches his brother sing, or fall in love, or struggle in despair. For the attentive and caring perceiver, "every gesture any human being makes is loaded" with meaning.[61]

Ultimately, the book we are reading, he confesses, is "a love song to my brother. It is an attempt to face both love and death."[62] In telling his brother's story, of course, he also tells his own. This, he says, was not his intent, but finally necessary. "I have had to try to strip myself naked. One does not like what one sees then, and one is afraid of what others will see: and do. To challenge one's deepest, most nameless fears, is, also, to challenge the heavens. It is to drag yourself, and everything and *everyone* you love, to the attention of the fiercest of the gods: who may not forgive your impertinence, who may not spare you. All that I can offer in extenuation of my boldness is my love."[63] Yet Hall recognizes the risks of such love. He worries about his brother constantly to the point of paranoia. "I worried about cops and billy clubs and pushers, jails, rooftops, basements, the river, the morgue: I moved like an advance scout in wicked and hostile territory, my whole life was a strategy and a prayer: I knew I could not live without my brother."[64] Was it healthy to be so involved in another person's life?

Was he "trapped" in the brother he adored? "Is adoration a blasphemy or the key to life?" he muses.[65] There was, after all, a "horrifying underside of adoration."[66] "If you're that taken up with someone else's life, it means that you're frightened of your own."[67]

Perhaps. But it is also true, Hall reminds himself (and his reader), "that we are all, forever, and every day, part of one another."[68] Part of understanding adoration, then, relies on tracing where it comes from and how it is enacted. For some of Arthur's fans, adoration is little more than objectification. They don't really want to *know* him, or the meanings of his songs. Applause, as Hall observes, can be interpreted as an act of appreciation, or as an attempt to "pacify, narcotize, the resulting violent and inescapable discomfort."[69] In this way, the singer, the song, and the listener are bound together; the nature of each performance—its meanings, its possibilities, its connections—is contingent on what each individual brings to the encounter. In one scene, for example, Arthur's shared intimacy with Crunch is referred to multiple times as "progress."[70] A term often ascribed to society as a whole and despised by Baldwin for its self-congratulatory, assimilationist undertones, it is re-conceived here as personalized, reciprocal love. As Arthur and Crunch lay in each other's arms, Arthur asks, "Do you think we making progress?" to which Crunch responds, "I'm with you."[71] Progress, in this way, takes on new valences. It is not a statistic, a law, or civil rights bill, but loving another human being against the odds.

Crossover

The term "crossover" first gained currency in the late 1950s and early 1960s as a way of describing black recording artists, performers, and entertainers who found success with "mainstream" white audiences in addition to black audiences. It wasn't a new concept, as forms of black art had appealed to large transracial, transatlantic audiences going back to minstrel shows and, perhaps most prominently in the twentieth century, during the Harlem Renaissance. The term was popularized, however, in the wake of the civil rights era, when it was perhaps best emblemized by Motown, a black-owned record company that achieved mass, multiracial appeal. Founded by Berry Gordy in Detroit in 1959, Motown transformed the formerly white-dominated "pop" charts with hits like "My Girl," "Baby Love," and "Dancing in the Street." It became, as the slogan proclaimed, the "sound of young America." The lineup of groups and artists under the Motown label are legendary: The Temptations, The Supremes, Gladys Knight and the Pips, Marvin Gaye, Smokey Robinson, Stevie Wonder, the Jackson 5.

The crossover phenomenon, however, was not confined to Motown or soul music. Like Arthur Montana, several major gospel singers "crossed over" in the second half of the twentieth century, including Mahalia Jackson and Ray Charles (two of Baldwin's favorite singers) and, later, Aretha Franklin and Sam Cooke. From "A Change Is Gonna Come" to "We Shall Overcome," gospel played a crucial role in the civil rights movement. Mahalia Jackson, in particular, played a large part in making gospel the soundtrack of the era, from her weekly CBS radio show to her many appearances at rallies and services, including the March on Washington. As Craig Werner writes: "If [Martin Luther] King gave the movement a vision, Mahalia Jackson gave it a voice."[72]

While Jackson remained mainly within the gospel tradition, other crossover artists began charting different paths from their roots in the church. Of all genres, black gospel, rooted not only in the sanctity of religious worship but also in the history of the spirituals, seemed antithetical to the commercial pressures of popular music. Yet in the age of late capitalism and mass media, it became increasingly difficult—and for many artists, unnecessary—to try to remain "pure." The gospel, after all, was meant to be heard. Its exodus from churches to radios and television screens happened gradually, as did the transformation of "pure" gospel to its various relatives and offspring: the blues, R&B, soul, and pop. Perhaps the most prominent early example of this shift was Ray Charles, who was both denounced and celebrated for his secular turn, symbolized by his 1954 hit, "I Got a Woman," which fused the sounds of gospel with the blues, and changed God-centered lyrics to an emphasis on relationships. "I was just being myself," Charles said in defense of the song. "Of course it created a lot of static from a lot of people. But then, on the other hand, it was a hit. It was a hit in the black community and the white community."[73] Baldwin saw such crossover artists as embodying something daring, "triumphant and liberating."[74] They bridged different sounds and genres as well as different races and nationalities. He also recognized, however, the risks and potential repercussions of their success.

By the 1980s, "crossover" had become so common to public discourse it was used to describe a wide range of popular black figures, from Bill Cosby to Michael Jordan, Whitney Houston to Oprah Winfrey, Prince to Eddie Murphy. These were figures who were not only perceived as having cross-racial appeal; whites made up a sizable portion of their audience. In no small part because of this, the term crossover often overlapped with "commercial," "selling out," "integrating," or in some way shedding or distancing oneself from one's racial heritage. "Crossover" artists were often perceived as opportunistic individualists assimilating to a white-dominated capitalist culture.

James Baldwin's novel was written and published at a time when the implications of crossover and integration were being fiercely debated. In his book *The Death of Rhythm and Blues*, Nelson George characterizes the period between 1975 and 1979 as both the age of "crossover" and the moment in which R&B died. As he writes:

> The struggle to overcome the overt apartheid of America had given blacks an energy, a motivating dream, that inspired the music's makers. By the mid-seventies, a segment of black America had beaten the odds, leaped over the barricade, and now lived in parts of the country they would have been lynched in a decade before. It struck many of them as time to remove the modifying adjective "black" from their lives. It was in that spirit that the term "crossover" came to dominate all discussion of black music and, eventually, the music itself. In the process, much of what had made the R&B world work was lost, perhaps some of it forever.[75]

George points to a number of disturbing signs that were emerging in the age of crossover, primary among them that (white) corporations were poaching off black artists, labels, businesses, and radio stations. On the other hand, however, being in the belly of the beast gave some black artists unprecedented resources and platforms. Some black artists, including Marvin Gaye and Stevie Wonder, had also reached new levels of acclaim and recognition. At the 1976 Grammy Awards, Paul Simon jokingly thanked Stevie Wonder for not releasing an album that year, given how many Grammys he had won in the preceding years. What did such inroads, such great popularity in mainstream America mean? Did it signify a new era of progress and understanding, or something, as Nelson George suggests, more ominous?

Such questions and tensions percolate throughout *Just Above My Head*. In a conversation at the Montana dinner table, they passionately debate early efforts at desegregation and the implications of integration for black communities. It is the late 1950s. The tone of the conversation is skeptical, particularly among the older generation. "They change their laws when their laws make them uncomfortable," says the father, Paul, "or when they think they can see some kind of advantage for them—we ain't, really, got nothing to do with it."[76] Arthur, however, contests his parent's bleak outlook. "Mama," he says, "you think they can't change?"[77] His mother, Florence, concedes that she's "known some white people who were beautiful and some black people who were rats," but that one cannot depend on white people to change society. "I hope they do," she says. "It might make life a little easier for you and a little better for them. But we're not really talking about them: we talking about us. Whatever they do, honey, you still got your life to live. I'm glad you don't have to ride in no Jim Crow car, like me and your daddy had to do. But, Jim Crow car or no Jim Crow car, we still had to raise you."[78] Florence encourages her son to "go on down, and test them waters," but presciently warns that once integration takes place, "how you going to look at them, how you going to look at yourself?"[79]

This question haunts Arthur's actualization of the American Dream. On the one hand, he can sense the power of his voice, of his music to transcend boundaries. "He sang, he had to sing, as though music could really accomplish the miracle of making the walls come tumbling down," Hall says.[80] Part of this self-belief comes from his lover, Jimmy. "It is very largely because of Jimmy," says Hall, "that Arthur became: a star."[81] Hall recognizes the paradox. Arthur's fame, after all, "was to become a part of Jimmy's [and Arthur's] agony: but I must let the statement stand."[82] Hall elaborates that Jimmy helped make Arthur a star, because his love "altered Arthur's estimate of himself, gave him a joy and a freedom he had never known before, invested him with a kind of incandescent wonder, and he carried this light on stage with him."[83] It was also Jimmy who encouraged Arthur to branch out from gospel and experiment with other genres—soul, R&B, jazz—"other music you got in you."[84] This, not surprisingly, his record company pushed in order to widen his audience.

This journey, which mirrors in so many ways the journeys of hundreds of black artists during the 1960s and 1970s, was both exhilarating and liberating for Arthur. He speaks of playing a show in Canada in which he "didn't see as many of *us* [black people]." "'I didn't see as many churches—their churches are different. I sang in civic centers, you know, and some *white* churches, and'—he laughed—'a football stadium, and, you know?'—his proud astonished eyes now searching mine—'it was full, that stadium was damn near full, there was ump-teen thousand people there, baby, and it was beautiful, I left them rocking to the gospel as I went off.'"[85] For Arthur, the experience offered enormous promise. "They hadn't seen nobody like me before" and "*I* hadn't seen anybody like *them*, either, and it was something, I think it was good for me, to sing before such a strange audience."[86] This indeed was a hope shared by many black artists of this time. Writes Mary Wilson of the Supremes: "Our tours made breakthroughs and helped weaken racial barriers. When it came to music, segregation didn't mean a thing in some of those towns, and if it did, black and white fans would ignore the local customs to attend the shows. To see crowds that were integrated—sometimes for the first time in a community—made me realize that Motown truly was the sound of young America."[87]

But there was a darker side to this success and to integration more broadly. Long before he becomes famous, Arthur's father, Paul, warns of his son's fate: "It's going to burn him up, burn him every hour that he lives, char the flesh from the bone, man."[88] Such statements, on the surface, seem counterintuitive. As Baldwin himself acknowledged, he could not have survived in obscurity; success was what allowed him to escape the traps that lay everywhere around him in Harlem; it allowed him some degree of safety and respect, and likely extended his life. But success and fame came with their own unique traps, particularly for black celebrities in a white industry—and in some ways were much more difficult to recognize. Looking back from the late 1970s, Hall muses that "thousands of black people cross the color line every year; become white Christians without even having to bob their noses, or change their names; they just change neighborhoods. No doubt, for this, they pay another price, a hidden price: but the price the country exacts from them for being white is exactly the price the country pays—for being white—and the price is incoherence."[89] Becoming white, as Hall describes it, is subscribing to the basic terms of the American Dream: to financial success, recognition, accolades, and safe, stratified neighborhoods. This indeed is what the Montana brothers experienced, along with hundreds of thousands of other black Americans in the 1960s and 1970s. Hall's first entry into this world comes through a job in advertising. "I could never, at bottom, take advertising seriously," confessed Hall. "I felt it as demeaning. It seemed to me to be really a shell game, based squarely on the sucker principle. One could scarcely respect the people who went for all this okeydoke, who were, indeed, addicted to it. The sense of life with which advertising imbued them—or vice versa—made reality, or the truth of life, unbearable, threatening, and, at last, above all, unreal: they preferred the gaudy image. . . . They did not know, and did not dare to know, what was in the package."[90] Nonetheless, Hall does his job. It pays the bills. He later switches jobs, working for an unnamed black magazine, but soon realizes he is, in essence, doing the same thing. "For, if my attitude toward advertising as concerned the great, white, faceless mass was, at best, ironic, my attitude toward advertising as concerned black people was very painfully ambivalent. I felt that black people had a sense of reality far more solid and arresting than the bubble-gum context in which we operated—though I had days, God knows, when I wondered about this, too."[91]

Like Hall, Julia makes a similar breakthrough, appearing on the cover of a magazine and establishing a career as a model. Hall is proud of her as he is of his brother. Still, he cannot help but wonder why "our breakthroughs seemed to occur only on those levels where we were most speedily expendable and most easily manipulated. And a 'breakthrough' to what? I was beginning to be wary of these breakthroughs, was not certain I wanted a lifetime pass to Disneyland."[92] Regardless of his misgivings, with Arthur's ascent, that is in essence what he gets. He is along for the ride, for better or worse. With Arthur's fame comes wealth, and a new life for him and Hall alike. Hall notes that "during one of Arthur's more spectacular years" he is able to buy a nice home in the affluent suburbs near Yonkers. He describes the suburbs as "a placid and terrifying landscape."[93] As he drives home, the bumper sticker on a car in front of him reads: AMERICA: LOVE IT OR LEAVE IT.[94] Observing the clean, quiet streets, he writes: "There is something unreal, then, about the reality of this beauty . . . a mask, a disguise, a lie. . . . [I]t was never intended that *we* should live here."[95]

Yet there they are, along with thousands of other middle- and upper-class African Americans throughout the country, trying to navigate their own version of the American Dream. In a revealing scene, the family is heading to the city to see a matinee showing of *The Wiz*.[96] The Broadway production of *The Wiz* was an African American re-telling of *The Wonderful Wizard of Oz*, featuring an all-black cast, with music and lyrics by Charlie Smalls. The 1975 Broadway production was popular among critics and the public alike, and received a number of awards, including Tony Awards for Best Musical and Best Original Score. It was subsequently adapted into a major motion picture in 1978, featuring Diana Ross, Michael Jackson, Lena Horne, and Richard Pryor, and a score by Quincy Jones. The film was co-produced by Motown Productions and Universal Pictures, and symbolized in many ways the possibility of cross-racial collaboration in Hollywood. While the film ultimately disappointed at the box office (for many reasons not entirely unrelated to race), it represented a significant cultural moment, ushering in a new era of black visibility on the screen.

It also took one of America's most beloved (white) classics in literature and film, and transformed it through a different context: in place of its original white, rural setting in Kansas, *The Wiz* is all-black, urban, and set in New York City, making the film a distinct experience, with different voices, music, and themes. In one of the more powerful scenes, a young Michael Jackson, playing scarecrow, hangs on a cross, surrounded by black crows, while singing, "You Can't Win," a song that directly addresses the American Dream from a black perspective. Jackson's character, much like Arthur, hears the voices around him, some taunting, some cautionary, about his prospects. "You can't win, Chile, no/ You can't break even/ You can't get out of the game." The "game" can be interpreted as the crossover dream. Of course, the voice singing these lines, Michael Jackson, achieved the cross-over dream in an unprecedented way, and paid the price for it, living his final decades mired in controversy and dying prematurely at age fifty. While the specific circumstances are as various as the individuals, numerous other iconic black singers have met similarly tragic fates, from Prince and Whitney Houston, to Billie Holiday, Otis Redding, Jimi Hendrix, Dorothy Dandridge, Sam Cooke, Donny Hathaway, and Marvin Gaye. This is part of the context for James Baldwin's Arthur Montana. Each of these artists pioneered and triumphed—they broke barriers, crossed over, integrated, sold millions of records and tickets, and brought multiracial audiences together across America and around the world. So did Arthur. Yet for Hall (and Baldwin), premature death brings with it a sense of betrayal and desperation. When Hall sees his brother lying in a pool of blood in the opening pages of the novel, he finds that language simply cannot do his brother's life or death justice:

> He had been found lying in a pool of blood—why does one say a pool?—a storm, a violence, a miracle of blood. . . . *My* blood, my brother's blood, *my* blood, Arthur's blood. . . . Oh. Oh. Oh. Arthur. Speak. Speak. Speak. I know, I know . . . how you jived the people—but that's not really true, you didn't

really jive the people, you sang, you sang, and if there was any jiving done, the people jived you, my brother, because they didn't know that *they* were the song and the price of the song and the glory of the song: you sang.[97]

The Beat

For Baldwin, black music was always inextricably bound to suffering, to the blues. "The music begins on the auction block," he wrote.[98] This was part of what made the music so powerful. What enraged him, however, was the prospect that tragedy would be compounded with the even greater tragedy of having one's life, one's story, one's song—and by extension, the story of black music in America—deleted or distorted. Yet by 1979, his words about how people respond to and write about music takes on a more political dimension. As Hall explains it: "To overhaul a history, or to attempt to redeem it—which effort may or may not justify it—is not at all the same thing as the descent one must make in order to excavate a history. To be forced to excavate a history is, also, to repudiate the concept of history, and the vocabulary in which history is written; for the written history is, and must be, merely the vocabulary of power, and power is history's most seductively attired false witness."[99]

Black music, for Baldwin, told the true story of black America. "Music is our witness, and our ally," he writes in his 1979 essay, "Of the Sorrow Songs." "The 'beat' is the confession which recognizes, changes and conquers time."[100] Yet this story was too often reduced and simplified in print. As he wrote of Stevie Wonder, perhaps the most successful black artist of the 1970s: "It will take a long time before white America can understand what his music is about at all; it's almost like a code. They don't really know what Stevie is singing about or what Stevie is saying. They can't afford to know."[101] *Just Above My Head* represents Baldwin's best attempt at cracking the code and revealing its multifaceted meanings.

This is the history Baldwin acts as witness to in his final novel: the history of black popular music. The crossover dream, he recognizes, is forever linked with both audacity and tragedy, just as Martin Luther King's dream of an integrated country was. "And when the dream was slaughtered," he writes, "and all that love and labor seemed to have come to nothing, we scattered. . . . We knew where we had been, what we had tried to do, who had cracked, gone mad, died, or been murdered around us."[102] But ultimately, the struggle continued—and continues. "Not everything is lost: responsibility cannot be lost, it can only be abdicated. If one refuses abdication, one begins again."[103]

This was Baldwin's message at the cusp of a new era in American history. Begin again. The music goes on. "The dream was repudiated: so be it."[104] Cynicism and disillusionment are understandable, but too easy, and too negligent of music's capacity for survival and struggle and pain and transcendence, if not triumph. "Now," reflects Hall, "watching my children grow, old enough to have some sense of where I've been, having suffered enough to be no longer terrified of suffering, and knowing something of joy, too, I know that we must attempt to be responsible for what we know. Only this action moves us, without fear, into what we do not know, and what we do not know is limitless."[105]

2

Freaks in the Reagan Era

Androgyny and the American Ideal of Manhood

> Oh, towering Ronnie Reagan . . .
> Deeply beloved, winning man-child of the
> yearning Republic,
> From diaper to football field to Warner
> Brothers sound-stages,
> Be thou our grinning, gently phallic, Big Boy
> of all the ages.
> —James Baldwin, "Staggerlee Wonders," 1983

In late 1984, James Baldwin submitted an essay, "Freaks and the American Ideal of Manhood," to Walter Lowe Jr., the first African American editor of *Playboy* magazine. Its radical thesis—that misguided notions of masculinity were at the root of America's moral quandary—was new for Baldwin (at least in emphasis) and a direct challenge to the magazine's primary demographic.

Founded in 1953 by Hugh Hefner, *Playboy* originally targeted and appealed to white, heterosexual, middle- and upper-class male consumers, depicting a life of glamor, status, sophistication, and sexual freedom. As Elizabeth Fraterrigo notes in *Playboy and the Making of the Good Life in Modern America*, in the postwar era the magazine was considered the "premier arbiter of American beauty" and possessed "tremendous cultural power."[1]

For its critics, however, the magazine's elevation of men as swinging bachelors and women as objects of lust made it an egregious example of sexism in the media. Gloria Steinem, feminist activist and founding editor of *Ms.* magazine, responded to Hugh Hefner's claim that *Playboy* celebrated the beauty of the female body by countering: "There are times when a woman reading *Playboy* feels a little like a Jew reading a Nazi manual."[2] Its popularity, however, was in many ways connected to its reliance on sexual conventions and "girl next door" fantasies as well as its subversion of traditional racial, sexual, and gender constrictions.

Hefner's sense of the magazine's social and cultural role developed gradually. It began for the express purpose of offering "a little diversion from the anxieties of the Atomic Age."[3] Yet it didn't take long for the magazine and its "brand" to assume other roles. Although *Playboy* featured white women exclusively as centerfolds in its first decade, its late-night television program, *Playboy's Penthouse*, frequently included black entertainers like Sammy Davis Jr., Nat King Cole, Ella Fitzgerald, Sara Vaughn, and Ray Charles.[4] In the 1960s, *Playboy* became a prominent platform for interviews with major black figures, including Miles Davis, Martin Luther King Jr., and Malcolm X. In 1965, the first black playmate, Jennifer Jackson, appeared in the magazine. By the late 1960s, *Playboy* had established itself, somewhat strangely, as one of the premier popular magazines in the country for serious journalism on civil rights issues, featuring work by Alex Haley, James Farmer, and James Baldwin (Baldwin's first essay in the magazine, "The Uses of the Blues," appeared in 1964). In the 1970s, realizing that while the magazine often covered black issues and featured black writers, it had no editors of color, Hefner directly ordered his human resources department to "go out and find a black editor."[5] They found Walter Lowe, a talented young writer and editor from Chicago. Not long after he was hired, Lowe reached out to James Baldwin. They would work together on three major articles in the 1980s (all of which I analyze in this book), including Baldwin's award-winning 1981 piece about the Atlanta child murders, "The Evidence of Things Not Seen."[6]

Playboy, then, offered an odd juxtaposition of titillation, fantasy, serious journalism, and cultural commentary, illustrating many of the paradoxical possibilities and seductive illusions inherent in American popular culture. Baldwin's "Freaks and the American Ideal of Manhood" appeared in the January 1985 issue, which featured actress Goldie Hawn on the cover. His subject matter was aimed squarely at the magazine's readership. What did it mean to be a man? How was masculinity represented in films, television, ads, and celebrity culture? How did it converge with race and sexuality? And what were its implications for the nation as a whole?

The article situates such questions in the context of the 1980s, offering a confessional account of Baldwin's own complicated sexual coming-of-age, framed by a broader social and cultural exploration of what it means to be a man in America. While not immediately recognized as such, "Freaks" has become one of his most widely regarded and cited essays. It offers some of the clearest evidence against the conventional wisdom that the author was in decline and no longer producing original work in the 1980s. Baldwin's interest in the subversive possibilities of androgyny aligned in many ways with the rising black feminist movement and anticipated subsequent developments in queer theory and cultural studies. Surveying the landscape of the Reagan era, he recognizes the tensions between the era's more traditional representations of masculinity (symbolized by President Reagan and many Hollywood blockbuster movies) and its queer alternatives (represented, among other ways, in the emerging New Pop Cinema). In place of America's longstanding myths about what a man should be, he calls for a new vision of identity, not constructed by fear of the Other or violent hierarchies, but by reciprocity, complexity, border crossing, and becoming.

Morning in America

"Masculinity," writes Abigail Solomon-Godeau, "however defined, is, like capitalism, *always* in crisis. And the real question is how both manage to restructure, refurbish, and resurrect themselves for the next historical turn."[7] It was certainly a relevant question at the dawn of the 1980s. By the end of the Carter presidency, the American ideal of manhood was perceived to be in trouble. Men had gone soft, the narrative went, and the nation, as a result, was weaker, more vulnerable, and uncertain. In the 1970s, explained Robert Bly, poet and leader of the mythopoetic men's movement, we "began to see all over the country a phenomenon that we might call the 'soft male.' . . . [T]hey're not interested in harming the earth or starting wars. There's a gentle attitude toward life in their whole being and style of living. But many of these men are not happy."[8] This unhappiness, Bly elaborated, had to do with no longer having role models, in the home or in popular culture, of strong, authentic masculinity. Instead, argued Bly, we saw everywhere domesticated, emasculated men. White men in particular felt anxious about their new roles in the wake of inroads by minorities, feminists, and gays. Far from being "Masters of the Universe," a term popularized in the 1980s to describe the hypermasculine hero (He-Man) of a children's cartoon series, as well as the Gordon Gekko–like characters in Tom Wolfe's novel *The Bonfire of the Vanities* (1987), many white men, in reality, no longer felt in control of the small orbit that was their lives. In 1979, film icon and conservative activist John Wayne died, symbolically representing the passing of a more traditional, triumphant vision of white masculinity.[9] What America lost and desperately needed again, Bly and others declared, were *real men*—men who reclaimed a "deep masculinity," a warrior mentality that had gone missing in post–civil rights culture.

For many, Ronald Reagan—voted the "most admired man in America" for eight consecutive years (1980–1988) in Gallup polls—answered the call.[10] Reagan's slogans called for a return to simpler times and ideals: traditional values, unambiguous strength, order and power. "No pale pastels," as he put it in a 1975 CPAC speech.[11] At home and abroad, clear distinctions were made between us and them, good and evil, tough and weak. It was a bridge back to an idealized, pre–civil rights Golden Age—before the Vietnam War and Watergate, before the assassinations, riots, and protests of the 1960s, before the inroads of the racial and sexual revolutions—to a time when men were men, when main streets were safe and white, and no one could doubt America's strength and power.[12] Reagan's famous 1984 campaign commercial declared that it was "morning in America"—only the morning was mythologized so as to be eternal and universal. This is the way things were, are, and should always be, it suggested. The reality it presented was exclusively white, suggesting whiteness was synonymous not only with wholesomeness, hard work, and integrity, but with Americanness itself. It also offered clearly demarcated, heteronormative gender roles, culminating in a traditional marriage between a white man and white woman. Reagan's America was "prouder and stronger and better," the ad declared, because it "returned" us to the way things were.[13]

For James Baldwin, seductive as this worldview might be, it was a fantasy—a fantasy America had been telling itself for decades while evading its more complex realities. "Reagan is a symptom of the American panic just as

Maggie Thatcher is a symptom of the British panic," he wrote. "They want to thrust themselves, you and me, back into the past."[14] Reagan's "Morning in America" was nowhere close to the world Baldwin grew up in, nor was it the reality Baldwin witnessed in the 1980s. "There is an unadmitted icy panic coiled beneath the scaffolding of these present days," he wrote in his 1984 preface to *Notes of a Native Son*.[15] The country, Baldwin recognized, had changed—just not in the ways most Americans assumed. For all of the country's institutional, sociopolitical, and technological advances, Baldwin contended that America's dominant narratives remained much the same.

Freaks

At the root of America's failure to mature as a country, Baldwin argues in "Freaks," are the mostly unacknowledged ways in which racial anxieties overlap with issues of gender, sexuality, desire, and power. "There seems to be a vast amount of confusion in the Western world concerning these matters," he writes.[16] Part of this confusion had to do with the tendency to reduce all concepts to simplistic either/or categories. For Baldwin, these binaries pervaded the American psyche and its resulting myths, narratives, and representations: there were "cowboys and Indians, good guys and bad guys, punks and studs, tough guys and softies, butch and faggot, black and white."[17] Such a rigidly bifurcated view of identity, Baldwin argues, is so "paralytically infantile that it is virtually forbidden—as an unpatriotic act—that the American boy evolve into the complexity of manhood."[18] How, he wondered, was it possible for a black man—indeed, any individual—to escape, resist, or reimagine these limiting types?

In a 1983 conversation with Audre Lorde at Hampshire College, excerpted in *Essence* in 1984, the two authors grappled with this very question. In a passionate but civil exchange, Lorde lays out some of the most pressing concerns of black feminists, directly challenging Baldwin and other black male writers to get on board. "I accept [the challenge]," Baldwin says.[19] While at times slipping into defensive, patriarchal positions, he shows a genuine desire to listen to women's concerns and tackle the problems accompanying American masculinity: "I don't quite know what to do about it, but I agree with you," he says. "And I understand exactly what you mean. You're quite right. We get confused with genders—you know, what the western notion of woman is, which is not necessarily what a woman is at all. It's certainly not the African notion of what a woman is. Or even the European notion of what a woman is. And there's certainly not a standard of masculinity in this country which anybody can respect. Part of the horror of being a Black American is being trapped into being an imitation of an imitation."[20] Lorde responds: "I can't tell you what I wished you would be doing. I can't redefine masculinity. I can't redefine Black masculinity certainly. I am in the business of redefining Black womanness. You are in the business of redefining Black masculinity. And I'm saying, 'Hey, please go on doing it,' because I don't know how much longer I can hold this fort, and I really feel that Black women are holding it and we're beginning to hold it in ways that are making this dialogue less possible."[21] In many ways this plea seems to be the direct inspiration for the subject matter of "Freaks and the American Ideal of Manhood," which was written soon after the conversation.

"Freaks," however, was also a kind of sequel to Baldwin's often-over-looked 1949 essay, "Preservation of Innocence," Baldwin's first text to deal primarily with homosexuality, gender labels, and the fallacy of "natural," essentialist roles. Indeed, while Baldwin frequently explored homosexuality in his fiction, "Freaks" and "Preservation of Innocence" are two of only three essays (the third, "The Male Prison," was originally published in the *New Leader* in 1954). Of the three, "Freaks" offers by far the most personal and developed analysis of sexuality and masculinity. It also offers his most compelling thesis: that in spite of received dualistic expectations about what it means to be a boy or girl, man or woman, we are all in fact *both*. This notion of "androgyny," as he terms it, does not obviously mean that everyone is biologically both male and female, but that the "hermaphrodite reveals in intimidating exaggeration, the truth concerning every human being—which is why the hermaphrodite is called a freak."[22] The androgyne, similarly, evokes both fascination and fear in American culture—fascination because she/he seems exotic and different, and fear because he/she feels uncomfortably familiar. In embodying a liminal space "in the middle," in ambiguity, the androgyne becomes problematic for those invested in protecting established borders of identity. Baldwin's essay, however, is not just about the androgynes we think we see. It doesn't require that a man wear eyeliner or a woman have short hair. Regardless of one's physical appearance or perceived characteristics, he argues, "there is a man in every woman and a woman in every man. . . . The last time you had a drink, whether you were alone or with another, you were having a drink with an androgynous human being."[23] That is, even the most masculine figures, whether or not they reveal or understand it, contain the "spiritual resources" of both genders. "I know," says Baldwin, "that the macho men—truck drivers, cops, football players—these people are far more complex than they want to realize."[24]

Baldwin transitions from this brief opening thesis on androgyny and its implications to relaying fragments of his own complicated past, and how he came to identify and be identified as a "freak." Growing up in Harlem, young Baldwin, we learn, was the victim of multiple forms of abuse. "My father," he writes, "beat me with an iron cord from the kitchen to the back room and back again, until I lay, half-conscious, on my belly on the floor."[25] Such experiences were among his first lessons about what it meant to be a man. Men were violent, and so too was America. "This violence, furthermore," reflects Baldwin, "is not merely literal and actual but appears to be admired and lusted after, and the key to the American imagination."[26] For Baldwin, then, the personal violence he experienced in his home and on the streets was intertwined with the violence that led to state-sanctioned brutality, nuclear standoffs, and imperialist wars.

At a young age, Baldwin was also made to feel ugly by his father and by the gaze of white society. His narrative of internalized insecurity about his physical appearance is a story that is typically gendered female (as in, for example, Toni Morrison's 1970 novel, *The Bluest Eye*). But Baldwin shows that such experiences are not confined to one gender. From very early in his life, he believed he was ugly and that his ugliness was critically linked to his identity and worth. "This meant that the idea of myself as a sexual possibility, or target, as a creature capable of desire, had never entered my mind," he writes.[27] It finally did enter his mind, he reveals, when he was molested as a young boy by a stranger who "lured me into a hallway, saying that he wanted to send me to the store."[28] It was the last time, Baldwin writes, he ever ran an errand for a stranger.

Baldwin's understanding of his sexual, gender, and racial identity continued under the menacing surveillance of society, for whom he was the "punch line of a dirty joke," a social pariah, a subhuman.[29] "The condition," he explains, "that is now called gay was then called queer. The operative word was *faggot* and, later, pussy, but those epithets really had nothing to do with the question of sexual preference: You were being told simply that you had no balls."[30] This emasculation had profound psychological effects. Young Baldwin was chased, bullied, and taunted. He was thrown out of cafeterias and rooming houses. He was told he was bad for the neighborhood. "The cops," Baldwin recalls, "watched all this with a smile, never making the faintest motion to protect me or to disperse my attackers; in fact, I was even more afraid of the cops than I was of the populace.[31] Later in life he was also stalked by the FBI; in one report, director J. Edgar Hoover describes Baldwin as a "well-known pervert."[32] In his youth, Baldwin remembers frequently being compared to a woman, usually by more demeaning synonyms. "It seemed to me," he writes, "that many of the people I met were making fun of women, and I didn't see why. I certainly needed all the friends I could get, male *or* female, and women had nothing to do with whatever my trouble might prove to be."[33]

At age sixteen, Baldwin reveals, he developed a close, intimate relationship with an older Spanish-Irish man in Harlem. The man listened to his poetry and treated him kindly. "I will be grateful to that man until the day I die," he writes, while acknowledging how strange it must have appeared to see "stingy-brimmed, mustachioed, razor-toting Poppa, and skinny, popeyed me" together in "various shady joints."[34] Later, he would meet and fall in love with an Italian man in Greenwich Village who became the model for Giovanni in his second novel, *Giovanni's Room* (1956), and bring him a certain degree of contentment and security.

But mostly these were years of great terror and confusion for Baldwin. "The mirrors," he writes, "threw back only brief and distorted fragments of myself."[35] He describes himself as "eager, vulnerable and lonely."[36] His relationships with women—mostly white women from the Village—seemed predetermined, for the most part, by social scripts. They "paralyzed me," wrote Baldwin, "because I simply did not know what, apart from my sex, they wanted."[37] The gay world, however, could be equally confusing and perilous. He writes about being preyed on by other young boys and men in darkened theaters and restrooms, parks, and bars. Many of these men, he writes, "far from being or resembling faggots, looked and sounded like the vigilantes who banded together on weekends to beat faggots up. . . . These men looked like cops, football players, soldiers, sailors, Marines or bank presidents, admen, boxers, construction workers; they had wives, mistresses, and children."[38]

The hypocrisy was striking and left a lasting imprint. The same men who publicly condemned and tormented him, privately "spoke very gently and wanted me to take them home and make love."[39] What Baldwin learned, among other things, was that love—whether homosexual, heterosexual, or bisexual—when denied and repressed, still surfaced, only often as something more cruel and grotesque. "The male desire for a male roams everywhere," he wrote, "avid, desperate, unimaginably lonely, culminating often in drugs, piety, madness or death. It was also dreadfully like watching myself at the end of a long, slow-moving line: Soon I would be next."[40] How was real love and connection—not just for gay men but for anyone—possible, he wondered, in a society that distorted, disciplined and punished its expression—indeed, the very idea of it? Baldwin "escaped," at least for the time being, by moving to Paris; but the problem of American masculinity, which, as he learned, was not disconnected from Europe, haunted him for the rest of his life.

The autobiographical passages of "Freaks" document a painful coming-of-age story. The result of such experiences, Baldwin writes, "is that all of the American categories of male and female, straight or not, black or white, were shattered, thank heaven, very early in my life."[41] Identity and desire, he asserts, are not the simple polarities the dominant culture pretends are "normal." The norm is, in reality, simply a cloak to disguise complexity and transgression (though its gatekeepers and police deny it). "That's why I call them infantile," said Baldwin in a 1984 interview. "They have needs which, for them, are literally inexpressible. They don't dare look into the mirror. And that is why they need faggots. They've created faggots in order to act out a sexual fantasy on the body of another man and not take any responsibility for it. . . . It's a way of controlling people."[42]

This control, however, comes at a great cost. While the subject may be able to resist, in certain ways, interpellation, "we all exist," he writes, "crucially in the eye of the beholder. . . . This judgment begins in the eyes of one's parents (the crucial, the definitive, the all-but everlasting judgment), and so we move, in the vast and claustrophobic gallery of Others, on up or down the line, to the eye of one's enemy or one's friend or one's lover."[43] Social transformation, that is, was contingent on psychological transformation, and vice versa, which revealed why the loop was so difficult to rupture.

After a deep dive into his past in the detailed middle portion of "Freaks," Baldwin explains that while he seems "to have strayed a long way" from his subject, his broader concern is "social and historical—and continuous."[44] The circumstances of his childhood, that is, were not disconnected from the cultural milieu of the 1980s. The same logic and forces he saw at work in his early childhood, he saw recirculating in films and TV shows, pageants, and media narratives. America, it seemed, was the nation that never grew up, and as Baldwin once warned, "anyone who insists on remaining in a state of innocence long after that innocence is dead turns himself into a monster."[45]

Hard Bodies/Soft Bodies

The late 1970s and early 1980s are often referred to as the "era of the blockbuster." Films such as *Jaws*, *Star Wars*, *Indiana Jones*, *Back to the Future*, and *Rambo* were not simply films; they were franchises with accompanying "product," from action figures to video games to amusement-park rides. From a corporate standpoint, the beauty of a blockbuster was in how many different ways it could be exploited for profit. The film itself was simply one stream of income. All of the ancillary markets had the potential to generate unprecedented amounts of revenue, not to mention cultural capital. This transformation had profound implications for the film industry in terms of distribution as well as content.

Film critics have generally characterized the blockbusters of the late 1970s and early 1980s as ideologically conservative, a sweeping assessment that has only recently begun to find critical dissent.[46] The conventional wisdom, however, isn't without basis. Many of the era's biggest films reinforced traditional notions of gender, race, and nation. The biggest box office stars of the period were figures like Clint Eastwood, Burt Reynolds, Harrison Ford, Sylvester Stallone, Bruce Willis, and Arnold Schwarzenegger. For the most part, they played cowboys and boxers, cops and renegades, military men and cyborg assassins. They toted guns and battled enemies. They exuded superhero-like strength. The common thread between all of these characters was their whiteness and their hypermasculinity.

In her 1993 book, *Hard Bodies: Hollywood Masculinity in the Reagan Era*, Susan Jeffords reads Hollywood's representations of men in the 1980s as a reflection of the president himself. Reagan presented himself as a stolid, wholesome, paternal figurehead; he and his conservative allies contrasted his masculine image with the soft, "feminine" Jimmy Carter. Where Carter was ineffectual, measured, and compassionate, conservatives argued, Reagan was a "real man": aggressive, straightforward, tough. "Reagan," writes Jeffords, "became the premiere masculine archetype for the 1980s."[47] Reagan, of course, was also a literal product of Hollywood, having acted in more than thirty Warner Bros. films in addition to numerous television appearances. As president, he frequently alluded to movies in his speeches, slogans, and policies, perhaps most notably in his characterization of the Soviet Union as the "Evil Empire," derived from *Star Wars*. His deftness at image making and storytelling earned him the nickname "the Great Communicator."

Reagan's manly, cowboy-like image and aggressive, "no pastels" policies both informed and were informed by a particular Hollywood vision of masculinity. As Jeffords puts it, "Ronald Reagan" and the "Reagan Revolution" became "sites" of a "national fantasy."[48] They spoke to how America—or at least many Americans—wanted to view themselves. The Reagan revolution wasn't just about policies; it was about images and narratives of strength, individualism, patriotic militarism, and unambiguous machismo. While Reagan embodied more than he *caused* such narratives to exist, the corresponding representations of hypermasculinity in major early- to mid-1980s films are pervasive and instructive. Films such as *Rambo*, *Indiana Jones*, *Rocky*, and *The Terminator* became iconic in the American imagination. Susan Jeffords describes these as "hard-body films" whose heroes' conquests, triumphs, and domination appealed to individuals, and a nation, who wanted to feel powerful again. "The Reagan America," writes Jeffords, "was to be a strong one, capable of confronting enemies rather than submitting to them, of battling 'evil empires' rather than allowing them to flourish, of using its hardened body—its renewed techno-military network—to impose its will on others rather than allow itself to be dictated to."[49] It is important to recognize the ubiquitous presence of these images and narratives in 1980s Hollywood cinema and the myths they sustained and perpetuated.

However, it is also important to recognize, as Baldwin does, alternative representations to these traditional American masculinities and how and what they signified. What was one to make, after all, of the presence of groups like Culture Club and the Eurythmics on mainstream radio and TV in an era supposedly dominated by Reagan archetypes? Or of the thoroughly gender-bending *Purple Rain* outperforming the hypermasculine *The Terminator* at the box office in 1985? The 1980s produced remarkably contradictory convergences of opposites, as, for example, when Boy George appeared on CBS's *Face the Nation* alongside Jerry Falwell in a 1984 special on "androgyny," "sexual ambiguity," and the "feminizing of society"; or when Michael Jackson visited the White House to receive an award from President Reagan for his efforts to prevent drunk driving.[50] The visual could not have been more striking: Reagan was old and white; Jackson was young and black. Reagan was dressed in a dark corporate suit, white shirt and tie; Jackson wore a sparkling blue French military jacket with gold trim, high-water black pants, white socks, aviator sunglasses, and, of course, his signature sequined glove. Reagan was unambiguously masculine; Jackson was the definition of androgyny.[51] The picture of the two icons side by side—probably the two most famous figures of the 1980s—illustrates the tensions, paradoxes, and competing visions of masculinity that persisted throughout the decade.

From Jackson and Boy George, to Prince, David Bowie, George Michael, and Freddie Mercury, the 1980s was a time of unprecedented mainstream "gender bending." Female artists such as Madonna, Annie Lennox, Grace Jones, Pat Benatar, and Janet Jackson also openly experimented with and transgressed gender expectations. For a wave of 1980s artists, the androgynous "look" and performance was a way of signifying a rejection of traditional roles and scripts. In "Freaks and the American Ideal of Manhood," Baldwin describes this new "androgynous craze" in positive terms. It was, he felt, an "attempt to be honest concerning one's nature," a symbolic outward demonstration of an internal reality not confined to eccentric pop stars, but to everyone.[52] "Such figures as Boy George," he writes, "do not disturb me nearly so much as do those relentlessly hetero (sexual?) keepers of the keys and seals, those who know what the world needs in the way of order and who are ready and willing to supply that order."[53]

In stark contrast to the muscular macho figures in *Rambo*, *Rocky*, and *The Terminator* (or the hypermasculine heroes of the Blaxploitation era), these "other" male leads were androgynous, theatrical, and lithe. In place of typical male uniforms, they wore an array of spectacular, colorful costumes; in place of guns and ammo, they wore eyeliner and rouge; in place of violence and aggression, they demonstrated vulnerability, sensitivity, and the value of creative resolution.

What appealed to Baldwin in particular about the wave of androgynous males was its de-emphasis of the actual act of sex, and its performance of gender as multifaceted, fluid, and individualized. He rejected the notion that one's identity was confined by static either/or categories (gay/straight, black/white, male/female), seeing subjectivity, like Stuart Hall, as an ever-mutating process of becoming, fashioned through "memory, fantasy, narrative and myth."[54] Physical androgyny became a kind of embodied resistance to dominant representations of masculinity and gender, allowing men and women alike to traverse socially circumscribed boundaries. Such performances came through less in traditional Hollywood films as in a particular new aesthetic of music videos and music films that exploded in the early 1980s: what I describe as the *New Pop Cinema*.

The New Pop Cinema was not simply an umbrella for every video that appeared on MTV. Many MTV videos, after all, reinforced the same problematic notions of race, gender, and sexuality as traditional Hollywood films. MTV initially refused to feature black artists on its network by policy.[55] It also featured numerous videos with degrading and misogynistic representations of women. The New Pop Cinema, however, transformed the visual space by placing African Americans, women, and queer artists at the forefront, including dynamic pop superstars like Michael Jackson, Madonna, Prince, Janet Jackson, and George Michael. As important as were their identities, the alternative idea(l)s they communicated and the alternative methods they used to communicate them were just as meaningful. Among the most crucial features of the New Pop Cinema was dance. Dance was the antithesis of rigidity, machismo, and conservatism. It was about movement, fluidity, liberation. Interestingly, the identity group most averse to dance as a legitimate element of film or music videos comprised heteronormative white men.[56] Indeed, in music, likewise, dance was largely absent from mainstream rock. Rock critics tended to look at dance music with condescension, while rock programmers found ways to marginalize it by race or gender and keep it off the AOR airwaves. Dance music, it was argued, lacked substance and authenticity. It was emotional, not cerebral. It appealed to blacks, gays, women, and other minorities. The New Pop Cinema accentuated dance, movement, and "queer" bodies. These performances were displayed in mostly short, five-minute clips, though some stretched as long as traditional feature films. They were in some ways the offspring of the old MGM musicals. What distinguished them, however, and gave them a younger, edgier feel was their hybridity: of different genres and styles; of race, gender, and sexuality; of high art and low art; of avant-garde experimentation and mass commercial appeal. While they signified on 1950s-era musicals, that is, they signified with a *difference*.

Perhaps the most well-known film of this movement, Michael Jackson's *Thriller* (1983) is often considered in relation to music videos and MTV, but it was also arguably the most successful black *film* in history. *Thriller* premiered at the Metro Crest Theatre in Los Angeles on November 14, 1983, attended by some of the biggest stars in Hollywood. Its television premiere was a cultural event, watched by people of all demographics across the country. A film that self-consciously explores the mutability of identity and identification, it presented a black man on screen in a way never seen before. In contrast to the respectable, liberal-integrationist, decidedly masculine characters played by actors like Sidney Poitier in the 1960s, or the violent, macho "hard body" Blaxploitation films that dominated the 1970s, Jackson's four-character performance in *Thriller*, alternately androgynous, graceful, grotesque, playful, queer, and mysterious, utterly destabilizes essentialist identities. It also, as Kobena Mercer notes in his excellent 1985 essay, "Monster Metaphors," "makes a mockery out of the menagerie of received images of masculinity," coyly playing with assumptions of gender and sexuality.[57] As Jackson himself famously acknowledges in the video, "I'm not like other guys." *Thriller* reached an unprecedented audience size—at least as much as the biggest blockbusters of the decade. Beyond its large and enthusiastic theater and cable television audiences, *The Making of Thriller* home video became the bestselling home video of all time, selling an estimated 10 million VHS copies.

One year later, in 1984, the full-length musical feature *Purple Rain*, starring Prince, reached number 1 at the box office and grossed over $80 million. With *Purple Rain*, Prince became the first artist since the Beatles to have the number 1 film, album, and single at the same time. Like *Thriller*, *Purple Rain* challenged traditional scripts for black masculinity, presenting a son trying to break the patriarchal pattern of abuse and domination set by his father. Prince's character ("The Kid") is a kind of modern-day dandy: unabashedly eccentric, spectacularly costumed, and fluidly moving from traditionally masculine to feminine traits. In his performance of the song, "I Would Die For U," he challenges the very idea of fixed gender roles, singing, "I'm not a woman/ I'm not a man/ I am something that you'll never understand." His stage performances, in which his relatively diminutive body is often exposed and exhibited, achieve the exact opposite of the "hard body" Hollywood blockbusters, expressing vulnerability, internal struggle, and passion over strength, power, and domination. In addition, Prince's band, the Revolution, in contrast to traditional homogenous rock bands, features women as well as men, black as well as white, gay as well as heterosexual (and members who, like Prince, blur the line between these categories). The New Pop Cinema, then, led by films like *Thriller* and *Purple Rain*, had a profound cultural impact and helped pioneer a new subversive film aesthetic in which blackness and queer masculinity played a central role.

Backlash

By 1985, however—the year Baldwin published "Freaks"—a severe backlash had begun against the "androgynous craze" that had invaded popular music and music videos. White America turned increasingly to "real," authentic, heteronormative rock icons like Bruce Springsteen, whose album *Born in the U.S.A.* became the bestselling album that year. While Springsteen was politically liberal, he fit more easily into traditional boxes of how men were supposed to look and act. He was white, straight, masculine, blue collar, had a raspy voice, and played guitar. On the cover of his 1984 album, Springsteen is depicted from behind, flanked by an American flag, wearing a white T-shirt (accentuating his biceps) and Levi's, with a faded red hat tucked in his rear pocket. Visually, he looked like he was pulled straight out of Reagan's "Morning in America" ad. Reagan must have thought the same thing as he began appropriating the singer—and his anthemic title track—as a patriotic rallying call for American pride (against Springsteen's wishes).[58] "There is not a smidgen of androgyny in Springsteen, who, rocketing around the stage in a T-shirt and headband, resembles Robert DeNiro in the combat scenes of *The Deerhunter*," championed conservative columnist George Will. "I have not got a clue about Springsteen's politics, if any, but flags get waved at his concerts while he sings songs about hard times. He is no whiner, and the recitation of closed factories and other problems always seems punctuated by a grand, cheerful affirmation: 'Born in the U.S.A.!'"[59] Regardless of Springsteen's intentions for the song, he became, as Bryan Garman observes, "for many Americans a white hard-bodied hero whose masculinity confirmed the values of patriarchy and patriotism, work ethic and rugged individualism, and who clearly demarcated the boundaries between men and women, black and white, heterosexual and homosexual."[60]

As Springsteen was elevated, Michael Jackson, who had become the most famous embodiment of androgyny, was dismantled. Evangelical leader Jerry Falwell claimed Jackson's "projection of a femaleness" presented "a very bad role model for the millions of children who literally idolize" him, and would cause "wreckage" in their lives.[61] Toward the end of 1984, Jackson was compelled to issue a public statement that pushed back against rumors that he was gay, that he had taken hormones to make his voice higher, and that he had undergone surgery to appear more like a woman (a prominent theory at the time was that he wanted to look like Diana Ross). The sudden contempt directed at Jackson, of course, wasn't just about his "feminine" persona. From 1980 to 1985, Jackson experienced one of the most stratospheric rises in entertainment history. Not only did he resurrect the dire financial prospects of CBS/Epic and MTV and generate a personal fortune through his own record-breaking albums, videos, and world tours, he also made shrewd business decisions, retaining full ownership of his master recordings and actively acquiring publishing rights, including the crown jewel of popular music, the ATV/Beatles catalog (purchased in 1985). According to *Forbes* journalist Zack O'Malley Greenburg, Jackson earned an estimated $1.1 billion over the course of his solo career ($2 billion adjusted for inflation) from record deals, publishing royalties, endorsements, and tours.[62]

Jackson, then, had become a major figure in the industry, and likely the most powerful black man in the history of American entertainment to that point. Observing this unprecedented rise and the early stages of the backlash, James Baldwin wrote in "Freaks" in 1985:

> The Michael Jackson cacophony is fascinating in that it is not about Jackson at all. I hope he has the good sense to know it and the good fortune to snatch his life out of the jaws of a carnivorous success. He will not swiftly be forgiven for having turned so many tables, for he damn sure grabbed the brass ring, and the man who broke the bank at Monte Carlo has nothing on Michael. All that noise is about America, as the dishonest custodian of black life and wealth; the blacks, especially males, in America; and the burning, buried American guilt; and sex and sexual roles and sexual panic; money, success and despair.[63]

Baldwin proved prophetic. It wasn't long after the successes of *Thriller* (including a record haul of eight Grammy Awards in February 1984) that the tide began to turn against Jackson for all the reasons Baldwin describes. In 1986, journalist Quincy Troupe (incidentally, the last person to interview James Baldwin) described the post-*Thriller* aftermath as "the most powerful backlash in the history of popular entertainment."[64] Having proved he was not merely in the show but in show business (to paraphrase James Brown's famous saying), Jackson could no longer be perceived as a mere innocent "man-child" or eccentric artist. What he came to represent, as Baldwin suggests, was enormously complicated. It was about money, status, and power, but it was also about race and race's convergence with queer masculinity and sexuality. For the "keepers of the keys and seals" Jackson was a "freak"; but he was a very powerful and influential freak. In his 1996 essay, "The Celebrity Freak: Michael Jackson's Grotesque Glory," David Yuan argues that Michael Jackson became the defining "freak" of the late twentieth century.[65] No other public figure evoked the same level of ridicule, scrutiny, and hyperinterrogation. "Jackson's queerness," observes Susan Fast, "was quickly turned from utopia to dystopia by the mass media; before any of it could be interrogated or celebrated, it was deemed pathological and then linked to criminality."[66] Indeed, if Reagan was the most "admired" man in America for eight consecutive years, Jackson was undoubtedly the most voyeuristically examined and pathologized. By the mid-1980s the media began referring to him as "Wacko Jacko," a diminutive title with racist roots.[67] Defying far too many scripts for a black man (or a black entertainer, for that matter), Jackson became, in the American imagination, a spectacle, a high-tech minstrel show.[68] In this way, he was, for Baldwin already in 1985, a tragic large-scale example of what results when a black subject defies his "place."

The backlash against Jackson and androgyny more generally, however, was not confined to white America. In a 1984 broadcast that made national news headlines, Louis Farrakhan warned that the image Jackson and other black androgynous artists like him projected "ruins young men and makes your young women have nothing to look up to as a *real man*."[69] Farrakhan conceded that Jackson was a "marvelous performer" but claimed his "female-acting, sissified-acting expression is not wholesome for our young boys, nor our young girls."[70] Farrakhan was not alone in this assessment. Many others in the black community, including prominent music critic Nelson George, expressed concerns about Jackson's (and Prince's) "disquieting androgyny," which he conflated with "racial treason."[71] For George, Jackson embodied an "alarmingly un-black, unmasculine figure" that signaled the death of traditional R&B.[72] In this way, racial authenticity was often intertwined with gender expectations.[73]

For Baldwin, then, the backlash to Jackson—coming from both black and white, male and female, conservative and liberal—was about far more than surface-level eccentricities or shifting tastes in music. It was even about far more than Michael Jackson. Rather, it was about what Jackson represented—and what (and who) his presence threatened. "Freaks," as Baldwin put it, "are called freaks and are treated as they are treated—in the main, abominably—because they are human beings who cause to echo, deep within us, our most profound terrors and desires."[74]

Here Be Dragons

To the end of his life, Baldwin attempted to force a confrontation between America's myths and realities. If the country were to change (a tenuous qualifier for Baldwin), it would not happen merely by moderate concessions in laws and institutions; its language, stories, images, and consciousness needed to change. His variation of "protest" required an insistence that the Other be recognized as more than a cause or a problem, a phantom of fear or projection of panic. As Baldwin explains by way of analogy in "Freaks":

> Ancient maps of the world—when the world was flat—inform us, concerning that void where America was waiting to be discovered, HERE BE DRAGONS. Dragons may not have been here then, but they are certainly here now, breathing fire, belching smoke; or, to be less literary and biblical about it, attempting to intimidate the mores, morals, and morality of this particular and peculiar time and place. Nor, since this country is the issue of the entire globe and is also the most powerful nation currently to be found on it, are we speaking only of this time and place. And it can be said that the monumental struggles being waged in our time and not only in this place resemble, in awesome ways, the ancient struggle between those who insisted that the world was flat and those who apprehended that it was round.[75]

Baldwin's "map" metaphor draws attention to the connections between race, masculinity, and nationalism. Powerful nations like America, he suggests, define themselves (like identities) by arbitrary and oppressive borders and by fear of the unknown ("Here be dragons!"). In shattering America's self-image as exceptional model (and distributor) of democratic values, he critiques imperialism as a white masculine delusion as misguided as "those who insisted that the world was flat."[76]

The "ancient struggle," for Baldwin, was finally about how reality was represented—both within and across borders—and this struggle, as Stuart Hall puts it, is always already unfolding, "subject to the continuous play of history, culture and power."[77] "It's a fascinating time to be living," Baldwin told an interviewer from the *Paris Review* in 1984. "There's a whole wide world which isn't now as it was when I was younger. When I was a kid the world was white, for all intents and purposes, and now it is struggling to *remain* white—a very different thing."[78] In "Freaks," Baldwin described and critiqued a nation also desperately struggling to remain—or rescue—its manhood. Those who crossed borders, those who occupied that liminal space "in between," incited panic precisely because they exposed the lie that propped up Reagan's black and white fantasy. But the inconvenient truth, Baldwin concludes, is that "we are all androgynous . . . each of us, helplessly and forever, contains the other—male in female, female in male, white in black and black in white. . . . We are part of each other."[79]

Photographed here in London's Hyde Park, Baldwin had fallen out of favor with critics in the post–civil right era. It was his work in the mid- to late 1960s and 1970s, however—including the photo-text book with Richard Avedon, *Nothing Personal* (1965), a screenplay on Malcolm X, and a book of film criticism, *The Devil Finds Work* (1976)—that marked his "cultural turn." That cultural focus remained the defining feature of his work in the 1980s. (Credit: Allan Warren, Creative Commons Attribution-ShareAlike 3.0 Unported [CC BY-SA 3.0] license)

Baldwin flashing his signature gap-toothed smile. While he acknowledged having many reasons to be bitter and was accused by critics of succumbing to pessimism, Baldwin said he remained optimistic about the 1980s—and the future more generally. "That doesn't mean it's going to be easy. But I'm far from being in despair. We cannot afford despair." (Credit: Allan Warren, Creative Commons Attribution-ShareAlike 3.0 Unported [CC BY-SA 3.0] license)

Baldwin speaking at Hampshire College in 1984. In 1983, Baldwin accepted a position as visiting professor of literature at the five-college consortium of liberal arts colleges in Western Massachusetts: Amherst, Hampshire, Mount Holyoke, Smith, and UMass Amherst. For the next three years—from 1983 to 1986—Baldwin lived primarily in Pelham, Massachusetts, and taught a variety of courses in alternating semesters, mostly at Hampshire College and UMass Amherst. (Credit: Hampshire College Archives & Special Collections)

Baldwin at Hampshire College. In spite of his waning health and personal challenges, Baldwin found working with students invigorating. (Credit: Michael Zide)

Baldwin said of his final years: "I would like to use the time that's left to change the world, to teach children or to convey to the people who have children that everything that lives is holy." (Credit: Michael Zide)

The official portrait of President Ronald Reagan. Reagan won massive electoral victories in 1980 and 1984, but his optimistic vision for America, for Baldwin, failed to acknowledge the realities on the ground. (Credit: Ronald Reagan Library)

Pictured here as a rugged cowboy, Ronald Reagan was voted the most admired man in America for eight consecutive years, from 1980 to 1988. Baldwin offered his most compelling critique of American masculinity in his 1985 essay, "Freaks and the American Ideal of Manhood." (Credit: Ronald Reagan Library)

Michael Jackson and Ronald Reagan emerge from the White House, where Jackson received an award for his efforts in support of a national campaign against drunk driving. The image of Reagan and Jackson not only highlights two of the era's most influential figures, but also offers two striking contrasts of masculinity. In "Freaks and the American Ideal of Manhood," Baldwin, predicting the backlash to Jackson's difference and power, predicted that the artist "will not swiftly be forgiven for having turned so many tables." (Credit: Ronald Reagan Library)

Rock Hudson with Ronald and Nancy Reagan in 1984. Fellow Hollywood stars, Hudson and Reagan were longtime friends. Just one year after this photo was taken, Hudson died of AIDS. His death marked a turning point in public awareness of the AIDS crisis. (Credit: Ronald Reagan Library)

Baldwin's home in Saint-Paul-de-Vence, France. The author purchased the home as a refuge following the assassinations of Martin Luther King Jr., Malcolm X, and Medgar Evers—not only for himself, but for his many guests. The home plays a key role in his unpublished play, *The Welcome Table*, in which visitors of all nationalities, races, classes, genders, and sexual orientations could find acceptance and "lay down their souls." (Credit: Daniel Salomons, Creative Commons CC0 1.0 Universal [CC0 1.0] Public Domain Dedication)

A 1986 Gay Pride Parade at city hall in San Francisco. As devastating as the AIDS crisis was, it galvanized the LGBTQ community. By the end of the 1980s, hundreds of support groups and political-action networks had emerged, HIV treatment had improved dramatically, and billions of dollars were raised for AIDS research, treatment, and education. (Credit: Alan Light, Creative Commons Attribution 2.0 Generic [CC BY 2.0] license)

Pictured here in 1996, the year it hosted the summer Olympics, Atlanta was heralded as a beacon of the "New South," a city, as one slogan put it, "too busy to hate." Beneath the surface, however, the picture was much darker and more complex. Baldwin believed the Atlanta child murders exposed the ugly truth, not only about Atlanta or the Deep South, but American cities more broadly in the Reagan era. (Credit: Joseph Pittelli, U.S. Air Force)

Perhaps the most influential figure from the religious Right, Jerry Falwell built a multimedia empire in the 1980s, founding Liberty University, the Moral Majority, the television and radio program *Old Time Gospel Hour*, and appearing regularly on prime time news shows. He also played an important role in Ronald Reagan's elections in 1980 and 1984. Baldwin saw him as part of a disturbing trend in born-again Christianity that resembled "the richest, most exclusive private club in the world, a club that the man from Galilee could not possibly hope—or wish—to enter." (Credit: Liberty University, Creative Commons Attribution-ShareAlike 3.0 Unported [CC BY-SA 3.0] license)

A friend of Martin Luther King Jr. and James Baldwin, Andrew Young became mayor of Atlanta in 1981 at the height of the Atlanta child murders. He faced scrutiny for putting Atlanta's image and business interests ahead of the lives of poor black children, as well as for allowing Wayne Williams to serve as a convenient scapegoat for all the murders. Baldwin believed Young and other black leaders had themselves become scapegoats but acknowledged the legitimate exasperation and growing, class-based divisions within the black community. (Credit: Library of Congress)

A protest in Ferguson, Missouri, following the death of Mike Brown. Ferguson ignited Black Lives Matter, a nationwide movement against police violence and the ongoing devaluation and expendability of black life in America. Perhaps none of Baldwin's books speaks to the Black Lives Matter movement better than *The Evidence of Things Not Seen*. (Credit: Jamelle Bouie, Creative Commons Attribution 2.0 Generic [CC BY 2.0] license)

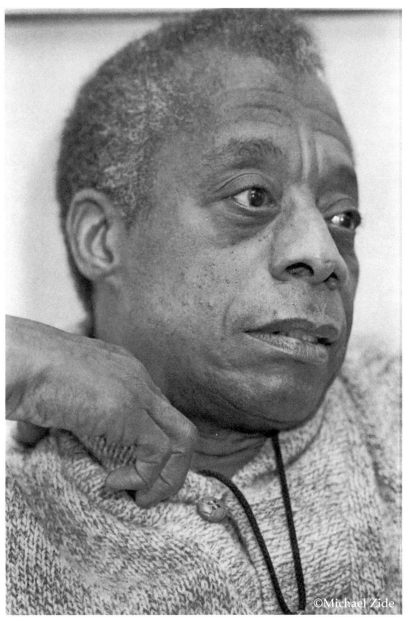

A close-up of Baldwin in 1984. As powerful as Reaganism was in the 1980s, Baldwin believed it was the responsibility of writers, artists, and conscientious citizens to offer their own "witness" of the America they saw and experienced. (Credit: Michael Zide)

3

The Welcome Table

Intimacy, AIDS, and Love

The theater will always remain a necessity.
One is not in the shadows, but responding to
one's flesh and blood: in the theater, we are
recreating each other.
—James Baldwin, *The Devil Finds Work*, 1976

Few events in the 1980s strained James Baldwin's inclusive vision in "Freaks and the American Ideal of Manhood" more than the AIDS epidemic. In the summer of 1981, the *New York Times* published its first article about the disease, claiming that "41 homosexuals" had been infected, and eight otherwise healthy gay men had already died.[1] The U.S. Centers for Disease Control (CDC) first called the disease GRID (gay-related immune deficiency); however, the name was soon changed to AIDS (acquired immune deficiency syndrome) to account for the fact that it was not found exclusively in gay men. The CDC listed four major risk groups: homosexual or bisexual males (75 percent); intravenous drug users (13 percent); hemophiliacs (0.3 percent); and Haitians (6 percent).[2] As more people in the gay community became aware of the seriousness of AIDS, they began searching for solutions. The Gay Men's Health Crisis was founded in 1982; in 1983, an AIDS clinic opened in San Francisco and U.S. Congress passed the first bill to include funding specifically targeted for AIDS research and treatment. That same year, the CDC created a hotline to respond to public inquiries about the disease. Still, by the middle of the decade, AIDS remained widely misunderstood, both within and without the gay community. There was great confusion about prevention and treatment, and increasing hysteria about the various ways the disease might be spread. It was the death of a celebrity—Hollywood actor Rock Hudson—that finally put the issue front and center in the national consciousness. In 1985, AIDS made the front page of both *Time* and *Newsweek*. "Now that the disease has come out of the closet, how far will it spread?" *Time*'s subhead asked ominously. The answer, tragically, was far and wide. By 1992, an estimated 230,000 Americans had died of the disease.[3] According to the World Health Organization, by 2016 more than 70 million people had been infected with the HIV virus globally and about 35 million people had died.[4]

What did James Baldwin have to say about the issue? As a prominent gay author, Baldwin has been criticized for his reluctance to be more outspoken about AIDS (and gay rights more generally) as he was for black civil rights in the 1960s. He was, however, abundantly clear about the legitimacy, dignity, and humanity of LGBTQ individuals. There was nothing wrong with us, he asserted; nothing immoral about our orientation or desires; nothing abnormal about loving another human being.[5] Asked if he believed gay couples should be parents, he responded: "Look, men have been sleeping with men for thousands of years—and raising tribes. This is a Western sickness, it really is. It's an artificial division. Men will be sleeping with each other when the trumpet sounds. It's only this infantile culture which has made such a big deal of it."[6] Asked why there was so much hatred directed at gays in America, Baldwin responded: "Terror, I suppose. Terror of the flesh. After all, we're supposed to mortify the flesh, a doctrine which has led to untold horrors."[7] This "terror of the flesh," of course, became amplified with the AIDS epidemic—suddenly anyone who was gay, or perceived as gay, was a social leper with whom any form of contact, many mistakenly believed, might lead to contamination.

While Baldwin denounced America's homophobia and fear of the Other, however, he insisted that sexuality, to him, was a private matter. His sexual orientation, of course, had not been much of a secret since at least the 1950s, when he released *Giovanni's Room*. For decades he had been disparagingly referred to as "Martin Luther Queen." Homosexual and bisexual relations remained a prominent theme in his fiction, from *Another Country* to *Just Above My Head*. In his work, he acknowledged, he felt a responsibility to act as a validating "witness" for other gay men (though, he was quick to note, not only for gay men). Yet at the same time, he remained adamant about his personal privacy. "I made a public announcement that we're private, if you see what I mean," he explained. He also acknowledged feeling like something of a "stranger" to the gay community; that he was "never at home in it."[8]

There were reasons for this ambivalence. For one, many of James Baldwin's intimate relationships were with men and women who did not identify as gay, including his longtime friend and lover Lucien Happersberger. "The people who were my lovers," says Baldwin, "the word 'gay' wouldn't have meant anything to them."[9] The fact that these individuals were intimate with Baldwin indicated to him that sexuality was not always a neat either/or box, but fluid, complex, and individual. Love, as he so often put it, was where you found it. Another reason for Baldwin's distance to the gay liberation movement had to do with the fact that, during the author's life, it was largely dominated by white men.[10] "The gay movement as such is no more prepared to accept black people than anywhere else in society," he claimed. "It's a very hermetically sealed group with very unattractive features, including racism."[11] Baldwin's critique was not unfounded. In a 1978 forum, the Washington, D.C., Coalition of Black Gays addressed widespread racism in the gay community, specifically highlighting *OUT* magazine's exclusion of black gay establishments and discrimination at white gay clubs via "carding."[12] In a Greenwich Village forum sponsored by the New York Chapter of Black and White Men Together (BWMT-NY) in 1981, Baldwin spoke of the hypocrisy within the white gay elite ranks, specifically mentioning that Gore Vidal, a celebrated gay writer, referred to him as a "jungle bunny."[13] When asked if he saw any possibilities of blacks and gays forging a political coalition, however, he responded affirmatively on the basis of "shared suffering, shared perceptions, shared hopes."[14] But that coalition, he stressed, would have to be based less on sexuality than on "human dignity."[15]

Part of Baldwin's resistance to the "gay" label was also his refusal to be boxed in. His impatience, he said, had to do with the way it "answered to a false argument, a false accusation . . . that you have no right to be here, that you have to prove your right to be here. I'm saying I have nothing to prove. The world also belongs to me."[16] Being interpolated as gay, for Baldwin, not only put him in a reactionary position, it also potentially diminished other parts of his identity. "The trick," he said, "is to say 'yes' to life. It's only this weird twentieth century which is so obsessed with the particular details of anybody's sex life. I don't think those details make any difference, and I will never be able to deny a certain power that I have had to deal with, which has dealt with me, which is called love—and love comes in very strange packages. I've loved a few men, I've loved a few women. And a few people have loved me. That's all that has saved my life."[17]

What, then, about Baldwin's views on AIDS? In a brief introduction to his 1984 *Village Voice* interview with Baldwin—which offers the most detailed published account we have of Baldwin's views on LGBTQ issues—Richard Goldstein expresses surprise at how little the author seemed to know about American gay life, specifically noting that Baldwin asked him about how AIDS was transmitted (strangely, given its focus on LGBTQ issues, Goldstein did not ask Baldwin about the AIDS crisis in the official interview). Still, this was 1984, and much remained unknown about the disease. Attending a Baldwin lecture in 1985, one audience member remembers a young man standing up and asking the author, "Why aren't you at the forefront in demanding that something be done about the AIDS epidemic?" According to this audience member, Baldwin's response was "quiet and filled with compassion, immediately calming the young man's accusatory behavior."[18] According to biographer David Leeming, Baldwin lost a lover to the disease in the mid-1980s. His "ashes, after his death from AIDS, were scattered in the garden" at Saint-Paul-de-Vence.[19] Why, then, wasn't AIDS mentioned in his work?

Unknown to all but a small coterie of Baldwin scholars and readers: it was. But that work has yet to be published. Throughout his final decade, Baldwin was working on a play titled *The Welcome Table*. Scholar and poet Ed Pavlic calls it "arguably [Baldwin's] single most important piece from the '80s."[20] At seventy-two pages, it represents Baldwin's most complete and significant unpublished work.[21] The play's reference to AIDS comes in act 1 in an extended dialogue between two of the play's main characters, Edith and Rob. While it is not referenced explicitly again, it serves as a significant backdrop to the events that follow. AIDS, that is, is not merely a trivial, passing reference in the text, but plays an important role as subtext and context. At its core, *The Welcome Table* is about intimacy and connection. In a climate of uncertainty, panic, ostracization, and tragedy, Baldwin's "welcome table" serves as a space in which people can have real conversations about their fears, desires, regrets, and dreams.

The play is similar to Baldwin's final novel, *Just Above My Head*, in its concern with how an African American star's life is understood, represented, and mediated. In this way, it continues to highlight Baldwin's interest in the intersections of media, celebrity, and popular culture. Yet it does so in a way that is much more elliptical than *Just Above My Head*. *The Welcome Table* is intentionally fragmented and incomplete. It is as much about what is not said, as what is said. This includes its handling of the looming AIDS epidemic. As Baldwin put it: "Nothing is resolved in the play. The play is simply a question posed—to all of us—'how are we going to live in this world?'"[22]

This chapter attempts to flesh out Baldwin's question by placing *The Welcome Table* within the social and cultural context of the 1980s, specifically amid the AIDS crisis. Since *The Welcome Table* remains unpublished and largely unavailable to the general public, the chapter also attempts to showcase a relatively unknown yet significant work from Baldwin's final decade that should add new dimensions to our understanding of the author and the 1980s.

The Epidemic

In early-1980s France, the setting of *The Welcome Table*, it was bad form to talk about AIDS. Some were skeptical that it was real; others doubted it singled out gay men. Very few people wanted to consider the possibility that all sexual activity might put one at risk of a deadly disease. The alarming news stories coming out of the United States in 1982 and 1983 were thus viewed with suspicion. Americans, after all, were prone to panics. "In Paris," writes author Edmund White in *The Farewell Symphony*, "AIDS was dismissed as an American phobia until French people started dying; then everyone said, 'Well, you have to die some way or another.' If Americans were hysterical and pragmatic, the French were fatalistic, depressed but determined to keep the party going."[23]

There was, of course, a great deal of denial in the United States as well in the early years. In a famous 1983 article published in the *New York Native*, titled "1,112 and Counting," gay activist Larry Kramer threw a grenade into the pervading apathy. "If this article doesn't scare the shit out of you," he wrote, "we're in real trouble. If this article doesn't rouse you to anger, fury, rage, and action, gay men may have no future on this earth. . . . Unless we fight for our lives we shall die. . . . Many of us are dying or dead already."[24] Kramer indicted New York mayor Ed Koch, the *New York Times*, the CDC, and even the gay community for refusing to face and deal with the crisis. "I am sick of everyone in this community who tells me to stop creating a panic. How many of us have to die before you get scared off your ass and into action?"[25] As Randy Shilts notes in his landmark book, *And the Band Played On*, "Larry Kramer's piece irrevocably altered the context in which AIDS was discussed in the gay community and, hence, in the nation."[26]

In April 1983, AIDS received its first major national coverage when it was featured as the cover story for *Newsweek*. "EPIDEMIC," read the cover line, "The Mysterious and Deadly Disease Called AIDS May Be the Public-Health Threat of the Century. How Did It Start? Can It Be Stopped?"[27] Following the *Newsweek* story, the United States saw a flood of news coverage on the disease. While these stories asked important questions, however, answers remained few and far between. By the end of 1983, there was still little clarity about the causes of the disease, how it was transmitted, and how it could be treated. The HIV virus was not identified until 1984; by that time nearly four thousand people had died, overwhelmingly gay men in New York City and San Francisco, and twice that many had contracted the disease. While the media tended to focus its attention on white gay men as the primary victims of the AIDS epidemic, people of color were disproportionately impacted.[28] As early as 1982, people of color made up more than 33 percent of all AIDS cases; by 2002, that number had risen to 62 percent.[29]

Still, in spite of its blind spots, the U.S. media became an important platform for spreading awareness about AIDS. A Gallup poll from June 1983 found that 77% of Americans had read about it.[30] The same could not be said, however, about the federal government. President Ronald Reagan infamously avoided mentioning AIDS until 1985. He wouldn't give a formal speech on the issue until May 31, 1987, when he accepted an invitation from actress Elizabeth Taylor to speak to the American Foundation for AIDS Research (AMFAR). In the late-80s, "silence = death" began appearing on posters and shirts around the country. By that time, the crisis was in full force, and the vacuum of silence on the issue had been filled by people like Reagan's communications director, Pat Buchanan, who argued that AIDS was "nature's revenge on gay men," and Moral Majority champion Jerry Falwell, who described the disease as "God's wrath on homosexuals."[31]

The tide began to turn with the diagnosis and eventual death of celebrity actor Rock Hudson. Hudson was not only beloved by millions of Americans, he was a friend to Ronald and Nancy Reagan. Hudson, for many people, gave the issue a familiar human face. "For decades," writes Randy Shilts, "Hudson had been among the handful of screen actors who personified wholesome American masculinity; now, in one stroke, he was revealed as both gay and suffering from the affliction of pariahs."[32] Doctors believed the Hudson announcement was "the single most important event in the history of the epidemic" in terms of raising awareness.[33] At a 1985 AIDS benefit organized by actress Elizabeth Taylor, Hudson acknowledged he was a reluctant spokesperson for the disease: "I am not happy that I am sick. I am not happy that I have AIDS. But if that is helping others, I can at least know that my own misfortune has had some positive worth."[34] While Reagan is often criticized for his seeming indifference as thousands of Americans died, his rhetoric on the issue, when he finally addressed it, fell in stark contrast to those on the far right. "What our citizens must know is this," he told the American Foundation for AIDS Research in 1987. "America faces a disease that is fatal and spreading. And this calls for urgency, not panic. It calls for compassion, not blame. And it calls for understanding, not ignorance. It's also important that America not reject those who have the disease, but care for them with dignity and kindness."[35] Reagan also increased federal spending on AIDS research, education, and treatment to half a billion dollars over the last five years of his presidency.[36] His critics argued that such efforts were the result of political pressure—and fears that the disease might spread outside the gay community—not genuine humane concern.

Yet regardless of Reagan's personal feelings on the issue, the transformation in public awareness and federal resources undoubtedly had to do with how the issue became humanized through the efforts of activists, journalists, and the stories of victims. In 1985, *People* magazine ran a series of sympathetic cover stories on Rock Hudson and the AIDS issue more broadly. "In some parts of Rock Hudson's America it is still a fairly radical proposition that someone can be both good and gay," read the cover article for August 12, 1985. "The ramifications of the dramatic announcement of Hudson's illness have galvanized both the gay and medical communities, which have been battling AIDS for more than four years."[37] William Hoffman, author of a Broadway play about AIDS called *As Is*, is quoted in the story as saying: "If Rock Hudson can have it, nice people can have it. It's just a disease, not a moral affliction."[38]

In addition to the awareness and compassion, however, the magazine also noted the growing panic throughout America—including in liberal Hollywood. "It is a town near hysteria," writes Scot Haller in a September 23, 1985, cover story for *People*. "Since Rock Hudson's confession, actresses have been shunning love scenes with gay co-stars. Two actors are starting private blood banks. In a world known for easy sexuality, even a social kiss is suspect. . . . Faced with spiraling statistics, few medical facts and many myths, Hollywood has reacted with both unreasoning fear and admirable courage. The danger is that fear could get the upper hand."[39] Haller goes on to compare Hollywood's response to the divisions that surfaced during McCarthyism in the 1950s. In spite of medical professionals' repeated assurances that AIDS could not be spread by casual contact, it changed the way people interacted. "At parties these days finger food is considered by some the sign of a thoughtless hostess," writes Haller. "On the town Joan Rivers now drinks her Perrier from a bottle instead of a glass. Shirlee Fonda wondered aloud recently if sweat on the mats at her exercise studio could put her at risk. Even some male hustlers are advertising their business in newspapers with a disclaimer: 'No contact.'"[40]

The impact on gay individuals (or those rumored to be gay)—whether they had HIV or not—was devastating. People worried they could be infected by handshakes, drinking fountains, saliva, sweat. "If a passing joint gets to a gay, that's where it dies," said Newt Dieter of the Gay Media Task Force in the *People* feature.[41] In the same article, actress-singer Cher admits: "I still kiss most of my friends on the mouth," says Cher. "But I don't think it would be wrong to say to some of my friends, 'Look, I love you but I am going to kiss you on the cheek because I want to protect myself.'"[42] Author Edmund White, who contracted HIV in 1985, remembers feeling like a leper: "Mothers didn't want me picking up their babies. People didn't want to kiss you on the cheek. People certainly didn't want to have sex with you, especially other gay people. It was very isolating and demeaning. That was a long battle."[43] Some legislators called for master lists for those with AIDS, while others demanded they be quarantined. In a 1986 article, renowned conservative writer William Buckley went so far as to argue that "everyone detected with AIDS should be tattooed in the upper forearm . . . and on the buttocks."[44]

The panic surrounding AIDS was epitomized in the story of Ryan White. A young boy from Kokomo, Indiana, Ryan was a hemophiliac who contracted HIV through a blood transfusion. When word surfaced that he had AIDS, he was ostracized, teased, and threatened by his fellow classmates and community. He found obscenities scrawled on his locker; some members of his church refused to shake his hand. Eventually, he was refused entry to his middle school. As more people became aware of his story, Ryan became, like Hudson, another important face for the AIDS crisis. Here was an ordinary kid who wanted nothing more than an ordinary life, yet he handled his diagnosis—and the publicity that came with it—with grace, tenacity, and courage. "After seeing a person like Ryan White—such a fine and loving and gentle person—it was hard for people to justify discrimination against people who suffer from this terrible disease," said Thomas Brandt, the spokesman for the National Commission on AIDS.[45] Indeed, in addition to the support he received from Americans across the country, a number of celebrities who heard about his story befriended Ryan, including Elton John, Elizabeth Taylor, and Michael Jackson, who dedicated the song and music video "Gone Too Soon" to Ryan and his struggle. Ryan White died in 1990.

Meanwhile, in France—James Baldwin's home away from home—the response to AIDS continued to lag. Whether sympathetic or sensationalized, AIDS coverage in the United States sold copy. It also quickly inspired activism, support groups, and research. In France, however, there remained a great deal of indifference. In his book *Queer in Europe: Contemporary Case Studies*, Robert Gillett notes that while some Parisian medical professionals were on the cutting edge of HIV/AIDS research, the French government and media were almost entirely silent on the issue in its first five years, where it was viewed as an American problem.[46] Indeed, in spite of the country's reputation for openness about sex, it was illegal to advertise condoms in France until 1987, let alone provide comprehensive education about AIDS prevention and treatment. "People didn't talk about things like that," recalls author Edmund White, who lived in Paris at the time. "If somebody became ill in Paris, they would go back to their village and die behind closed shutters."[47] White recalls talking to renowned French scholar Michel Foucault about AIDS in the early 1980s and learning that the author was skeptical. "'Oh that's perfect Edmund: you American puritans, you're always inventing diseases. And one that singles out blacks, drug users and gays—how perfect!'"[48]

Foucault, tragically, would die of the disease just a few years later in 1984.[49] The French newspapers refused to identify his cause of death as AIDS, instead citing "maladies of the nervous system" and "cerebral suppuration." The French paper *Libération* pushed back hard against the "viciousness of the rumor [that Foucault died of AIDS]. . . . As if Foucault must have died shamefully."[50] It wasn't until 1986, in a gay American weekly, *The Advocate*, that the rumors were confirmed by his longtime partner, Daniel Defert, who subsequently founded Association AIDES in Foucault's memory. In the wake of Foucault's death and the mounting death toll from AIDS, serious debates emerged about what the gay community—and gay individuals—should do. Some suggested that the 1980s marked the end of the "Golden Age of Promiscuity"—that it was time for a safer, more responsible era. "I am sick of guys who moan that giving up careless sex until this blows over is worse than death," wrote Larry Kramer. "How can they value life so little and cocks and asses so much? Come with me, guys, while I visit a few of our friends in Intensive Care at NYU. Notice the looks in their eyes, guys. They'd give up sex forever if you could promise them life."[51] Two gay men living with AIDS in New York City, Michael Callen and Richard Berkowitz, published *How to Have Sex in an Epidemic*, which attempted to spread awareness about safe and responsible practices. "Safe sex" became a new catch phrase in public-health advertising and popular discourse, in the gay community and beyond. Some doctors and gay rights activists believed gay bathhouses had a responsibility to distribute AIDS pamphlets and be strictly regulated. Yet others argued that a disease should not—and could not—simply stop people from seeking pleasure and enjoying their lives as they saw fit. They did not want the bathhouses closed or regulated; and they did not want people telling them how to have sex. As Konstantin Berlandt, co-chair of the gay parade board of directors, put it: "I didn't become a homosexual so I could use condoms. Of course, we're concerned about spreading a disease. But what should we do? Take our bodily fluids and put them in barrels off the Farallons?"[52]

As one might expect from the self-proclaimed "maverick," Baldwin embraced neither the fear and hysteria nor the reckless denial and fatalism that represented two of the more common responses to the crisis in America and France. Rather, he was interested in figuring out how one might live—and love—in an era when sex had become intertwined with tragedy. What was the meaning of intimacy in the wake of AIDS?

There's a Man Going 'Round Taking Names

It is within this context that Baldwin wrote *The Welcome Table*. The opening scene takes place in a Paris hotel room, where a journalist named Peter has arrived from the United States. He has come to France to interview the play's central character, Edith, a famous actress and singer. After the opening scene, the remainder of the play takes place in the "ancient rambling stone house" of Edith Hemings, in the South of France, at a party for ninety-three-year-old Algerian exile Mlle LaFarge.[53]

Edith brings up the specter of AIDS in act 1. Her current lover, Rob, a white American in his late twenties, is living with her in France. Their commitment to each other is strained, however, by the visit of Rob's longtime former lover, Mark. Sensing her discomfort with his presence (and perhaps her jealousy as well), Rob asks Edith if there is "a problem."[54] "Well, hell, yes," she responds, "and there may be more than one. There's a man going 'round taking names, you know."[55] Edith's line references lyrics from a Lead Belly song about death. But she is alluding more specifically to the AIDS epidemic (and perhaps the widespread fear of a mandatory quarantine or master list for those tested positive for HIV), an implication Rob picks up on immediately. "You're talking about the plague," he replies. "—it's striking everywhere—you're talking about AIDS—because of Mark?"[56] As the play unfolds, it is clear Rob and Mark still have strong feelings for each other—although it is also revealed that Rob—in part because of his attraction to women—has been unable to fully commit to their relationship. "You don't know where Mark's been, who he's been with, since you and he—haven't been together," says Edith. Rob defends Mark; he says he "trusted him."[57] That's all one can do in a relationship. One can never know for certain; one must trust (and be trustworthy)—although Rob concedes that he wasn't always trustworthy himself.

Yet it is clear that the looming presence of AIDS has caused both Edith and Rob to grapple not only with how it might affect their relationship but also with the very idea of a relationship. "I think it's great," Rob says, "—the plague strikes: right in the middle of the joyless orgy—and fraudulent libertines, like me, can finally stop all the push-ups and curl up in the arms of one person. Wow. As they say over here: *enfin!*"[58] Rob's response obviously contains some sarcasm, riffing on the conservative line that AIDS was the result of hedonistic behavior. Baldwin, however, doesn't allow the play to make the same conflation. AIDS is never presented as a punishment for sin or reckless activity but rather as an impetus for self-reflection and honest conversation. The conversation between Rob and Edith makes clear that all relationships are "untidy." Edith expresses reservations about Rob's sincerity: "I can't believe I'm hearing this from you."[59] She also suggests that Rob has been far more sexually active than she has been. "I wasn't in the middle of an orgy. I was in the middle of rehearsals and found myself falling in love with you."[60] Edith, however, acknowledges she is being self-righteous—that Mark's presence has made her feel insecure. Regardless of his past, Mark, like everyone else in the play, is welcomed in the home.

What Rob and Edith are ultimately wrestling with are their responsibilities to each other. Rob's reference to the "joyless orgy" seems to indicate a certain disillusionment with the sexual revolution. The post-Stonewall ethos was: the more sex, the better. Greenwich Village in New York City and the Castro district in San Francisco became free-love havens, with many gay men reporting hundreds of sexual partners per year, many of them anonymous. Yet like some gay men, Rob expresses a certain weariness with this lifestyle and a yearning for something more stable and fulfilling. He indicts himself as a "fraudulent libertine" who is finally ready to "stop all the push-ups and curl up in the arms of one person." What he expresses, that is, is a desire for a deep, committed, lasting relationship. "For me," he tells Edith, "it just means that we are going to have to take seriously—what we always claimed to take seriously—our responsibility for each other."[61]

To what degree these characters reflect Baldwin's own views is of course debatable. Yet some of these sentiments seem consistent with Baldwin's prior fiction, essays, and interviews. The author was by no means puritanical, but he believed relationships were about more than mere pleasure. In *Giovanni's Room*, after David's first sexual experience with Giovanni, he proclaims:

Now, from this night, from this coming morning, no matter how many beds I find myself in between now and my final bed, I shall never be able to have any more of those boyish, zestful affairs—which are, really, when one thinks of it, a kind of higher, or, anyway, more pretentious masturbation. People are too various to be treated so lightly.[62]

Sex, that is, for Baldwin, cannot be separated from responsibility. People, regardless of sexual orientation, must ultimately grow up, and this growth is contingent on how we see and treat one another. In his 1984 *Village Voice* interview, Richard Goldstein notes that Baldwin, on this point, sounded like literary critic Leslie Fiedler (to which Baldwin responds, laughing, "I hope not!").[63] Yet there are similarities. In his provocative classic, *Love and Death in the American Novel*, Fiedler argues that American literature reveals a persistent refusal to let go of innocence and embrace maturity, experience, and responsibility. From *The Adventures of Huckleberry Finn* to *Moby Dick*, writes Fiedler,

The typical male protagonist of our fiction has been a man on the run, harried into the forest and out to sea, down the river or into combat—anywhere to avoid "civilization," which is to say, the confrontation of a man and woman which leads to the fall to sex, marriage and responsibility. One of the factors that determine theme and form in our great books is this strategy of evasion, this retreat to nature and childhood which makes our literature (and life!) so charmingly and infuriatingly "boyish."[64]

As a result, writes Fiedler, "The great works of American fiction are notoriously at home in the children's section of the library."[65] Yet while Fiedler saw American literature as fundamentally childish and sexless, Baldwin saw postmodern America as, more often, sex obsessed, yet still unable to openly deal with it or understand it—in its most fulfilling expression—as a reciprocal act of love. In his 1984 interview with Goldstein, Baldwin describes the primary concern of *Giovanni's Room* as "what happens to you if you're afraid to love anybody."[66] He probes a similar theme in *The Welcome Table*, only now the question is pursued in the wake of the AIDS epidemic. Now, more than ever, Baldwin seems to suggest, it is imperative that one not be afraid of love—that one embrace not only the pleasure but also the "stink of love." Life, particularly for gay men in the 1980s, was too fragile and tenuous to live without it. With the plague "striking everywhere," love was the only thing left to cling to.

Somebody's Calling My Name

Given the intimate, physical relationship it allowed between audience and characters, a play was the perfect vehicle for Baldwin to pursue such themes. According to biographer David Leeming, James Baldwin began conceptualizing *The Welcome Table* as early as the late 1960s, while living in Turkey.[67] It was resurrected in the early 1980s after Baldwin saw Walter Dallas's production of his 1954 play, *The Amen Corner*. Dallas remembers Baldwin reading an early draft of *The Welcome Table* in a hotel room in Atlanta. He was excited but nervous about it. In March 1984 he sent Dallas a revised copy of the play with a brief letter:

> Dear Walter:
> Here it is.
> I find I have absolutely nothing to say about it: but hope to hear from you.
>
> Love,
>
> Jimmy[68]

Baldwin continued thinking about it, tinkering with it, and making revisions until the last week of his life. In a letter to Dallas dated July 4, 1987, Baldwin writes: "I don't think there's any point in my attempting to do anymore with it before you take it over."[69] Baldwin notes that the final draft has "been cut by about twenty pages. I didn't realize this until I typed it for the last time—I don't know if that's a good sign or a bad sign: to drop twenty pages and not even realize it."[70]

Yet he said he was focusing on the "coherence and precision" of his characters. He conceived of the play as being about "exiles and alienation." The "welcome table" was a symbolic refuge where outsiders and outcasts "could lay down their souls," at least for a moment. The impetus, Baldwin said, came "out of a need to get away from it [the horror of our time], to ventilate, to look at the horror from some other point of view."[71]

A refuge from horror, indeed, was in large part what his home in Saint-Paul-de-Vence represented. The author decided to purchase the house, he revealed in a 1987 interview with *Architectural Digest*, after the assassination of Martin Luther King Jr. "devastated his universe." It offered a certain peace: a beautiful fortress, surrounded by cobblestone streets, rolling hills, and the Mediterranean Sea, far from the madness of America. The old home, he said, always had "something in need of repair or renewal or burial. But this exasperating rigor is good for the soul, for it means that one can never suppose one's work is done."[72] Indeed, while the Saint-Paul-de-Vence home certainly offered refuge, Baldwin never mistook it for Eden—he, and his many visitors, brought their histories, experiences, struggles, and pain with them.

This reality is reflected in *The Welcome Table*. Each character's identity comes into view gradually through fragments of conversation, confessions of their respective pasts. The cast is diverse in every way imaginable: by race, by gender, by sexual orientation, by nationality, by class. Indeed, in his description of the photographer character, Terry, Baldwin simply writes: "Terry is male or female, Black or White." Magdalena Zaborowska defines Baldwin's welcome table as "a meeting space for those who transcend boundaries and divisions of identity."[73] Baldwin based many characters on visitors to his home. Mlle LaFarge was modeled after Mlle Faure; the journalist, Peter Davis, is modeled after Henry Louis Gates Jr.; Daniel, the former Black Panther and aspiring playwright, was inspired by Cecil Brown; Regina, an alcoholic who has recently lost her husband, is based on Baldwin's longtime friend, Mary Painter; LaVerne is modeled after the dancer Bernard Hassell, who lived with Baldwin and managed Baldwin's house for many years; and Rob and Mark seem to draw inspiration from former Baldwin lovers, including Lucien Happersberger. Yet as David Leeming notes, these characters and the house itself are also "a metaphor for Baldwin's mind, for his many selves gathering around and finally attempting to face the welcome table, where everything will have to come together."[74]

At the center of the play is Edith Hemings, the Creole star actress/singer, modeled in part after Baldwin's famous friends, Josephine Baker and Nina Simone. In his final weeks Baldwin insisted that Hollywood actress Lena Horne play the role of Edith. Yet as a famous expatriate artist grappling with fame, alcoholism, and elusive love, Edith also, as Magdalena Zaborowska observes, serves as "an intriguing transgender figuration of Baldwin."[75] That Baldwin might inhabit, or at least explore parts of himself, in a female character is not surprising given the trajectory of his interest in gender identity. Leeming points out that "the female within the male had long fascinated Baldwin," not only as an abstract concept in his writing, but in his life.[76] "For much of his life," writes Leeming, "Baldwin avoided flamboyant clothes because he believed it was important not to 'signify' a particular sexual stereotype. Yet by the 1980s he had long since given into a love of silk, of the recklessly thrown scarf, the overcoat draped stole-like over the shoulders, the large and exotic ring, bracelet, or neckpiece. Even his movements assumed a more feminine character."[77] Androgyny and gender identity, of course, were also the animating concerns of his 1985 essay, "Freaks and the American Ideal of Manhood."

What does Edith reveal about how Baldwin understood himself in his final decade? She is a complex, flawed, and tragic character. In part because of her celebrity, she is also enigmatic. At the beginning of scene 2, Peter calls to arrange his interview with her, but the star "is not available." Acting as intermediary is her cousin LaVerne. When Peter tells LaVerne that he has been promised an "exclusive interview," she responds: "for that, people have practically walked the Sahara."[78] Peter explains that he has, in fact, come all the way from Detroit. What is significant here is that Edith is clearly somewhat shielded and insulated from the outside world. Her schedule is made for her; visitors are screened. "Lord, if she didn't have me here to hold her hand—!" LaVerne complains.[79] Many of those closest to her work for her. Besides LaVerne, her other "help" in the house includes a gardener (Mohammed) and cook and housekeeper (Angelina). Her fame ensures that millions of people know her, but very few can actually reach her. And even if they are allowed in—like Peter—they must try somehow to get beyond a calculated performance.

The audience first sees Edith in her role as singer. She is at the piano, crooning to an old bluesy tune. The song is "Hush, Hush, Somebody's Calling My Name"—a spiritual with double meaning once sung by slaves.[80] On the surface, it is about an individual calling out to Jesus, asking for spiritual guidance ("Oh, my Lord, what shall I do?"). Yet it was also used by slaves on the Underground Railroad as code to lay low on the dangerous journey to freedom. In the context of the play, it is impregnated with additional meanings. Somebody (Peter) is, quite literally, calling her name, as he seeks to interview—and unveil—the "true" identity of the star. The song signals that the play may in fact do just that, but only to those who are attentive enough to read—or listen and hear—between the lines.

In conversation with former black revolutionary, Daniel, Edith confesses, "[I am not] as happy in front of my mirror as I [think I] used to be."[81] It is not just her physical appearance (although she does express misgivings about aging on multiple occasions)—it is a certain sadness and doubt about who she is. When her housekeeper Angelina expresses admiration for her seemingly glamorous, cosmopolitan life, Edith responds with self-deprecation: "You can get the best of me at the box-office for the price of two metro tickets—before inflation, anyway."[82] Her longtime (recently widowed) friend, Regina, sees Edith from a nearly opposite perspective. "It was astounding to watch you on screen," she says. "Or on that box. I thought to myself, I know her! She's not like that at all! And, then, I would think, But I guess I don't know her. Maybe we never know each other.—I don't know if I ever knew my husband."[83] Edith responds: "I was so twisted and possessed—I was alive when I was being someone else. What can anyone do with such a creature? How can anyone find, let alone love—someone who is always someone else?"[84] Such questions are at the core of the play. On the one hand, she suggests to Angelina that the star on the screen is an illusion, a commercial product; yet on the other hand, she tells Regina that she felt most alive while performing. This paradox, however, leaves her with a kind of identity crisis, particularly when it comes to finding and giving love.

Many of those around her sense this confusion, and fear she is dealing with the loneliness and self-doubt by drinking too much. When LaVerne mentions it, Edith retorts, "[I don't] want anybody to take care of me."[85] When Daniel brings it up, she responds: "Oh, child—you are young. I drink a lot too much. But I know what I'm doing when I'm up on that stage. I never bump into the equipment or the furniture or the crew and I always knew where the camera is."[86] Edith seems to recognize that she is an alcoholic, but she takes pride in her professionalism—and her ability to fool people. By knowing where the camera is, she can present what she wants to present—and conceal what she wants to conceal. Yet the camera is juxtaposed with the mirror—which reveals an image of herself that makes her feel much less comfortable and confident.

Act 2 begins with Edith being photographed and Peter interviewing, not Edith, but Edith's friend Regina. As in act 1, getting to Edith requires a process of intermediaries. In Regina, Peter catches glimpses of Edith—not only is she Edith's friend, they share a similar sense of sadness and loss. Perhaps because Regina feels she knows the "real" Edith, she is suspicious and protective of her friend. "Do you have a personal interest in this interview?" she asks Peter, "or is it just another assignment?" Peter deflects the question, but Regina persists: "What is the point of an interview?" "Well," Peter responds, "for the people who hire me—it's business—it sells papers, you know, magazines, whatever—but for me——"[87] Before he is able to finish his sentence, Peter is cut off by the entrance of Terry, the photographer, leaving his intent suspended in tension. When Edith and Peter finally meet in person, Edith says that something about Peter reminds her of a surgeon she had. She is vague about the reason for the surgery, but it was clearly a profound experience for Edith. "I didn't know if I'd ever see anyone again," she says.[88] Why does Peter remind her of this experience? Edith seems to sense that the interview, like the surgery, may demand great vulnerability. It may reveal something about her she did not know—or did not want to know. It may make her feel exposed. Or it may make her feel better. She doesn't know.

Later in act 2, Peter finally reveals that he believes an interview, at its best, can be a kind of "mutual confession."[89] Edith begins to let down her guard a bit. She speaks of her childhood—of sneaking to the local whorehouse and becoming friends with the brothel keeper, a black woman named Lady Jones. "I loved the way she looked," says Edith, but "we were Creoles—and we were supposed to be better—and—I didn't really understand what was *wrong*. . . . That fucked with my mind for a long time."[90] Edith also opens up about an abortion. She still feels conflicted about it. It seems to represent a life that might have been, but she is uncertain if that life ever had a chance. When asked why she made the choice, she says, "I was alone."[91] Peter asks her why she is still alone, and she responds: "I don't know why!" But Peter believes *he* does. He makes his own confession: He used to work in advertising, and was making good money. He thought he was providing a good, safe, middle-class life for his family. But one day his son asked him if "what [he] was writing was true."[92] "Trust your Daddy, son," he replied.[93] But his son eventually grew up and saw his father as a hypocrite and a fraud. Peter ended up in jail, and then in a clinic, "kicking his habit."[94] Peter's insinuation seems to be that refusing to be honest about yourself—and to others—does not ultimately protect you. It may, in fact, destroy you.

Why, Peter finally asks, does someone as accomplished as Edith feel like a disappointment? Edith answers that women are always considered and treated as disappointments, but Peter doesn't find this answer satisfying. "You're funny," says Edith. "We've spent hours, now, with you hoping to make me tell the truth—or to come somewhere near it—and the moment I do, you start howling like one of my Papa's hogs at hog-killing time."[95]

He Ran Away

Over the course of the play, Edith's greatest disappointment, we learn, is that love has somehow eluded her. Her relationship with her current lover, Rob, is complicated in a number of ways. For one, as she reminds him, she is old enough to be his mother.[96] This doesn't seem to bother Rob. More significant, however, are the ways in which their past experiences (and lovers) still haunt them. Rob acknowledges that when he fell in love with Edith, he "still saw Mark—everywhere."[97] This, no doubt, is why Edith feels suspicious of Mark. At one point, Rob admits that he sometimes wonders what it would be like if Mark were a girl—"you know, with tits and all, instead of—what he's got."[98] Edith initially doesn't know how to respond to this revelation. It seems, however, that Rob feels comfortable being open and honest with Edith about it. He continues: "That will always have a certain power over me, no matter what happens; no matter how long I live. There shouldn't be any confusion about it—and no grounds for jealousy. Love is where you find it."[99] To this, Edith responds: "I damn sure can't argue that. Not when I remember some of the places I've found it—and lost it, too."[100]

Yet Rob's complex sexual orientation—and the presence of his former lover, Mark—does risk his relationship with Edith. At the party, when Rob and Mark finally have the chance to speak alone, it is immediately apparent that they still have feelings for each other. While he is happy to see Rob, Mark finds it difficult to simply be friends. "I'm not like you," he says. "I've got to get away from you." Rob responds: "We've said that before. We've tried it before—and what happens? Sooner or later, we always end up back with each other."[101] Mark, however, doesn't see it this way. "You mean, I always come back—to you. And you're always glad to see me and you're always very nice about making room for me in your busy schedule."[102] This account angers Rob. "Will you come down off that suffering faggot bull-shit! I don't make room for you. You're not some fucking guest on my property—you live in me!"[103]

It becomes clear, however, over the course of their exchange that they have different expectations. Mark feels Rob is more "normal" than he is—or at least has chosen a more "normal" life by being in a heterosexual relationship. Yet Rob cautions him: "Don't be too sure I have Edith. The Lady's not for burning. She's a star. A lot connects us. A lot divides us, too."[104] This is

a fascinating confession from Rob. He seems to recognize inherent limitations to his relationship with Edith—in part, because of her fame, but
in part, we soon learn, because of Mark. "I might have five old ladies and
seventeen children and I'd still be crazy about you."[105] Mark, however, is
not happy with this arrangement. "Look," he says, "you've got me standing
at the end of the line . . . And what do you want me to do—between mar-
riages and births and baptisms?"[106] "Celebrate them with me," says Rob.[107]
Mark's point, however, is that they will never really be partners under these
circumstances. Rather, Rob will have his family, and Mark will be the lover
to the side, outside the official portrait. Rob wants to have it both ways,
while Mark feels, for him, that such a setup is impossible.

The dynamic is further complicated by Edith's own personal history.
When she was young, she reveals to Peter, she fell in love with a man, a
track star who was "the color of ginger-bread."[108] "His name—do you believe
this?—was Romeo. Really. Romeo Clarke."[109] While it has been years since
they were together, it left a deep imprint. Edith is vague about what happened to the relationship. "He—moved—away," she says. "One morning,
he was gone."[110] Edith says she doesn't know why he left, or why they never
looked for each other after. But later she ascribes part of it to her life as
a celebrity. "My life just became a matter of: Hello. Good-bye. See you—:
when? Of airports and airplanes and crowds and stages."[111] Somehow, amid
the busyness of life, the need for love become secondary. Yet, she confides,
"Every time I stepped from the ramp onto that plane, something in me
thought: from earth to heaven. I thought of the Lady Jones—how she used
to say, sometimes, this may be the last time to talk with you."[112] Edith's
confession is a tender and beautiful recognition of the transience of life.

The interview, like so many conversations in the play, is left hanging.
When the conversation resumes, Edith simply says: "He ran away"—with
no further explanation.[113] "Is that the end of the interview?" asks Peter.
"Only for a moment," says Edith.[114] What we learn about Edith, by the end
of the play, is intentionally incomplete—as is our knowledge of Peter, Rob,
Mark, and the other characters. Conversations are interrupted or bleed
into each other. Stories are left unresolved, missing crucial details. Baldwin
was inspired, in part, by Russian playwright Anton Chekhov, renowned
for his elliptical style in which conventional action is replaced with mood
and subtext. What is left unsaid is as important as what is said. As Martin Esslin writes: "It was Chekhov who first deliberately wrote dialogue in

which the mainstream of emotional action ran underneath the surface. It was he who articulated the notion that human beings hardly ever speak in explicit terms among each other about their deepest emotions, that the great tragic, climactic moments are often happening beneath outwardly trivial conversation."[115]

This style is crucial to understanding the play. The audience is left with a slice of life: one day in one house, in which various identities and stories intersect, but, as Baldwin put it, "nothing is resolved"; gaps are intentionally left unfilled. Peter does not get the interview he expected—he is, perhaps, left with far more questions than answers. Edith is not easy to understand—and cannot be reduced to a simple profile. Yet the incomplete portrait that emerges feels fully human and reveals a character not unlike Baldwin himself—beset with flaws, insecurities, and challenges, surrounded by plagues, horrors, and tragedies—searching for that most elusive, but valuable thing: love.

Welcome Home

In one of his last letters, dated July 4, 1987, Baldwin wrote to Walter Dallas that he was "convalescent," but that this was "infinitely preferable, obviously, to not being convalescent."[116] Still, his illness and age made him reflective about his life:

> Well. Everything is new. *And* old. *And* frightening. One's body refuses to be taken for granted. This is a great shock, and, with the body's stubborn recalcitrance, a new sense of reality begins. It is difficult to describe this, and this sense must vary incredibly from one person to another. The key, I suppose, at bottom, is one's reaction to one's life, whether it strikes one, finally, as a matter of regret or a matter of rejoicing (For it is certain that the time which stretches behind you is longer than the time stretches before you) Well. I certainly fucked up often enough and my hope seemed frequently to turn to ashes and poison but I don't think I have any real regrets. It's awful (not to say awkward) that it takes so long to learn so little but there's nothing anyone can do about that. So, I don't feel noways tired.[117]

A similar reflectiveness comes through in *The Welcome Table*. Death haunts the play from beginning to end. "There's a man going 'round taking names."[118] AIDS could take anyone at any time, even healthy young men like Mark and Rob, or stars like Edith. Everyone is vulnerable. Not just because of AIDS, but because life is fragile and fleeting. Edith reflects on how, every time she stepped on a plane, she thought about how it might be the last time she talked with someone; she reflects on how, when she underwent surgery, she thought it might be the last time she saw anyone. Baldwin's own health issues and anxieties about death are an obvious subtext. In the period he wrote the play, his body began deteriorating—slowly at first, and then rapidly in the final year. While Baldwin died of cancer, not AIDS, he could certainly empathize with the thousands who were dying of AIDS in the 1980s. When journalist Quincy Troupe visited Saint-Paul-de-Vence in the fall of 1987, he was "shocked by [Baldwin's] frail and weakened condition."[119] "I held him close for a long moment," writes Troupe, "partly because I didn't want him to notice the sadness that had welled up in my eyes. . . . I will never forget that image of Jimmy weakly sitting there, the feel of his now-wispy hair scratching my face when I hugged him, the birdlike frailty of his ravaged body and the parting telescopic image of him dressed in a red and green plaid robe that all but swallowed him, his large head lolling from one side to the other as his longtime friend [and lover], painter Lucien Happersberger, lifted him to put him to bed."[120]

In the third and final act, Edith lights the candles in the dining room for Mlle LaFarge's birthday. It is a celebration, of course. But there is also a sadness about the occasion, as it is clear that the life that made the home possible will soon end. Mlle LaFarge has turned ninety-three. "It is your night," says Edith. "Indeed. One of my last," says Mlle LaFarge.[121] Baldwin based Mlle LaFarge on Mlle Jean Faure, an Algerian exile from whom Baldwin rented and eventually bought his home in Saint-Paul-de-Vence. Her unusual relationship to Baldwin underscores the possibilities of connection Edith and Mlle LaFarge represent. As Josiah Ulysses Young observes: "That an Algerian-born French imperialist and a Harlem-born anti-imperialist would become soul mates seems improbable; yet their friendship indicates that the artificial barriers people erect and institutionalize to protect themselves from each other dissolved between these two. Their friendship also bears witness to what Baldwin thought to be a fact: human beings are one family."[122]

This philosophy of an inclusive human family or community is clear throughout the play. The characters come from all over the world. They are American, French, and Algerian; Muslim, Jewish, and Christian; black, white, and Creole; gay, straight, and bi-sexual. The barriers of nationalism are replaced by the open doors of cosmopolitanism. "Who needs flags?" says Mark, to which Regina responds: "I hope to God I never see another flag as long as I live. I would like to burn them all—burn every passport, abolish every border."[123] This openness was, indeed, the governing philosophy of Baldwin's actual home. As biographer David Leeming writes: "There had always been an unwritten law in Jimmy's households that people greet each other with a kiss on each cheek at the first encounter of the day. This applied to men and women, to the maid, the gardener, the doctor, and even to those who might have had a terrible dispute the night before. Such arguments were commonplace around the welcome table, but the house demanded the recognition of community in the ritual kiss."[124] Likewise, in *The Welcome Table*, a sense of community and intimacy pervades the play, even among former strangers. The gardener, Mohammed, speaks to African American expatriate Daniel about how in Algeria "the people, they are more—everywhere—more to be touched—with hands, with eyes, with everything—more clear!"[125] Intimacy, Mohammed suggests, is feared in America, and even in France. But it is a way of life in Algeria; it offers clarity.

Indeed, it is a display of such intimacy, between former strangers, that concludes the play. In the final scene, Peter and Edith sit together by the piano. Throughout the play, he has tried to somehow get beyond her many walls but has managed to glean only glimpses of her story. Now the official interview is over. It is late in the evening, but Peter isn't in a hurry. "We got time," he says. Edith responds: "You want to spend it listening to me?" "Yes," Peter says.[126] Suddenly the distant interviewer/interviewee dynamic dissolves. He touches her face, very gently. Instead of language, they begin a more sensual, intimate form of communication, through physical touch and music. "I'll play something for you," Edith says, and as the song begins, the curtain falls.[127]

The context for this connection matters. As Edith's conversation with Rob makes clear, fears about AIDS dominated the decade. It changed the way people thought about sex, intimacy, and love. It also changed the way many people thought about LGBTQ individuals. As Jonathan Engel writes, "While homosexuality had never been broadly accepted in the general population, AIDS seemed to galvanize many people's disdain for homosexual practices, and for homosexuals in general. *Time* magazine reported in 1985 that it was 'open season on gays,' while a *Los Angeles Times* poll found that even in the nation's most tolerant cities—New York and Los Angeles—over 60 percent of surveyed adults found homosexuality 'wrong.'"[128] From 1982 to 1985, hate crimes against gays more than tripled, as right-wing activists brandished signs that called to "quarantine the queers."[129] In this context, Baldwin, by contrast, created a play in which characters interact freely across borders. Concerns and misunderstandings exist—but they are the catalyst for discussion and confession, not division and ostracization. Characters connect (or try to connect), regardless of sexual orientation or disease. With death claiming the lives of too many too soon, Baldwin believed, the world could not afford the greater tragedy of conceding love for fear.

4

"To Crush the Serpent"

The Religious Right and the Moral Minority

> We're supposed to mortify the flesh, a
> doctrine which has led to untold terrors. This
> is a very biblical culture; people believe the
> wages of sin is death. In fact, the wages of sin
> *is* death, but not the way the moral guardians
> of this time and place understand it."
> —James Baldwin, "Go the Way Your Blood
>   Beats," 1984

At some point in the 1980s, James Baldwin must have been flipping through channels on TV and stumbled upon an appearance of Jerry Falwell on *Nightline*, or perhaps Pat Robertson's talk show, *The 700 Club*, or maybe Jim and Tammy Faye Bakker's Praise the Lord (PTL) network. These figures were so ubiquitous during the Reagan era, it would have been difficult not to. While we may never know the full range of thoughts looming behind those large, inquisitive eyes, Baldwin, fortunately, did leave behind a written record on the subject that offers important insights into the author's evolving thoughts on religion, salvation, and transgression from the final decade of his life.

Religion was always a major theme in James Baldwin's work. From his first 1953 novel, *Go Tell It on the Mountain*, to his last in 1979, *Just Above My*

Head, it served as a crucial vehicle in which his characters struggled, connected, explored, and evolved. Religion was also the language in which his prose moved: its rhythms, cadences, and vocabulary. A survey of Baldwin's work finds constant references to spirituals, gospel songs, Bible stories, proverbs, and adages. While Baldwin personally left the church and his role as preacher in adolescence, he remained, even in his final years, fascinated by it. As Joanna Brooks observes: "What Baldwin could not be, think, say, or do in the church he did in his writing, even as he carried forward in his writing spiritual, moral, aesthetic, and rhetorical impulses he first learned at church."[1]

Yet in spite of its significance to the author's life and work, as Douglas Field notes, the renaissance in Baldwin studies has in many ways ignored or marginalized the religious dimensions in his work in favor of more popular theoretical discussions of race, gender, and sexuality.[2] There are, of course, some notable exceptions, including two substantial theological studies: Clarence Hardy's *James Baldwin's God: Sex, Hope, and Crisis in Black Holiness Culture* (2003) and Josiah Ulysses Young's *James Baldwin's Understanding of God* (2014). There have also been a handful of important chapters and articles, including Douglas Field's excellent chapter, "James Baldwin's Religion," from *All Those Strangers* (2015).

Part of the neglect, Field suggests, may have to do with Baldwin himself, "who steered readers away" from such criticism due to his scathing attacks on religion's efficacy and moral authority.[3] Baldwin could be ruthlessly adept at cutting through religion's hypocrisies. "Being in the pulpit was like being in the theatre," he writes in *The Fire Next Time*. "I was behind the scenes and knew how the illusion was worked. . . . I knew how to work on a congregation until the last dime was surrendered—it was not very hard to do—and I knew where the money for 'the Lord's work' went."[4] It was not merely that the ministers acquired big houses and Cadillacs while the congregation wallowed in poverty, Baldwin explains. It was religion's failure to even come near to addressing the realities of day-to-day life. "The transfiguring power of the Holy Ghost ended when the service ended, and salvation stopped at the church door."[5] Baldwin characterizes institutional Christianity as arrogant, intolerant, and cruel. "It is not too much to say that whoever wishes to become a truly moral human being," he writes, "must first divorce himself from all the prohibitions, crimes, and hypocrisies of the Christian church. If the concept of God has any validity or any use, it can only be to make us larger, freer, and more loving. If God cannot do this, then it is time we got rid of Him."[6]

In addition to such blunt critiques, however, he also recognized the richness and communal power religion could offer.[7] In one of the better-known passages from *The Fire Next Time*, he describes the palpable ecstasy of the black Pentecostal Church:

> There is no music like that music, no drama like the drama of the saints rejoicing, the sinners moaning, the tambourines racing, and all those voices coming together and crying holy unto the Lord. There is still, for me, no pathos quite like the pathos of those multicolored, worn, somehow triumphant and transfigured faces, speaking from the depths of a visible, tangible, continuing despair of the goodness of the Lord. I have never seen anything to equal the fire and excitement that sometimes, without warning, fill a church, causing the church, as Lead-belly and so many others have testified, to "rock." Nothing that has happened to me since equals the power and the glory that I sometimes felt when, in the middle of a sermon, I knew that I was somehow, by some miracle, really carrying, as they said, "the Word"—when the church and I were one. Their pain and joy were mine, and mine were theirs.[8]

This intimate relationship with the black Pentecostal Church continues in his later works, perhaps most notably in his 1979 novel, *Just Above My Head*.[9] In his final decade, however, another important dimension emerges in Baldwin's commentary on religion: his direct engagement with the new, mass-mediated, predominantly white, born-again Christian movement. By the 1980s, Baldwin recognized, a major transformation had occurred in the sociopolitical functions of religion. His critique adapted accordingly, focusing on the ways in which religion—particularly white evangelical Christianity—had morphed into a movement deeply enmeshed with mass media, politics, and late capitalism. Religion in the Reagan era was being leveraged, sold, and consumed in ways never before seen, from charismatic televangelists to Christian-themed amusement parks to megachurches. "The people who call themselves 'born again' today," wrote Baldwin, "have simply become members of the richest, most exclusive private club in the world, a club that the man from Galilee could not possibly hope—or wish—to enter."[10] The new movement was often characterized as the "religious Right" or the "Moral Majority" and was central to Reagan's political coalition as well as the broader culture wars.[11]

For Baldwin, this development had wide-ranging ramifications for society and the individual, from Christian-fueled militarism to the so-called "prosperity gospel." In "To Crush the Serpent" he focuses particularly on the definitions and uses of the sinner or transgressor in the context of Reagan-era obsessions with the body and sexuality. The title references a prophecy from Genesis 3:15, from the Garden of Eden: "And I will put enmity between you and the woman, and between your offspring and hers; he will crush your head, and you will strike his heel." How might this prophecy be interpreted? Who or what does the serpent represent? Why should it be crushed? For Baldwin, the answer has to do with shame, guilt, and terror. To crush the serpent is to crush desire, and, therefore, to crush the putative transgressor. Lurking behind this impulse to police and punish, Baldwin believed, was self-loathing and terror of the flesh. "This accounts for the violence of our TV screen and cinema, a violence far more dangerous than pornography," he writes. "What we are watching is a compulsive reliving of the American crimes; what we are watching with the [Jerry] Falwells and [Pat] Robertsons is an attempt to exorcise ourselves."[12]

Despite significant new contributions highlighting Baldwin's relationship to Pentecostalism and the Holiness movement, there has been no focused critical examination on Baldwin's engagement with Christianity in the 1980s, or on "To Crush the Serpent," the last major article published before his death in 1987. This chapter attempts to fill this gap with a historicized reading of Baldwin's article in the context of the rise of the religious Right.

The Electric Church

To fully understand Baldwin's critique of born-again Christianity in "To Crush the Serpent," it is helpful to flesh out the context. Born-again Christianity not only shaped the 1980s; it changed America in ways that are still being felt today. A direct line can be traced from George W. Bush's evangelical base or today's Tea Party back to the fundamentalist-Christian renaissance that emerged at the cusp of the Reagan era. A coalition of like-minded sects intent on "re-taking America," the religious Right was, as Lauren Winner puts it, "a political force to be reckoned with."[13] A less-prominent presence on the political stage for much of the twentieth century, the Christian Right began to mobilize in the 1960s and 1970s around social issues and "family values." Richard Nixon famously identified part of this growing constituency as the "silent majority" in a 1969 speech defending the Vietnam War.[14] For Nixon, however, the silent majority was not yet specifically identified as Christian; rather, it was an appeal to "middle America" and to a general wariness of the growing counterculture.

The political rise of born-again Christians first revealed itself—ironically, given its subsequent loyalty to the Republican party—with the candidacy of a Democratic president: Jimmy Carter. A Southern Baptist from Plains, Georgia, Carter often taught Sunday School in his hometown even after becoming governor of his home state. His story was compelling: a peanut farmer who, through pluck and hard work, worked his way up the political ladder and realized the American Dream. Following the political corruption and disillusionment of the previous decade, he based his campaign on religiously infused moral principles of honesty, humility, human rights, and care for the poor. In the 1976 election, Carter managed to garner nearly half the evangelical vote to become the first born-again president. *Newsweek* called 1976 the "Year of the Evangelical."[15]

Carter's ascendance was remarkable on a number of levels, not the least of which was the diverse coalition he put together to defeat Republican incumbent Gerald Ford. Even James Baldwin, notoriously scathing in his criticism of elected officials, tenuously supported Carter. In an open letter published in the *New York Times* in January 1977, Baldwin documented some of the issues the new president must confront. "I am not so much trying to bring your mind to the suffering of a despised people," he wrote "—a very comforting notion, after all, for most Americans—as the state and the fate of a nation of which you are the elected leader. . . . Too many of us are in jail, my friend; too many of us are starving, too many of us can find no door open."[16] He concludes his letter: "I must add, in honor, that I write to you because I love our country: And you, in my lifetime, are the only president to whom I would have written."[17]

Carter had not even been sworn into office, however, before his coalition began to break apart, starting with born-again Christians. In a now-infamous 1976 interview with *Playboy* magazine, Carter confessed to having lusted in his heart. "I've looked on a lot of women with lust," he revealed. "I've committed adultery in my heart many times. This is something that God recognizes I will do—and I have done it—and God forgives me for it."[18] Carter's remarks set off a media frenzy. Among conservative Christians, such candor was met with outrage. Beyond his comments, the very fact that he gave an interview to a putatively pornographic magazine like *Playboy* caused some to question his faith and morality. Following the interview, Carter dropped fifteen points in the polls.[19] More significant, over the long haul, evangelicals began a mass exodus from the Democratic Party that has remained largely unchanged to this day.

The political messiah to lead Christians out of the liberal wilderness turned out to be a man named Ronald Reagan. A twice-divorced former Hollywood actor, Reagan was not, on the surface, a natural fit for evangelicals. He did not have a miraculous conversion story, and he rarely spoke at any length about his theological views. As Steven P. Miller writes, "Ronald Reagan was more an evangelical's president than an evangelical president."[20] But he did share many of the same ideological sensibilities and figured out quickly how to communicate whose side he was on in the emerging culture wars.[21] "I know you can't endorse *me*," he famously told born-again Christians at a 1980 rally in Dallas, Texas. "But I want you to know that I endorse *you* and what you are doing."[22] As it turned out, evangelicals *did* endorse Reagan in a paradigmatic shift in American politics.

Reagan's 1979–80 campaign for the presidency began just as the religious Right was coalescing. In a 1980 "Washington for Jesus" rally attended by more than two hundred thousand people, Pat Robertson proclaimed, "We have together, with the Protestants and the Catholics, enough votes to run the country. And when the people say, 'We've had enough,' we are going to take over."[23] By this time, Robertson had become an enormously influential figure in the Christian community, having established the Christian Broadcasting Network (CBN) in the 1960s, and later *The 700 Club*, which, by the 1980s, aired on more than two hundred television stations.[24] A former Southern Baptist minister from Lexington, Virginia, Robertson was telegenic and understood how to use new media to spread his message in an accessible way to a mass audience. In 1979 he laid out an "Action Plan for the 1980s," calling for a "profound moral revival" based on "Biblical Christianity."[25] In the plan, he specifically highlights the "awesome power of the media to mold our moral and political consensus."[26] Robertson advocates that Christians "do everything in their power to get involved in media (radio, television, newspapers, magazines) . . . [to] learn motion picture techniques, produce drama, write music, publish books—anything to produce a climate of righteousness and godliness."[27]

Robertson had a major ally in this effort in Reverend Jerry Falwell. Like Robertson, Falwell was media savvy and deft in his ability to shape public discourse for mass audiences. Millions of viewers across America watched his television show, "Old-Time Gospel Hour." In addition, in the 1980s he often appeared on mainstream television shows like *Nightline* and *Face the Nation*. Like Robertson, Falwell had a Reagan conversion story, claiming that he left a 1980 meeting with Reagan "with a fire burning" in his heart. "In answer to prayer and hard work, God had given us a great leader."[28] Perhaps the most prominent and influential voice of the religious Right in the Reagan era, Falwell was born and raised in Lynchburg, Virginia, where, under his pastorship at the Thomas Road Baptist Church, membership exploded to over seventeen thousand people, making it one of the nation's first megachurches. In 1971, he also established Liberty University, which would become the largest evangelical Christian university in the world. He founded the political action group, the Moral Majority, in 1979, whose purpose was to wed conservative Christian social values, often described as "family values," with politics. In this way, it was ideologically aligned with the religious Right—indeed, the two terms would often be used interchangeably in the 1980s to describe the broader cultural Christian movement.

Falwell's political activism, like that of many white, Southern, born-again Christians, was largely a response to cultural changes in America. As a young minister, he believed the roles of religious leaders and elected officials were fundamentally different. "Preachers are not called to be politicians, but soul winners," he said in 1965.[29] In the intervening years, however, as major shifts in American culture took place—including the Civil Rights Act, the Equal Rights Amendment, and *Roe v. Wade*—Falwell had a change of heart. "God is angry with us as a nation," he declared. "I have a divine mandate to go right into the halls of Congress and fight for laws that will save America."[30] Not so coincidentally, Falwell's first dip into political waters was an attempt to protect the status quo on issues of race. Like most white Southern evangelicals, Falwell was enraged by changes to Jim Crow and refused to support Lyndon B. Johnson's civil rights bills specifically, and any efforts at integration more broadly. "It is a terrible violation of human and private property rights," he claimed. "It should be considered civil wrongs rather than civil rights."[31] In 1968 he opened his pulpit to George Wallace, former governor of Alabama, perhaps best known for his intransigent "Segregation Now, Segregation Tomorrow, Segregation Forever" speech.[32]

In the 1970s Richard Nixon's "Southern Strategy" used code, euphemism, or "dog whistles" to activate white conservative fears about race, gender, sexuality, and the loss of traditional values. While "moderate" conservative politicians like Nixon and Reagan used this strategy effectively, culture warriors like Falwell and Robertson could be more blunt. By the 1980s, the religious Right latched onto a range of social causes that would define the decade's culture wars: prayer in classrooms, pornography, language arts curriculum, gender roles, homosexuality, AIDS, the war on drugs, and abortion. All of these issues, Falwell believed, were indicative of America's social and moral decline; his responses were often aggressive, uncompromising, and inflammatory. "Though they claim to be another poorly treated minority," he said of gays, "homosexuals are involved in open immorality as they practice perversion . . . they are not a minority any more than murderers, rapists or other sinners are a minority. Since they cannot reproduce, they proselyte."[33] In concert with Reagan's campaign for the presidency, Falwell rallied the evangelical troops, casting the culture wars as a holy war. By the time Reagan was elected in 1980, Falwell was described as a "political kingmaker."[34] Not surprisingly, he was among the first visitors invited to Reagan's White House. Meanwhile, the rise of the Moral Majority and the religious Right became one of the top political stories of 1980.

As the Reagan era continued, some journalists began describing the emerging evangelical media infrastructure—which included TV and radio shows, telethons, direct-mail campaigns, magazines, Bible schools, colleges, and Christian-themed amusement parks—as the "Electric Church."[35] This movement was invigorated by Ronald Reagan's landmark elimination of the Fairness Doctrine, a longstanding policy signed into law by Harry Truman in 1949 whose aim was to ensure fairness and balance on the airwaves. Without regulation by the Federal Communications Commission (FCC), the floodgates opened for more polemic religious and conservative content on television and radio. The Electric Church also benefited from the births of cable television and VHS home video. Fewer than twenty million Americans had cable in 1980, approximately 10 percent of the population; the share was 70 percent by the end of the decade.[36] While some of those channels—most prominently, HBO and MTV—featured content that infuriated the religious Right, conservatives were not about to cede control of the powerful new medium to the secular Left. An ABC News report found that by the late 1980s, there were more than sixteen hundred television minsters generating an astounding $1.5 billion per year.[37] Many new channels, including CBN, featured Christian content exclusively. VHS home videos likewise went from expensive novelties in the late 1970s to near-ubiquity by the end of the 1980s. The format became a crucial platform for the religious Right, offering the individual more control about when, where, and how often they could watch content.

The booming market of television ministers and preachers, often referred to as "televangelists," took advantage of these new media platforms. Among the most popular in the 1980s were Jim and Tammy Faye Bakker. While the Bakkers were much less explicitly political than Jerry Falwell and Pat Robertson, they possessed the same media savvy and were perhaps the best example of purveyors of the so-called "prosperity gospel" preached by many televangelists. The prosperity gospel, which promised financial rewards to the righteous, was a perfect fit for the Reagan era. In a time of yuppie excess and admonitions to "shop 'til you drop," it also did nothing to discourage conspicuous consumption. God wanted people to live the good life, televangelists promised. Increasingly, according to this logic, money could be viewed as evidence of righteousness. God had blessed the rich; otherwise, they would not be rich.

Jim and Tammy Faye Bakker began working for Pat Robertson's Christian Broadcasting Network in the 1960s; by the 1970s they had created a television channel of their own: the Praise the Lord (PTL) Club, which featured a variety of programs and was broadcast twenty-four hours a day. It was like MTV for evangelical Christians. In the late 1970s they opened Heritage USA, a Christian amusement park that, as journalist Emily Johnson observes, "combined the Bakkers' growing televangelism empire with theme-park hedonism, offering an immersive experience in the sights, sounds, and practices of American conservative evangelicalism."[38] The theme park included an enormous waterpark, a Disneyland-like train, a campground, luxury hotels and condos, and a full-scale replica of ancient Jerusalem for shopping. At approximately twenty-three hundred acres, it was more than ten times larger than Disneyland.[39] In the 1980s, the Bakkers' television shows, theme park, and ministry were so successful, they were bringing in more than $100 million annually and did little to hide their resulting extravagant lifestyles.[40] "If we're called to be fishers of men, which we are, we're simply using better bait," Jim Bakker boasted of his multimedia approach.[41]

Ultimately, the Bakkers' empire came crumbling down when news broke that Jim Bakker was engaged in an affair with a twenty-one-year-old church secretary named Jessica Hahn and had committed multiple acts of fraud and conspiracy.[42] Other televangelist stories of excess and corruption followed, including popular preacher Jimmy Swaggart's televised confession that he had sexual relations with a prostitute in 1988. Many critics felt that by the end of the 1980s the religious Right was waning in the wake of several high-profile scandals. While certain figures rose and fell, however, the movement proved a resilient force in American politics. In the Obama era, Pat Robertson's *The 700 Club* still aired on ABC Family, while two major 2016 presidential contenders, Donald Trump and Bernie Sanders, paid visits to Jerry Falwell's Liberty University. New media-savvy ministers continue to thrive: evangelical pastor Rick Warren, whose book *The Purpose Driven Life* (2002) sold in excess of forty million copies, was invited to offer the prayer at President Obama's 2008 inauguration, while Joel Osteen's televised sermons draw more than 20 million viewers each month.[43] Meanwhile, high-profile conservative evangelical politicians, including Mike Huckabee and Ted Cruz, staged viable national campaigns for the presidency in 2008 and 2016, respectively, while Donald Trump won the 2016 election with unprecedented white evangelical support. Such examples speak to the powerful presence evangelical Christianity still has on all facets of American life. Its defining features, issues, and political activism are rooted in the 1980s, a period in which the role of religion in American society fundamentally changed.

Power, Prosperity, and Protest

In this context, James Baldwin's critique of American Christianity is fascinating for a number of reasons, including the paradox that while he came out of a strain of the born-again tradition, he was in many ways the embodiment of all it feared and despised, being black, gay, and relentlessly critical of organized religion, nationalism, and capitalism. Baldwin's characterization of the religious Right as "members of the richest, most exclusive private club in the world" cuts right to the core of the "prosperity gospel," as well as the overarching ethos of the Reagan era.[44] Perhaps the most notable feature of domestic policy in the 1980s was its top-down economic vision, often described as Reaganomics. Ronald Reagan promised to cut taxes, eliminate regulations, and set Wall Street loose. Over his two terms in office, he did just that, and while the stock market soared, the gap between the rich and the poor widened. Inner-city poverty, homelessness, and crime all peaked during the Reagan era.[45] By the end of the 1980s, nearly 50 percent of black children were living below the poverty line. "The great, vast, shining Republic knows nothing about them and cares nothing about them," wrote Baldwin in *The Evidence of Things Not Seen*, "recognizes their existence only in times of stress, as during a military adventure, say, or an election year, or when their dangerous situation erupts into what the Republic generally calls a 'riot.'"[46]

What was the Christian response to this growing inequality and poverty? By and large, the religious Right not only passively accepted Reaganomics but actively embraced it. Increasingly, the messaging of religion, government, and corporate America were in perfect harmony. What was the message? As the character Gordon Gekko famously put it in the 1987 movie *Wall Street*: "Greed, for lack of a better word, is good. Greed is right. Greed works. Greed clarifies and cuts through to the essence of the evolutionary spirit."[47] This was the spirit in which born-again Christianity thrived in the 1980s. Trickle-down economics replaced the widow's mite; congregations became consumers; pastors became millionaire media moguls; and Jesus's famous renunciation of wealth was replaced with the prosperity gospel. "It is scarcely worth comparing the material well-being—or material aspirations—of these latter-day apostles with the poverty of Jesus," writes Baldwin. "Whereas Jesus and his disciples were distrusted by the state largely because they respected the poor and shared everything, the fundamentalists of the present hour would appear not to know that the poor exist."[48] Indeed, the wealth of televangelists like the Bakkers', ironically, derived primarily from the cynical exploitation of poor and lower-middle-class whites. Such member-consumers, Baldwin writes, are manipulated to believe that they too can be saved, receive forgiveness, and become financially prosperous. They must only write another check to learn how. Of the leaders of this "new" commodified Christianity, Baldwin asserts: "They have taken the man from Galilee as hostage. He does not know them and they do not know him."[49]

Such hypocrisy, of course, did not come out of a vacuum. It had roots. While white Christians and black Christians theoretically worshipped the same God, they were shaped by different histories. Baldwin reminds readers that chattel slavery was justified by many white Christian sects and survived by many black Christians.[50] The practice of not only treating people as inferior based on race but actually *owning* them was supported by appeals to the Bible, including the Old Testament curse laid on the sons of Ham, as well as Paul's admonition for servants to obey their masters. Baldwin became aware of such religious-based rationales for oppression at a young age, and he writes that "it was impossible not to sense in this a self-serving moral cowardice" which caused him to "regard white Christians and, especially, white ministers with a profound and troubled contempt."[51] Such self-serving rationales for slavery, and later for Jim Crow, Baldwin suggests, are not unconnected to the prosperity gospel of the 1980s. It is simply the latest attempt to protect and advance power and security by and through white Christian doctrine.

Of course, Baldwin also witnessed greed, hypocrisy, and moral cowardice in his own Church. How was it different from or similar to the white born-again movement that now permeated American culture and politics? For Baldwin, the answer had to do with positioning. Among his greatest frustrations with Christianity in the context of the black community was its pacifying effect, its complacency with injustice in the present by the promise of salvation in the next life. "When I faced a congregation," writes Baldwin in *The Fire Next Time*, "it began to take all the strength I had not to stammer, not to curse, not to tell them to throw away their Bibles and get off their knees and go home and organize, for example, a rent strike."[52] Yet for all his misgivings about black Christianity's susceptibility to simply reinforce the status quo, he recognized there was more to the picture. The black Church, in all of its various strands, was also a site of resistance; its songs were documents of strength, solidarity, resilience, and beauty. As susceptible as it might be to the problems that infected white Christianity, then, its historical positioning made it different. For Baldwin, speaking in general terms, white Christianity in America, by and large, spoke from a position of power; black Christianity from a position of struggle, resistance, and survival. While working with similar Gods, texts, and stories, then, these were translated through different languages, voices, histories, experiences, and intent.

Moreover, within black Christianity, as Douglas Field notes, Black Pentecostalism—the faith of Baldwin's youth—was even further marginalized and animated by the protest tradition. Its identity was oppositional, anti-establishment, and averse to materialism—even if individual leaders sometimes fell prey to greed.[53] Baldwin retained much of the radical, individualist spirit of his Pentecostal faith, while finally rejecting what he saw as its fatal flaw: its fear of love. "There was no love in the church," writes Baldwin. "It was a mask for hatred and self-hatred and despair. . . . When we were told to love everybody, I had thought that meant *everybody*. But no. It applied only to those who believed as we did."[54] This exclusion and fear of the other, shared and inflated by many white Christian groups, including the Moral Majority, began with hatred of the body.

Terror of the Flesh

The body, thus, becomes the starting point for Baldwin's exploration of modern Christianity in "To Crush the Serpent." Baldwin's youth was a time of great confusion, he admits, in no small part because of his Church's teachings about sexuality. This confusion was compounded in adolescence when he became more aware of his own body. "Until adolescence," he writes, "one's body is simply there, like one's shadow or the weather. With adolescence, this body becomes a malevolently unpredictable enemy, and it also becomes, for the first time, appallingly *visible*."[55] Baldwin's point in describing this physical transformation is to demonstrate what religion often attempts to do with this self-awareness. The body, according to the dominant strain of Christian theology, is the enemy. It is filthy, impure, prone to all sorts of limitations, diseases, and deviant impulses. "The carnal mind," reads Romans 8:7, "*is* enmity against God." For Baldwin, this self-hatred was further reinforced by his race and sexual orientation. Everything about him was wrong.

The beauty of the pulpit, Baldwin writes, is that it allowed him, at least for a fleeting moment, to feel cleansed. He could temporarily deny his flesh, abandon his impure thoughts, and find acceptance. "I threw all my anguish and terror into my sermons," he writes, recognizing in retrospect that "the salvation I was preaching to others was fueled by the hope of my own."[56] But in the end, after the service was done, "nothing was obliterated: I was still a boy in trouble with himself and the streets around him."[57] Baldwin ultimately decided to leave the pulpit and the Church, he writes, because "I did not want to become a liar. I did not want my love to become manipulation. I did not want my fear of my own desires to transform itself into power—into power, precisely, over those who feared and were therefore at the mercy of their own desires."[58]

Such a revelation seemed never to have occurred to those who made up the modern religious Right—or perhaps it had occurred to them, but they made a different calculation. Nearly all of the issues that animated the Christian Right were rooted in fear and hatred of the body, from homosexuality to pornography, to women's liberation, to AIDS. "AIDS is not just God's punishment for homosexuals," proclaimed Jerry Falwell. "It is God's punishment for the society that tolerates homosexuals."[59] Not so coincidentally, it was nearly always "sins of the flesh" that surfaced in the scandals of shamed ministers and televangelists, some of whom ultimately turned on and blackmailed each other. Due to this blatant discrepancy between their actions and words, writes Baldwin, "I cannot take seriously—not, at least, as Christian ministers—the present-day gang that calls itself the Moral Majority, or its tongue-speaking relatives such as follow the Right Reverend Robertson."[60] He could not take them seriously, that is, because of how clearly their gospel of sexual repression and fear of the body was a projection of power rather than a genuine personal commitment. Moreover, Baldwin found the sexless, Puritan gospel theologically and historically bankrupt. The scriptural Jesus, he contends, had nothing much to say about carnality. His sermons on sexuality do not exist, nor does his condemnation of women controlling their own bodies. "Not one of the present-day white fundamentalist preachers would have had the humility, the courage, the sheer presence of mind to have said to the mob surrounding the woman taken in adultery, 'He that is without sin, let him first cast a stone,' or the depth of perception that informs 'Neither do I condemn thee: Go, and sin no more.'"[61] The scriptural Jesus, in other words, did not condemn the body.

Baldwin traces the division between flesh and spirit back to the apostle Paul, whom, as Josiah Ulysses Young notes, "Baldwin dislikes more than any other Biblical figure."[62] Young elaborates: "For Baldwin, the [alabaster Lord's] power has to do with Paul's classical distinction between the flesh and the spirit. The former is to sin as the latter is to grace. Given that ancient dualism, white American Protestants, Baldwin asserts, have thought that the black body has been to the flesh as the white body has been to the spirit."[63] This critique is crucial to Baldwin's alternative gospel; not only does he see a harmful division between body and spirit, as did, for example, the Romantic poet William Blake, a writer with whom Craig Werner persuasively documents some striking theological similarities.[64] He also recognizes the racial prisms of body and spirit—the ways, that is, in which racialized bodies come to signify this duality. As cultural scholar Richard Dyer puts it, "To represent people is to represent bodies."[65] In Western culture, such representations are always already racialized: black people are often reduced to the corporal—the "race" of their bodies—while white people are often raceless, colorless, universal, transcendent. A black author is described as a black author while a white author is simply called an author. To be white is to be pure, clean, and innocent, while to be black is to be defiled, corrupt, marked. It is this mythology that underpins D. W. Griffith's influential film, *The Birth of a Nation* (1915), which enacts onscreen a kind of cosmic war against the black body. For Griffith, the black body is portrayed as corrupting or defiling the white body—particularly the body of the angelic white woman. The myth of the black male as corporal, sexual beast and the white woman as ethereal victim remains one of the most persistent, deeply embedded terrors in American culture.[66]

These intersections of religion, race, gender and sexuality, writes Baldwin, "are fearfully entangled in the guts of this nation, so profoundly that to speak of the one is to conjure up the other. One cannot speak of sin without referring to blackness, and blackness stalks our history and our streets."[67] Playing on such myths and fears, indeed, was the purpose of the infamous Willie Horton ad in 1988, one year after Baldwin's essay was published. The commercial was orchestrated by Republican strategists Lee Atwater and Roger Ailes and actively supported by the religious Right. Before airing the ad, George H. W. Bush was running seventeen points behind his opponent, former Massachusetts governor Michael Dukakis. The ad, however, proved disturbingly effective. Not only would it portray Dukakis as soft on crime, it would effectively exploit the specter of race. Horton, who was serving a life sentence for murder, was out of prison via Dukakis's furlough program, during which time he raped a white woman. Horton became the embodiment of America's fears about black men. His image was darkened to accentuate what he was intended to conjure: fear, rape, violence, and corruption. As Susan Estrich, Dukakis's campaign manager, writes: "There is no stronger metaphor for racial hatred in our country than the black man raping the white woman. If you were going to run a campaign of fear and smear and appeal to racial hatred you could not have picked a better case to use than this one."[68] Bush ended up winning the 1988 election by a landslide.

While in theory, all flesh—all bodies—were at odds with the spirit according to traditional Christian theology, Baldwin recognized that *black bodies* were particular targets of both the state and Christianity. Indeed, these institutions often worked hand in hand to perpetuate the devaluation of the black body. Consequently, what the actions and obsessions of the political and religious Right reveal more than anything, Baldwin contends, is a desire for *control*. Like their ancestors, many white Christians believe they must define, police, and control black bodies for the good of society. He compares the ministers of the religious Right to deputies he encountered throughout America. "They both believe they are responsible . . . to define and privileged to impose law and order; and both, historically and actually, know that law and order are meant to keep me in my place."[69]

The need to repress and control the body—particularly the body of the other—results in many grotesque and dangerous outcomes for black and white alike. For one, writes Baldwin, it makes "the possibility of the private life as fugitive as that of a fleeing nigger."[70] Yet it also results in a kind of psychological slavery. Hating the body means hating oneself; violence against the body is also violence against oneself. As a former preacher, Baldwin recalls its effects even on the minister preaching fire and damnation. "Joy was not even, to judge from the endless empty plain behind their eyes, a memory. And they could recognize, in others, joy or the possibility of joy only as a mighty threat—as something, as they put it, obscene."[71] In a strange counterintuitive reversal, that is, religion taught its members to fear joy and pleasure, to hate the body, to view intimate contact as a threat.

Ultimately, Baldwin concluded that such a belief system could not be his home. "*My* salvation could not be achieved that way," he writes.[72] Upon leaving church one day—his last day—he remembers an old white woman from his congregation pulling him aside and warning of the eternal torment that awaited boys like him. "Her face and her eyes seemed purple," he writes. "Her lips seemed to be chewing and spitting out the air. . . . And, all the time, her grip on my arm tightened."[73] Love had nothing to do with such an encounter, Baldwin writes. "The motive was buried deep within that woman, the decomposing corpse of her human possibilities fouling the air."[74] This description—the decomposing corpse of her human possibilities fouling the air—can be interpreted as Baldwin's symbolic embodiment of the moral outcomes of the religious Right. It was a gospel based on fear, rejection, and exclusion. Yet as Baldwin writes: "Those ladders to fire—the burning of the witch, the heretic, the Jew, the nigger, the faggot—have always failed to redeem, or even to change in any way whatever, the mob. They merely epiphanize and force their connection on the only plain on which the mob can meet: The charred bones connect its members and give them a reason to speak to one another, for the charred bones are the sum total of their individual self-hatred, externalized."[75]

Moral Minority

Baldwin's alternative gospel had to do with re-examining assumptions about the body and desire. If William Blake's theology married heaven and hell, Baldwin's reunited body and spirit.[76] "True to his credo," writes Josiah Ulysses Young, "he rejects any 'God' that would cause him, or anybody else, to put down the flesh and lift up the spirit, thus tearing the two asunder."[77] While the religious Right marked, policed, and condemned the body, Baldwin retorts that "sin is not limited to carnal activity, nor are the sins of the flesh the most crucial or reverberating of our sins."[78] Sin, for Baldwin, goes deeper than the flesh. "Carnal activity" can be grotesque, mundane, or sublime. For sex to be sacred, it must be about genuine, reciprocal connection. Thus, "salvation," for Baldwin, "is not flight from the wrath of God. . . . Salvation is not separation. It is the beginning of union with all that is or has been or will ever be."[79] This is Baldwin's gospel of love. Douglas Field clarifies that the author's emphasis on love is not to be confused with sentimentality, which Baldwin abhorred. Love, for Baldwin, was an active spiritual and political force, "something more like a fire . . . something which can change you."[80] Love did not deny the body or sexuality; it embraced it. "Rather than transfiguring the religious into the sexual," writes Field, "Baldwin urges his readers to reexamine what is generally held sacred. This entails, far from a repudiation of the sacred, a need to accept the sensual side of religion."[81] Baldwin's "new spirituality" thus includes all bodies and all forms of love.[82]

Such a revision of traditional Christianity compels one to interrogate the language used to describe the sinner or transgressor. The meaning of the word "transgressor," argues Baldwin, is much different than we suppose. His reassessment of the label's true meaning was, he writes, the "key to [his] journey through the Bible."[83] This reappraisal begins by understanding that transgressors, in many cases, are the *moral minority*. Jesus, Baldwin reminds, was one such transgressor, as were many of the people with whom he surrounded himself. Historically, Baldwin argues, "transgressors" include those who opposed Hitler in Germany; they include Rosa Parks and Martin Luther King Jr. To transgress, that is, can be a courageous and *moral* act. It is a society's minorities, not the majority, who so frequently act as its conscience.

Whether Jerry Falwell's Moral Majority and the religious Right did in fact represent a majority of Americans is debatable. But certainly the worldview they espoused—Manichean, militaristic, capitalist, white, heteronormative, suspicious, and at times outrightly violent toward difference—was carried triumphantly in two landslide elections for Ronald Reagan. Like Foucault, Baldwin recognized that power was not simply enacted by the government or the Church or any other institution; rather, it was deeply embedded in all aspects of society. Foucault used the term *episteme* to describe a set of assumptions, ideas, attitudes, and procedures that construct our reality in a given culture and time.[84] The episteme determines what is moral and immoral, and who is normal and abnormal. In this way, the language of the religious Right represented the dominant *episteme* of the Reagan era. In political parlance, it controlled the narrative.

The religious Right's power and influence, however, did not make it moral. Morality required a willingness to challenge tradition, power, and authority; it required unpopular "disturbers of the peace" and visionary "transgressors." As Baldwin put it in his 1962 essay, "The Creative Process": "Societies never know it, but the war of an artist with his society is a lover's war, and he does, at his best, what lovers do, which is to reveal the beloved to himself, and with that revelation, make freedom real."[85] For Baldwin, the Moral Majority, replete with Thou Shalt Nots, Scarlet As, and repressed desires, represented an easier, less evolved understanding of morality and salvation. It demanded fear and condemnation. But to condemn the other, he writes, "obliterates the possibility of salvation, since condemnation is fueled by terror and self-hatred."[86] This is the destructive epistemic loop—on the individual and society—of traditional organized religion: there must always be queer, threatening bodies to justify one's own righteous, superior identity. This impulse, indeed, was one of the driving forces behind Donald Trump's presidential campaign, and white evangelicals approved of it, or looked past it, in overwhelming numbers. According to 2016 election exit polls, white evangelicals made up an unprecedented 26 percent of the electorate; more than 80 percent supported Trump—a higher percentage than supported Mitt Romney in 2012, John McCain in 2008, or even George W. Bush in 2000 and 2004.[87] The numbers surprised many political analysts who assumed religious individuals would defect from the Republican Party's standard-bearer, given Trump's hate-filled rhetoric and moral deficiencies. As it turned out, many of his most bigoted campaign promises—banning Muslim immigrants, building a wall on the southern border to prevent Mexicans from entry, criminalizing abortion, repealing the Affordable Care Act, and revitalizing "law and order" in predominantly African American cities—were the very issues that won him evangelical support. As Baldwin observed in the 1980s, such rhetoric and policies bear little resemblance to those of Jesus found in scripture. Rather, it exposes the values of the modern, white, religious Right, which remain deeply drenched in fear, racism, violence, and exclusion.

By contrast, writes Baldwin, in perhaps the most eloquent encapsulation of his alternative theology,

> Salvation is as real, as mighty, and as impersonal as the rain, and it is yet as private as the rain in one's face. It is never accomplished; it is to be reaffirmed every day and every hour. There is absolutely no salvation without love: this is the wheel in the middle of the wheel. Salvation does not divide. Salvation connects, so that one sees oneself in others and others in oneself. It is not the exclusive property of any dogma, creed, or church. It keeps the channel open between oneself and however one wishes to name That which is greater than oneself. It has absolutely nothing to do with one's fortunes or one's circumstances in one's passage through this world. It is a mighty fortress, even in the teeth of ruin or at the gates of death.[88]

Salvation, that is, is not achieved in some distant heaven through the verdict of some scrutinizing deity. It is not achieved by escaping damnation or being cleansed of one's desires or sins. Rather, it comes through intimacy, love, and connection, through "seeing oneself in others and others in oneself."[89] For Baldwin, if we are saved, finally, it will not be by God, but by each other.

5

Things Not Seen

Covering Tragedy, from the Terror in Atlanta to Black Lives Matter

> History, I contend, is the present—*we*, with every breath we take, every move we make, *are* History—and what goes around, comes around."
>
> —James Baldwin, *The Evidence of Things Not Seen*, 1985

"Am I next?" read signs held by young black men in Ferguson, Missouri, in late August 2014.[1] Days earlier, Michael Brown, age seventeen, was shot and killed by a white police officer. According to reports, Brown was walking home with a friend when police approached and ordered them off the street and onto the sidewalk. What happened next is disputed, but according to multiple eyewitness accounts, it ended with Brown raising his hands in the air, saying, "Don't shoot!" and the officer proceeding to fire. According to Brown's friend, Dorian Johnson, after being shot once, Brown "stopped running, his hands went immediately in the air and he turned around towards the officer, face-to-face. He started to tell the officer he was unarmed and that you should stop shooting me. Before he [could] get his second sentence out, the officer fired several more shots into his head and chest areas. . . . It was like being shot like an animal."[2]

Brown's death ignited a national movement. How could racial violence be worsening when a black man was sitting in the Oval Office? Why was black life so devalued and expendable in the twenty-first century? The Ferguson incident came on the heels of several other high-profile killings of young black men, including those of Oscar Grant, Trayvon Martin, and Jordan Davis, and followed by many more: Tamir Rice in Cleveland, Freddie Gray in Baltimore, Walter Scott in South Carolina, and Laquan McDonald in Chicago. According to a 2014 report, on a national scale black males were nearly ten times more likely to be victims of homicide than white males.[3] Black males were also far more likely to be pulled over, stopped and frisked, or otherwise profiled by police. Yet while statistically, black males are far more likely to be the victims than the perpetrators of violence, in the American imaginary they remain synonymous with criminality, danger, and fear.[4] Such perceptions include young black boys. As the American Psychological Association notes, "Black boys as young as ten may not be viewed in the same light of childhood innocence as their white peers, but are instead more likely to be mistaken as older, be perceived as guilty and face police violence if accused of a crime."[5] This indeed was the case with Tamir Rice, a twelve-year-old African American boy who was playing alone at a park on November 23, 2014, when a neighbor called the police about a suspicious figure "pointing a gun at people."[6] The gun turned out to be a toy. That did not prevent him from being shot dead within seconds of police officers arriving on the scene.

We have become all too familiar with the conventional media coverage in the wake of such tragedies. A predictable cycle ensues in which the dead black victim is further scrutinized—*Did he deserve to die? What did he do to elicit such an outcome? Was he a delinquent, a thug?*—and in which the dead black victim is mourned. In some cases, the pain, anger, and outrage translates into peaceful protests and, in some cases, riots. Sometimes, as in the cases of Ferguson and Baltimore, we see both. The news media shows up when the situation is hot, or when the story is compelling. The more volatile and violent the circumstances, the higher the ratings. Rarely, however, does the coverage delve deeper.

Where, then, does one look for better answers? Or even the right questions? One would be hard pressed to find an author who Black Lives Matter have referenced as much as they have James Baldwin. His words speak to the present in ways that seem not only relevant but also prophetic. Baldwin would be the first to lament this relevance, at least insofar as it speaks to the country's inability to move forward on issues of race and violence. But his work nonetheless remains as timely as ever. There are, of course, numerous works by the author one can turn to for insight on the present moment. Yet arguably none is as connected to the issues animating the Black Lives Matter movement as Baldwin's final nonfiction book, *The Evidence of Things Not Seen* (1985).

Written in response to what became known alternately as the "Terror in Atlanta" or the "Atlanta Child Murders," Baldwin's book is a piercing examination of antiblack violence in America, why it persisted after the "gains" of the civil rights era, and why it would likely continue unless deep-rooted structural and psychic changes occurred. Published at the height of the Reagan era in 1985, *The Evidence of Things Not Seen* was a sequel of sorts to his 1963 civil rights era classic, *The Fire Next Time*. In sharp contrast to *Fire*, a national bestseller, however, *Evidence*—both upon publication and today—is likely his most overlooked book. To date, *Evidence* has been reprinted once, on its tenth anniversary in 1995, by Owl Books. At the time of its first publication, in spite of the nation's abiding interest in the case, Baldwin found the book difficult to publish. His longtime publisher, Dial Press, passed it over. It was picked up in England and France before it finally found a home—and modest print run—in the United States via Holt, Rinehart and Winston. There are several possible reasons for this sudden indifference, perhaps most significant that the tone of *Evidence* was out of step with the "colorblind," optimistic ethos of the Reagan era. As David Leeming observes, "White people wanted to be told that the 'new South,' that the existence of black mayors and police chiefs in American cities, the presence of blacks as television anchors, and the emergence of black men and women as 'successful' authors, meant that the civil rights movement had worked and that America was on its way to 'glory.' Baldwin, always the Jeremiah, always the disturber of the peace, let it be known in *Evidence* that they were wrong."[7]

The book has begun to receive some limited critical attention over the past decade.[8] Among the most noteworthy analyses is Richard Schur's astute chapter, "Unseen or Unspeakable? Racial Evidence in Baldwin's and Morrison's Nonfiction," which appears in *James Baldwin and Toni Morrison: Comparative Critical and Theoretical Texts*, edited by Lovalerie King and Lynn Orilla Scott, and focuses on the legal implications of Baldwin's book alongside Toni Morrison's "Friday on the Potomac" (1992). In both texts, he argues, the authors "recast legalized racism as a sensory problem, rather than one of rationality" in which the "meaning and operation [of race] have changed due to the growth of neoliberal rhetoric and policies during the post–civil rights era."[9] D. Quentin Miller builds on Schur's work in chapter 5 of *A Criminal Power: James Baldwin and the Law* (2013), reading *Evidence* as an attempt to use legal rhetoric to challenge the law itself. "Critics who complained that Baldwin was merely rehashing old ideas . . . completely miss the point," writes Miller, "that he was trying, in all earnestness, to change with the times as well as to change the times."[10] Miller's assessment of the book's value is precisely right: while it remains one of his most overlooked and undervalued works, *Evidence* reveals an author both adapting to and challenging the new realities, and rhetoric, of the Reagan era.

This chapter adds to the small but growing body of scholarship on *Evidence* by examining how Baldwin's article and book act as correctives to sensationalist media accounts of the Atlanta child murders and simplistic gloss-overs of the New South—and, by extension, post–civil rights America—more broadly. The Terror in Atlanta was a national media sensation and, for the vast majority of Americans, a mediated experience. People learned about what was happening from TV, newspapers, magazine articles—and later, made-for-TV movies, documentaries, and bestselling books. "Black death has never elicited so much attention," marveled Baldwin.[11] There were, of course, many different reasons for this, some humane, some voyeuristic. In most media narratives, the intrigue sprang primarily from the crime drama. Who was the killer? What were his motives? Why did it take so long for him to be caught? How many more children would he murder? When Wayne Williams was finally arrested in the summer of 1981, the media finally had their serial-killing monster and, before long, their headline-spawning trial. With its potent combination of race, sex, and violence, the Wayne Williams trial was a precursor in many ways to the OJ Simpson trial in 1995. For Baldwin, however, Williams was a convenient scapegoat, and the trial more a postmodern circus than an attempt to deliver justice. Who was really responsible for the murder of so many innocent black children? The answer, Baldwin asserts, is not one individual but "what our history has made of us."[12] For all the media hype, he contends, "We were not really confronting a Jack the Ripper fantasy, or an Agatha Christie puzzle: we were being confronted with the concrete result of the choices we had made."[13]

Holding up this mirror to America was the impetus for his original article, published in *Playboy* in 1981, and his purpose for ultimately developing the piece into a full-length book, published in 1985. He saw himself as a witness—and the book as a lasting document—against the media accounts that dominated headlines for years. In doing so, he not only provided one of the most penetrating portraits of urban America in the Reagan era, he also traced its historical context back several decades and presciently anticipated the "post-racial" violence that continues in the Obama era and beyond.

The Spectacle of Black Death

It was not mere coincidence that the Terror in Atlanta (1979–1981) coincided with the birth of cable news. CNN launched in the summer of 1980, becoming America's first twenty-four-hour news network. It marked a new era—and new approach—to news media. Media mogul Ted Turner, CNN's founder, conceived of it as an alternative to the limitations of the major news networks: CBS, ABC, and NBC. On cable news, events could unfold live. It wasn't scripted—the unpredictable might happen. A story could be followed day after day, week after week, like a television series. It was tailor-made, that is, for high-drama, human-interest stories like the Iranian hostage crisis, the attempted assassination of Ronald Reagan, and the Atlanta child murders. CNN reached the second-highest ratings in its history in 1982, the year of the Wayne Williams trial (the network's peak ratings came in 1991, the year of the Rodney King beating and the Gulf War).[14]

Until the 1980s, many assumed that problems such as racism, poverty, and crime persisted because they remained invisible. Indeed, one of the biggest criticisms of Ronald Reagan was his refusal to even acknowledge the so-called "reign of terror in American cities," instead presenting a wholesome, prosperous America in which drugs, violence, AIDS, and poor people did not exist.[15] Yet the 1980s saw a transition from invisibility and neglect to occasional bursts of media-driven national obsession. Following the story in its early stages from his home in Saint-Paul-de-Vence, France, Baldwin was initially confused by all the interest. Why did America suddenly care so much about black death? Certainly, as he wrote in his 1981 article, there was "nothing new in this city or state or nation about black bodies floating finally to the surface of the river."[16]

One of his primary concerns in *Evidence*, then, was the meaning and impact of this transition from invisibility and denial to saturation and exploitation (a pattern which would proliferate in the 1990s and 2000s with the advent of the internet, video recording devices, smartphones, and social media). The Atlanta child murders turned out reporters in droves. "Many of those out-of-town reporters," writes *Los Angeles Times* journalist Howard Rosenberg, "popped into Atlanta for ratings-sweeps quickies and stayed just long enough to form capsule impressions, which distorted the meanings of the slayings and the image of a city known for being coolheaded during the civil rights violence of the '60s. Stations would bring in a crew, do the 'Atlanta: City of Fear' theme, interview an official and then blow town."[17] In this way, the media coverage is not unlike that surrounding the tragedies of the Black Lives Matter era, in which death is often presented as a spectacle: a spectacle that incites a range of responses to be sure—sympathy, fascination, fear, voyeurism—but a spectacle nonetheless. In early-1980s Atlanta, with each new headline—"They Found Another Body"—the plot continued and the media was on the scene, snapping pictures of lifeless children. Prior to the 1980s, it seemed if only people were more aware, if only the media would report on what was actually happening in poor areas, change would occur. After the Atlanta child murders, Baldwin wasn't so sure.

Ironically, the Atlanta child murders would have likely remained under the radar if not for the persistent efforts of grief-stricken mothers, desperate to find answers about their missing children. Edward Hope Smith was the first boy to go missing, in July 1979. Eight days later he was found dead in a wooded area. He had been shot. He was fourteen years old. Then Alfred Evans, age thirteen. Then Milton Harvey, age fourteen. Then Yusuf Bell, age nine. Bell was last seen getting into a blue car; his body turned up in a deteriorated elementary school. The list went on and on. From the summer of 1979 to the spring of 1981, at least twenty-nine children and young adults were killed in the city. These were just the deaths that became part of the official "list," conforming to a particular "pattern."[18] All were African American; all were from the inner city; and all but two were male. Some were strangled, some were stabbed, some were shot. They were discovered dead in rivers and woods, off the sides of roads and in abandoned buildings. It wasn't until July 1980, after fourteen children had been killed, that the media and police began to recognize they had a crisis on their hands. "It was a Black woman, Ms. Camille Bell," notes Baldwin, "who blew this whistle in Atlanta. That whistle forced Authority to enter, control, and close a case concerning slaughtered Black children, most of them males, a banality with which (and I am a witness) they had never, previously, been remotely concerned."[19] Led by Camille Bell—whose son Yusuf was lost at just nine years old—several mothers of missing children formed the Committee to Stop the Children's Murders and publicly chastised the police and city officials for their lackluster efforts to stop the violence and apprehend the killer(s). This led to an official Atlanta police task force and eventually to an FBI investigation.

Shortly after mothers came forward with their stories, "The Terror in Atlanta" exploded into a national story. People marched to show support, wore green ribbons in solidarity, and sent letters of condolence from all over the country. President Reagan called it "one of the most tragic situations that has ever confronted an American community," promising his administration would be "totally colorblind" in offering resources and support.[20] Sammy Davis Jr. and Frank Sinatra, meanwhile, teamed up for a benefit concert that raised more than $250,000. In July 1981, The Jacksons swung by on their Triumph Tour, raising $100,000 for the Atlanta Children's Foundation. That same year, Muhammad Ali pledged $400,000 in reward money to try to find the killer(s) and stop the murders. So ubiquitous was the story in national news, the artist Prince even alluded to it in his 1981 song, "Annie Christian." "Once the media packaged the 'Atlanta Child Murders,'" writes historian Gil Troy, "modern America demonstrated its odd mix of mawkishness and generosity."[21]

Yet there were also more grotesque aspects to the media interest. Funerals were turned into movie sets. The "ghettos" were infiltrated by reporters and camera crews, making some local citizens feel like zoo animals. "Most repugnant of all," writes the *Los Angeles Times*' Howard Rosenberg, "was the Atlanta TV crew that camped outside the home of a slain youth to televise police breaking the news to his parents."[22] This all preceded the media circus that unfolded once Wayne Williams was identified as a suspect and, later, when he was indicted and the trial got underway.

Yet before Williams became Public Enemy No. 1, for nearly two years—from 1979 to the summer of 1981—there were no serious suspects, leaving motives and identities to the imagination. In the black community, some believed that it was a conspiracy carried out by the Ku Klux Klan, the CIA, or the FBI. Prominent comedian and activist Dick Gregory argued that it was part of a federal experiment carried about by the Centers for Disease Control and Prevention to harvest interferon from black bodies to cure cancer. Many others claimed it was most likely a black man from the community because of the seeming ease with which he was able to lure children in predominantly black neighborhoods. Perhaps the most common media narrative was that the culprit was "a black homosexual," or a ring of black child predators, who were kidnapping, raping, and killing the children. The evidence for this theory was thin at best. The victims' bodies showed no signs of sexual assault, and there were no indications that a seedy house in Northwest Atlanta noted for prostitution was swallowing up children. Yet in story after story, reporting speculated on the theory of "organized homosexual activity." In the spring of 1981 the *New York Times*, CBS, ABC, and NBC ran stories with the "black homosexual" angle featured prominently. The police and FBI reportedly found it compelling as well, yet they had no serious suspects to arrest. "We don't have any evidence of sexual abuse," acknowledged Dr. John Feegel, associate medical examiner for Fulton County, "but when you find a teenage boy in his underwear, you can construe that there's probably a sexual motive."[23] Baldwin did not doubt there was a sexual motive for some of the victims. Indeed, for Baldwin, "the murder of a child is a sexual performance, whether or not the child's body bears any of the more obvious marks (apart from being strangled) of sexual aggression."[24] What disturbed him was the ease with which the media conflated child rape and murder with homosexuality and blackness. Why was this story so compelling to media and law enforcement? What did being black and gay have to do with killing little boys (and some girls)? All that was certain was that black children were disappearing at an alarming rate, primarily young boys between the ages of nine and fifteen.

The response from the police and city was slow and tepid, in part out of a desire to protect the city's image. By the 1980s, Atlanta had become the undisputed capital of the "New South." The PR proclaimed it a booming, vibrant, integrated "city too busy to hate." Once a key location in the civil rights movement and home to Martin Luther King Jr., Andrew Young, and Jimmy Carter, it was now a sort of microcosm for the paradoxes that characterized black life in the 1980s. On the one hand, it represented a power center for wealthy and middle-class African Americans; yet on the other hand, it had the highest murder rate and overall crime rate in America. Poverty was rampant.

As more blacks moved into the city in the 1960s and 1970s, whites (and eventually many middle-class blacks) fled to the suburbs. This class-based segregation had the practical effect of wiping out many black-owned businesses and institutions and isolating and abandoning the inner city, where a substantial portion of people were poor, powerless, and unable to find work. With the middle class gone, schools began to crumble and social services diminished as the money left the city. By the early 1980s, Atlanta's public schools were, for all intents and purposes, segregated and unequal again. The same was true for housing. "With sunset each day," explained Baldwin, "the city became a black enclave. The whites flee by way of the bristling system of freeways—known as the 'ring around the Congo.'"[25] Middle-class African Americans, meanwhile, were in "a kind of limbo. They cannot move further out and they cannot move back in."[26]

Mayor Maynard Jackson was in his second term when the Atlanta child murders began in 1979. Many black men and women occupied other leadership positions in the city, including Public Safety Commissioner Lee Brown (who replaced Reginald Eaves in 1978). The presence of black authority became a key part of the narrative surrounding the missing children. It was, in the eyes of many white Georgians and white Americans, bluntly put: a *black* problem. Black parents didn't watch out for their children; black police botched the investigation; and black leaders proved unable to govern and make the city safe. Such oversimplified narratives allowed whites to conveniently avoid any responsibility or culpability for the tragedy and added to the spectacle.

For Baldwin, it was crucial to witness against such narratives, even if it did little to change the present. History, Baldwin asserted, was never static; it was always being reimagined and reinterpreted. Years after Wayne Williams was convicted and the Atlanta police department's task force was closed, new, contested representations of the Terror in Atlanta continued to emerge. To understand the valuable contribution of Baldwin's book, one must understand it in relation to these other narratives. In 1985, the controversial made-for-TV crime drama *The Atlanta Child Murders* aired on CBS. It featured an all-star cast, including Morgan Freeman, James

Earl Jones, Martin Sheen, Jason Robards, Gloria Foster, Bill Paxton, and Ruby Dee. The three-series, four-hour movie was directed by John Erman, who had previously worked on the groundbreaking *Roots* (1977) television series, and produced by Academy Award-winning screenwriter Abby Mann, perhaps best known for his work on the film *Judgment at Nuremberg* (1961) and a friend of James Baldwin's. The series was nominated for two primetime Emmy Awards and does a surprisingly deft job of capturing many of the Terror's complexities and ambiguities. It also features stand-out performances from Freeman as a lower-middle-class police officer with conflicted loyalties, and Jason Robards as Wayne Williams's charismatic defense attorney, Alvin Binder. Perhaps most significantly, it calls into serious doubt the case against Williams. It also portrays city leadership as more concerned about its image and economic interests (particularly its convention business) than getting to the root of the murders. Indeed, the film's representation of Atlanta's police and government is so critical, it prompted active resistance from city authorities, who described the movie as an unfair distortion.

In *Evidence*, Baldwin praises Mann as "indisputably alert" and well-intentioned. He took issue, however, with the film's representation of black authority, particularly its representation of the city's mayor and chief of police.[27] Baldwin concedes that, over his time in Atlanta, there was serious mistrust and even anger between the city's poor black citizens and its mostly black leadership, and more broadly between the black lower and middle classes. However, he believed the widespread characterization of black leaders as uniquely selfish, indifferent, and incompetent was a self-serving media invention. It allowed white people to say, "See what happens when you let black people run things?" In one of the most memorable scenes, Camille Bell (played by Gloria Foster), laments: "We've got black everything. We've got ourselves a black mayor, we've got ourselves a black commissioner of public safety, black councilman. We've got everything black from top to bottom! We got everything—but protection for our black children." What such a statement missed, according to Baldwin, is context. Atlanta existed within a state and country (and history) in which blacks clearly did not have "everything." While Baldwin appreciated Mann's effort, and certain aspects of the film, then, he ultimately believed it fell "irresponsibly wide of the mark."[28]

Just a year after the trial, in 1983, another narrative emerged in the form of a 514-page book called *The List*, written by former police detective Chet Dettlinger (played by Martin Sheen in the 1985 movie) and *Los Angeles Times* journalist Jeff Prugh. Like the movie, *The List* strongly contested the conviction of Wayne Williams, offering an exhaustively detailed break-down of how the case was mishandled by the government, police, court, and press. Dettlinger and Prugh's primary thesis was that the infamous "list" of victims, which was created by a special police task force formed in response to community pressure in the summer of 1980, was arbitrary in every way imaginable, yet went largely unexamined. "Contrary to popular belief," writes Dettlinger, "Atlanta's murders did not stop with the arrest of Wayne Williams in June of 1981. The police stopped counting, and the press stopped reporting."[29] Dettlinger and Prugh's account became a bestseller in 1984 and was nominated for a Pulitzer Prize.

Such representations made important contributions to the public's un-derstanding of what actually happened in Atlanta and why, and in certain ways, contested traditional news media narratives. Still, Baldwin felt the broader sociohistorical context for the violence was missing. Indeed, while numerous other representations of the Terror in Atlanta have surfaced over the years, including several books, a major CNN documentary, and the made-for-TV movie *Who Killed Atlanta's Children?* (2000)—*Evidence* stands apart as the only narrative with substantial context. For all the crime drama and courtroom intrigue, the only way the real story could be understood, Baldwin believed, was to situate it within a city, a country, and a history. That is where *Evidence* begins.

The New South

Baldwin's original impetus for revisiting Atlanta was an assignment from the *New Yorker* in which he was to assess the New South and reflect on the legacy of the civil rights movement. In 1980, he, along with English film-maker Dick Fontaine and African-American actress Pat Hartley, who were married, visited historical sites of struggle as Baldwin both narrated the story and interviewed people who lived through it. Baldwin's *New Yorker* piece never materialized. However, the resulting film, *I Heard It Through the Grapevine*, was released in 1982, and its bleak tone foreshadowed the material that would become "Atlanta: The Evidence of Things Not Seen," which *Playboy* published in December 1981, and eventually, the full-length book, *The Evidence of Things Not Seen.*

"Forget everything you may have heard, or may wish to believe, concerning the New South," Baldwin announces in his 1981 article.[30] Baldwin's alternative narrative sought to set the historical record straight. The *Playboy* article was an assignment from African American editor Walter Lowe Jr., with whom Baldwin would work on four major articles over the course of his final decade. Baldwin somewhat reluctantly accepted the assignment in the spring of 1981 and made multiple trips to the city in the ensuing months and years. The work was difficult for Baldwin in numerous ways. "I have never in all my journeys felt more of an interloper, a stranger," he reflected, "than I felt in Atlanta in connection with this case, and I sometimes cursed the editor whose brainstorm this had been."[31]

Yet even after his article was complete, Baldwin found he could not let the story—and city—go. "I have a peculiar relationship to [Atlanta]," he confessed. "It has hounded me, I sometimes feel, like mysteriously unfinished business, some terrifying and inescapable rendezvous."[32] Even after the media interest died down, he returned to Atlanta, grappling with its contradictions, its troubled history, its changing economic apparatus and spatial shifts, and its attempts to brand for itself a progressive image.

The article ultimately transformed into the book. Yet in many ways the two are quite different. Most obviously, there is no mention of Wayne Williams in the article, as he had yet to become the focal point of the investigation when Baldwin was writing. The article also puts much greater emphasis on growing divisions in the African American community. What Baldwin heard from the black poor in Atlanta was exasperation with black leaders, and with the black middle class more generally, who the underclass believed had abandoned them. Baldwin did not believe this sentiment was entirely accurate or fair, but he understood that middle-class blacks, himself included, had a responsibility to bridge the divide. "The terror in Atlanta," he writes, "begins to alter, or to reveal, the relationships among black people. The black middle class of Atlanta believes itself to be the oldest and noblest in the South—which means the nation—and it probably is; and who cares? I mean, who gives a flying fuck about all this genteel house-nigger ancestry if it cannot save our children or clarify a town?"[33] In the post–civil rights era, Baldwin sensed, the fault lines in the black community had changed and deepened. More cities might have African Americans in positions of power, but that did not immediately end inner-city poverty. *The Cosby Show* may have been the No. 1 sitcom on television, but the reality it presented was foreign in many ways to black families in inner-city Atlanta, or Los Angeles, or Chicago. This gap led to an increase in resentment, anger, and misunderstanding. "Somewhere, in the brutal Western desert, in the long American night," writes Baldwin, "the blacks of this nation began to lose faith in what had produced and sustained us."[34] The sentence did not make it into the book, nor did the poignant conclusion. Numerous other passages—some excellent—do not transfer from article to book. It is unclear why.[35] What is evident in comparing the two texts is that Baldwin was constantly re-evaluating what to emphasize, what to include and excise, what mattered most in the story.

One emphasis that remains constant in both article and book is the significance of how a place—in this case, the South, and more specifically, Atlanta—is understood and represented. In spite of all the media hype about progress, color-blindness, and integration, Baldwin warns, "Do not come down here looking for it."[36] That version of the South did not exist. The New South, for Baldwin, was as much a myth as the Old South. Only now its tactics and propaganda were more subtle and sophisticated. In place of overt racism was a Reaganesque fantasy in which all the gains of white America seemed earned, and the pains of black America seemed deserved. In *Evidence*, Baldwin states unequivocally: "I would like to have this on my record, that the Reagan vote was an anti-Black/Black vote."[37] This assertion, however, had far less to do with Reagan himself as it reflects the systemic and cultural logic of the post–civil rights era. As Richard Schur observes, "The transition to the post–civil rights era transformed the grammar and syntax of racism, racialization, and white supremacy. . . . If political leaders previously relied on conscious racist language to keep African Americans 'in their place,' the 1970s and 1980s saw a resurgence of property rights and state's rights rhetoric that evaded overt references to race while tapping into racialized fears."[38] Thus, Reagan could claim to be, and may in fact believe himself to be, "totally color-blind" in response to the Atlanta murders; he could allocate millions of dollars, even as he supported policies, practices, and people that ensured the status quo would continue. Indeed, such color-blind practices were a big part of the so-called "Southern Strategy" that lifted Reagan into office in the first place and that resurfaced throughout his presidency. As Michelle Alexander writes:

> When we think of racism we think of Governor Wallace of Alabama block-ing the schoolhouse door; we think of water hoses, lynchings, racial epi-thets, and "whites only" signs. These images make it easy to forget that many wonderful, goodhearted white people who were generous to others, respectful of their neighbors, and even kind to their black maids, garden-ers, or shoe shiners—and wished them well—nevertheless went to the polls and voted for racial segregation. . . . Our understanding of racism is therefore shaped by the most extreme expressions of individual bigotry, not by the way in which it functions naturally, almost invisibly (and some-times with genuinely benign intent), when it is embedded in the structure of a social system.[39]

The South in the 1980s, then, was only "new" insofar as it had found new, more sophisticated and discreet ways of maintaining white supremacy. Baldwin, not surprisingly, saw through the veneer. "What is meant by the New South," he writes, "is as aggressively visible and superbly photogenic as a Cecil B. DeMille extravaganza, or the wonderful world of Walt Disney, or *The Birth of a Nation*, or Tara. It is a brutally mercantile endeavor, created for commerce and the camera."[40] The mention of these entertainers, films, and filmmakers is significant (elsewhere Baldwin references *Gone with the Wind*); these narratives, Baldwin recognizes, are largely responsible for how Americans understand the past and present. It is further reinforced by other media narratives "created for commerce and camera." Yet this mythology, for Baldwin, is precisely what allows a situation like the Atlanta child murders to occur. To fully understand the present, one must go back and trace the city's—and region's—less enchanting histories.

Baldwin had first visited Atlanta in 1957; at the time, he felt a deep con-nection to the city—as he put it, "a profound acceptance, an unfamiliar peace, almost as though, after despairing and debilitating journeys, I had, at last, come home."[41] Yet he also sensed the heavy burden this "home" carried. "Atlanta," he reflected in the title essay for *Nobody Knows My Name* (1961), "*is* the South."[42] Its "bitter interracial history" is "written in the faces of the people and one feels it in the air."[43] It was upon arriving in Atlanta, Baldwin recalls, that he first felt how the southern landscape—the trees, the silence, the liquid heat, and the fact that one always seems to be traveling great distances—seems designed for violence, seems, almost, to demand it. What passions cannot be unleashed on a dark road in a Southern night! Everything seems so sensual, so languid, and so private. Desire can be acted out here; over this fence, behind that tree, in the darkness, there; and no one will see, no one will ever know. Only the night is watching and the night was made for desire.[44]

Baldwin's vivid description draws a crucial connection between desire, violence, and secrecy that would become central to the events of *Evidence*.

In the 1950s, Atlanta was just beginning to establish itself as the capital of the Deep South, a title contested only by nearby Birmingham, which had a similar population of 350,000. Atlanta, however, was seen as a more moderate city, boasted a relatively large black middle class. It was a segregated city; but it was a city on the rise, a former railroad town turned bustling commercial hub. The 1950s and 1960s saw a flurry of construction—hotels, convention centers, and malls, as well as an elaborate new freeway system; the city also approved funding a new, world-class airport and rail system. In the 1960s, public schools were integrated and housing restrictions loosened; by 1970, more than half of the city was black. Soon after, in 1974, Maynard Jackson became the first African American mayor elected in a major American city. Changes in key leadership positions throughout Atlanta followed. Such changes were offered as "evidence" that Atlanta had "overcome" the South's troubled racial past. Many believed, with its growing African American presence, Atlanta would soon transform into America's best example of post–civil rights success and possibility.

As early as the late 1950s, however, Baldwin was skeptical. He saw "the myth of integration" as a trap.[45] Whatever its intentions or ideals, it "attacked and began to unravel a tightly woven social fabric" in the black community.[46] "Integration," writes Baldwin, "was never considered a two-way street. Blacks went downtown, but whites did not come uptown."[47] Moreover, he asserted, power was (and would be) still firmly within the hands of the state of Georgia (and therefore white and conservative), regardless of demographic changes, or even leadership changes, in the city. "The optimistic ferocity of this cosmetic job is the principle, if not the only reason for the presence of the Black Mayor," writes Baldwin. "It is a concession masking the face of power, which remains White."[48] The black wealthy and middle class were making inroads, to be sure. But their standing was still precarious. "The safety of their children is comparative," writes Baldwin. "It is all that their comparative strength as a class has bought them so far; and they are not safe, really, as long as the bulk of Atlanta's Negroes live in such darkness. On any night in that other part of town, a policeman may beat up one Negro too many, or some Negro or some white man may simply go berserk. That is all it takes to drive so delicately balanced a city mad."[49]

Atlanta, then, was a complicated city: a city with a deep and turbulent history, a city of contradictions and divisions, and certainly, in the early 1980s, a city plagued with poverty, violence, unofficial segregation, and unfulfilled promises. Against this backdrop, then, came the terror of the Atlanta child murders, a terror which, as Baldwin put it, "did not so much alter the climate of Atlanta as reveal, or, as it were, epiphanize it."[50]

That Child Was Myself

James Baldwin would have preferred not to write about the Atlanta child murders. "I certainly don't want to be here," he confessed, "and I could have many reasons for being sorry that I came. I don't, on the other hand, quite see how I could possibly have avoided being here, and indeed, precisely at this moment."[51] Baldwin came to Atlanta, that is, because he felt responsible. He was not merely connected to the city in an abstract historical sense; he felt linked to the community; he had close friends there with children. The reports he heard on the news were heartbreaking. "Human life, and especially a child's life," he declared, "is our most important gift, our only real responsibility, and is more sacred than any temple or any doctrine, anywhere."[52]

Still, it was difficult to process the horror. "No degree of imagination or disciplined power of rehearsal," he writes, "can prepare anyone for the unspeakable; and there can be nothing more unspeakable—nor, alas, very probably, more common—than the violence inflicted on children."[53] For more than two years, black families in the city lived in a state of perpetual fear. "It's 11:00 in Atlanta," warned the ominous public-service announcement. "Do you know where your children are?"

Baldwin, of course, did not have children of his own. But he spent considerable time helping raise siblings, nieces, and nephews. In Atlanta, he listened to black children describe the terror in their own words. "Sometimes I think that I'll be coming home from (baseball or football) practice," one boy told Baldwin, "and somebody's car will come behind me and I'll be thrown into the trunk of the car and it will be dark and he'll drive the car away and I'll never be found again."[54] It was a haunting statement that illuminates the sense of fear that prevailed in the city.

For Baldwin, the horror was further magnified by his own identification with these children and their circumstances. "That child," he writes, "*was* myself."[55] Baldwin remembered all too clearly what it meant to grow up black in America—particularly black and poor. He explains:

> If I say that the poor are strangers to safety, it is not only because others look on the poor with such defensive disdain, it is also because the poor cannot bear the condescension and pity they see in the eyes of others. . . . You smell your odor, as it were, in the eyes of others. And this is intolerably compounded if you are poor, young, and black. . . . To be poor and black in a country so rich and white is to judge oneself very harshly and it means that one has nothing to lose. Why not get into the friendly car? What's the worst that can happen? For a poor child is, also, a very lonely child.[56]

This reality is something the predominantly white media had difficulty comprehending. "The missing children were, for a while, lumped together as runaways, or 'hustlers,'" observes Baldwin.[57] Such designations, he believed, were euphemisms for poor black children whom society simply did not value or understand. If they were simply "street kids" from "broken homes," with histories of illicit behavior, middle-class America could still feel relatively safe—and dismiss the horror as a problem of the poor inner city's own making. Yet Camille Bell, mother of nine-year-old Yusuf Bell, took exception to this narrative. Her son was well-behaved and bright. He was simply running an errand for a neighbor when he was kidnapped and killed. Labeling such a child a "hustler" or "runaway" only further compounded the injustice of his death. "It takes 28 blacks to make up one white boy," claimed Camille Bell. "No one cares if [black] children die."[58]

Yet the strange paradox was that after the story of the Atlanta child murders finally broke, the "interest" was significant. People *seemed* to care. The deaths of black children, for so long relegated to the back pages of newspapers, was now front-page news. Yet for Baldwin, the interest was deceptive; "the violently publicized murders" became part of the problem—indeed, may have made the problem worse. "The attention, the publicity given to the slaughter," he writes, "becomes, itself, one more aspect of an unforgivable violation."[59] This violation takes place on a number of fronts: the aforementioned funerals-turned-TV-spectacles; the exploitation stories; the gruesome photos splashed on tabloid papers and network news; the misrepresentation of both the children and the suspects. Was it progress for invisible black children to be suddenly visible and dead? Who were the narrators of their life stories?

"The Atlanta air rings and stings of twenty-eight murders," writes Baldwin.[60] But this was not a new terror, Baldwin was quick to point out; nor was it particularly surprising. This was simply another episode of American history—from slavery to Emmett Till to the bombing of Sixteenth Street Baptist Church in Alabama, to thousands of other less-documented deaths. "We all came here as candidates for the slaughter of innocents."[61] What Baldwin remembered from his own boyhood, he writes, was a kind of ubiquitous terror—a terror that destroys (or threatens to destroy) one's identity and one's memory. Somehow, he survived. It was not pleasant to re-visit that fear and vulnerability—to re-imagine himself as a child, to look back on all the potential traps, all the likely outcomes. The national media interest in the dead children of Atlanta, then, was a cruel paradox: Invisible in life, visible in death. The city "became, for a season, a kind of grotesque Disneyland," writes Baldwin.[62] What constituted "justice," in these circumstances? What was the media's purpose? Yes, they were, at least for a time, on the scene in Atlanta. But what exactly were they covering?

Patterns and Profiles

It was not until June 1981 that a suspect was arrested: a twenty-three-year-old African American man named Wayne B. Williams. "ATLANTA MONSTER SEIZED," blazed the June 4, 1981, headline for the *New York Post*. A month earlier, Williams was pulled over near a bridge after a police officer reportedly heard an unusual splash in the Chattahoochee River. Williams said he was on his way to audition a singer, Cheryl Johnson, who police subsequently discovered did not exist. Two days later the body of Nathaniel Cater, age twenty-seven, was found less than a mile downriver from the bridge. The evidence that Williams murdered Cater was compelling, if not conclusive. One witness claimed he saw Williams holding hands with Cater outside a theater just days before the murder (four other witnesses, however, claimed to have seen Cater alive a day after Williams was pulled over by the bridge). Central to the prosecution's case against Williams were trilobal green carpet fibers and dog hairs found on Cater—and several other victims—that seemed to match those from Williams's parents' home. This scientific evidence supposedly "proved" that Williams murdered the victims.[63] Williams also failed a polygraph test in which he was questioned specifically about Cater.

James Baldwin was uncertain whether Williams was innocent or guilty of the two murders for which he was charged, but he felt the case against Williams was circumstantial and deeply flawed. What disturbed him most is that while Williams was only legally indicted (and eventually convicted) for the deaths of two adults—Nathaniel Cater and Jimmy Ray Payne—he was assumed responsible for all (or at least most) of the deaths of more than two dozen children, a point he drives home repeatedly in *Evidence*. Following Williams's conviction, the Atlanta police claimed Williams was guilty of at least twenty-four of the thirty murders and that those cases, while untried, were considered "solved" and closed. The state claimed a clear "pattern" connected each of the murders on the "official list." While they didn't have enough evidence to try each of them, they were confident the "pattern cases" were all the act of one individual and that individual was Wayne Williams.

This belief—that because Williams may have killed two adult men, he must have also killed twenty-six others (more than twenty of whom were younger than age sixteen)—was profoundly revealing to Baldwin. "It is the emotional climate of Atlanta," he wrote, " . . . that creates, permits, this 'link.' For, without this 'link,' it is perfectly possible—indeed, it is likely—that the last two murders of two anonymous drifters, would not have been noticed at all, especially, I must repeat, in the Deep South. Hence, the connection of the two murders with the previous twenty-six has absolutely no legal validity. No one has been tried for these murders and no one, therefore, can be condemned."[64]

What exactly was the "pattern"? he asked. Some of the children were shot, some stabbed, some strangled. Some were naked, some were clothed, some were put in different clothes. None, as far as could be ascertained, were sexually assaulted (an important point, since Williams was assumed to be a pedophile). What, then, connected the murder of twenty-seven-year-old Cater with a seven-year-old boy, Yusuf Bell, with a nine-year-old girl,

Latonya Wilson? If anything, the common thread between the victims was that they were all black, all from the Atlanta area, and mostly from disadvantaged backgrounds. But did these facts point obviously to Williams or even to the notion of one serial murderer? What constituted a pattern, and who determined it? How did one delineate the beginning and end, since murders of black youth preceded the "terror" and continued after Williams's arrest? Why was laying all the deaths at the feet of one monstrous black gay man so satisfying, such a relief to the city of Atlanta and the country as a whole?

There was little evidence to connect Williams to all the murders, which is why, no doubt, the prosecution decided to officially charge him in only two cases. As Dettlinger and Prugh note in *The List*, there were plenty of other potential suspects. At one point, police narrowed in on a "Vietnam veteran type."[65] In the case of thirteen-year-old Clifford Jones, five eyewitnesses identified a suspect who was the manager of a local laundromat. According to FBI records, the suspect failed two polygraph tests. That suspect, however, was not arrested, and Jones's death was eventually charged, without evidence or a trial, to Williams.[66] Years after Williams's trial, the Associated Press reported that Charles T. Sanders, an Atlanta-based white supremacist whose brother Don Sanders was a Ku Klux Klan leader, told a Georgia Bureau of Investigation informant in 1981 that "the KKK was responsible for a series of slayings of black youths in Atlanta that began in the late 1970s."[67] On since-destroyed tapes, Sanders reportedly told the informant that the killer had "wiped out a thousand future generations of niggers," and that they planned to continue to kill one more each month.[68] More specifically, two police informants claimed Sanders admitted to killing or threatening to kill fourteen-year-old Lubie Geter, who went missing outside a mall near Sanders's home in January 1981. Descriptions of the truck witnesses saw Geter entering closely matched that of Sanders's truck. A police report by a University of Georgia veterinarian also concluded that dog hairs found on the victim's body came from a Siberian husky or an Alaskan malamute. Sanders owned a Siberian husky.[69] While the public had no knowledge of this evidence in the early 1980s, the police did. An internal police memo referred to Charles Sanders as "the main suspect" during much of the investigation.[70]

That was, however, before Wayne Williams emerged on the radar. Williams was, in many ways, the ideal scapegoat: he was black and queer (at least by perception). He was also seen by many as arrogant, narcissistic, and defensive. Williams came from a middle-class background, the only child of parents who were teachers, and he'd attended college for nearly four years before dropping out to start a radio station. He had ambitions of being a music producer and talent manager. Perhaps most relevant to the trial, the prosecution strongly suggested that Williams was gay and a pedophile (labels that were used almost interchangeably) and that he had a deep contempt for his own race. These two claims—both of which Williams denied—became central to the prosecution's case in terms of establishing character and motive. Crucially, the judge in the Williams trial, who was African American, decided to allow "prior acts" to be admitted, meaning Williams's entire life before the murders could be scrutinized for "patterns." Likewise, his personality on and off the stand could be mined and pathologized for clues about his identity. He was judged, then, not simply by what he did or did not do, but by who he was and how he was perceived.

Baldwin was fascinated by Wayne Williams, seeing in his public "image" the embodiment of so many of America's contradictions, hypocrisies, and failures—"the creation and object of a racist civilization."[71] "He struck me," Baldwin wrote, "as a spoiled, lost, and vindictive child."[72] In another passage he refers to him as an "odd creature," less likely to be gay than simply an isolated man who had bought into the American Dream of success and dominance over emotional (or sexual) intimacy. But these were simply impressions, Baldwin acknowledges, from a distance. None of Williams's perceived character flaws, or failed relationships, or personality quirks "proved" he was a serial murderer. "The State has failed," Baldwin writes, "to prove Wayne Williams guilty. But this archaic incompetence cannot be said to prove him innocent. For the State, his guilt or innocence is a matter of convenience, but for us, this question—involving, as it does, complicity—must be more urgent and more personal."[73]

For Baldwin, then, what we perceived in Williams—what role we needed him to play in the Atlanta child murders—was of utmost significance. "Patterns" are inevitably poisoned by expectations, assumptions, prejudices, and power. "There is nothing," writes Baldwin, "that won't, under pressure, establish a 'pattern,' and, once one begins looking for a 'pattern,' this 'pattern' will prove anything you want it to prove."[74] Ultimately, Wayne Williams placated the public's anxieties. He was different, enigmatic, black, gay (at least by perception)—a freak. The evidence that he was in fact a prolific serial murderer might not have been strong, but this *profile* proved good enough. On February 27, 1982, after eleven hours of deliberation, a jury of eight whites and four blacks determined him guilty on two counts of first degree murder, effectively ending the Atlanta child murder saga, though certainly not ending the loss of black life in the city and other cities throughout America.

Beyond the trial, however, Baldwin begged his readers to look deeper. We—all of us—who followed the story were implicated. "The circus and the audience are absolutely indispensable to the hygiene of the state," he asserted.[75] Our interest, that is, could be—and was—exploited for particular purposes and manipulated into particular narratives. "The cowardice," he wrote, "of this time and place—this era—is nowhere more clearly revealed than in the perpetual attempt to make the public and social disaster the result, or the issue, of a single demented creature."[76] That creature—in this case, Wayne Williams—offered a kind of relief and closure to middle-class Atlanta (and middle-class America). The national media left, conventions continued, and the "magic of the marketplace" hummed on. The "crisis" was officially over. But the root causes of twenty-eight deaths remained unsolved.

A Dream Deferred

Baldwin's book was met with mostly poor reviews, if not silence. *The New York Times* described it as a "lackluster account of a complex, nightmarish event that demands more thorough treatment."[77] The expectation seemed to be that Baldwin provide a more strictly journalistic account, which he was uninterested in doing. Moreover, Baldwin's book lacked a clear thesis or solution or call to arms. In his 1981 *Playboy* article, he concluded with a short vignette of a child—his nephew—watching the author being interviewed on the TV screen, then seeing the "real" James Baldwin sitting beside him. "He kept looking from the TV screen into my face," writes Baldwin, "and the only way he could frame his enormous question was continuously to ask me, *Where you been?* I think we'd better take it from there."[78] It was meant to demonstrate one's responsibility not only for one's own child, but for extended families, communities, classes, and generations.

In place of this story, Baldwin's conclusion in *Evidence* wanders and weaves its way to a finish that is at once more elaborate and elusive. In

Gatsby-esque fashion he riffs on the American Dream. But the dream presented here is not pure, and then corrupted. It was toxic from the beginning. The sooner we recognize this, Baldwin implores, the better. "There are no more oceans to cross, no savage territories to be conquered, no more natives to be converted (and those for sale have been bought)."[79] The Reagan vision of winners and losers, strength and dominance had proved itself a failure. One need look no further than inner cities across the country, where crime, poverty, and violence showed no signs of abating—to the contrary, conditions had grown worse, in most cases, since the 1960s.

Baldwin's alternate vision of America has to do with community: "our endless connection with, and responsibility for, each other."[80] In his original article he references Toni Morrison's notion that it takes a village to raise a child. While that particular sentence is excised from the book, he continues to emphasize its point. "In the twentieth century, and in the modern State," he laments, "the idea—the sense—of community has been submerged for a very long time."[81] Baldwin's final paragraphs take on a sermonic tone that harks back to *The Fire Next Time*; yet here it does not quite work the same. The center cannot hold. The rhythm is disrupted. There is no satisfying crescendo and release. It is an appropriate end for a book filled with contradictions: a 125-page examination of a new era that is alternately indignant, vulnerable, hopeful, dark, bleak, unflinching, uncertain; a book that is full of stream-of-consciousness dives and detours; that is at times precise and eloquent, at others, repetitive and weary; that provides social history, autobiography, journalism, legal commentary, psychological analysis, political salvos, and cultural and media criticism.

As Baldwin finished work on *Evidence*, the nation was commemorating the twenty-year anniversary of Martin Luther King Jr.'s "I Have a Dream" speech at the March on Washington in 1963. It had now been calcified as the triumphant moment of the civil rights movement, the moment America's conscience was pricked, the tide finally turning with regard to issues of racial and social injustice. But Baldwin, surveying the outcomes of those battles in King's hometown, was not in a celebratory mood. "I would like to point out," he wrote, "that Martin Luther King, Jr., for the people whom he loved and served, was not a (pious) martyr. . . . Nor was he a victim. He was not even a *hero*. These terms are meant to distract one from, and, as it were, justify the obscenity of the publicly and privately willed event that transformed him into a *corpse*."[82] Baldwin's still-visceral anger and sadness had to do with loss, certainly, but also the meaning of King's legacy in the post–civil rights era. King was not merely an icon to him, but a friend and ally. Baldwin still wore a watch given to him by Coretta Scott King with the Reverend's face and the incantatory words, *I have a dream*. "Martin is dead," wrote Baldwin, "because he was our witness—still is, for that matter."[83]

In *Evidence*, Baldwin attempted to honor King's struggle—and the struggle of hundreds of thousands of others—by pushing beyond the surfaces and slogans and media narratives of the Reagan era, by being honest about what he observed. King's dream, Baldwin lamented, remained unfulfilled. Atlanta was evidence of this. The Beloved Community required more than a change in leadership or laws, but "a movement of the human soul." "This dream," he writes, "must, alas, be disentangled from whatever nightmare controls this fearfully White Republic."[84]

In many ways, this disentanglement was more challenging in the post–civil rights era than it was in the 1950s and 1960s. It may be, in certain ways, more challenging still in the so-called "post-racial" era, in which covering black death in the national media has become a near-weekly ritual. "The inescapable and irreducible danger of being a black man or black woman in this country," writes Baldwin, "is being forced to live with so vast a horror, day in and day out, that one finally ceases to be able to react to it. *Another man done gone*; and one clicks on the television set."[85] Over fifty years now since the March on Washington, and over thirty-five years since the Atlanta child murders, the disentanglement between King's dream and the American Dream continues in Cleveland and Chicago, Ferguson and Atlanta (the latter of which continues to boast a large black middle class but still has a homicide rate that ranks in the top 10 for U.S. cities). It is, as President Obama put it shortly after the Trayvon Martin verdict, "a history that doesn't go away." That is not to say that it is deterministic but, rather, that we are responsible for understanding the connections between 1619 and 1955, 1981 and 2016, or we remain trapped in a destructive cycle. In *Evidence*, Baldwin insists that the Terror in Atlanta be more than a mere media spectacle or crime story. He insists, amid all the noise and distractions, beyond the PR of the "city too busy to hate," against a thousand narratives about hustlers, runaways, and predatory gays, that the children deserve better from their country: that, as the movement of the present moment puts it, black lives matter.

Epilogue

One of Baldwin's final public speeches came at the National Press Club in Washington, D.C., in December 1986. He was sixty-two years old. In less than a year, he would die of stomach cancer. In his extemporized speech, "The World I Never Made," he rehearsed mostly familiar riffs about his concerns for America, followed by a brief Q&A (Baldwin called it a "rap session"). He seemed tired. His remarks lacked the incisive punch and dramatic power that once mesmerized audiences and elevated him to celebrity status. Yet even in this less-than-inspired talk, there were flashes of brilliance. "A few weeks ago," he reflected,

> I happened to have the TV set on . . . and I was flicking it, aimlessly for a while . . . and then I started doing it deliberately. And what was I watching? I was watching a series of images, all of them bloody. Guns, all kinds of weapons, corpses, cowboys and Indians, good guys and bad guys, and for a moment it seemed to me that these compulsive set of images . . . that I was watching a person, a human being, who was very, very, very ill. And he was trapped in these images; he could not be released from these images.[1]

The metaphor of a television set as a window into the mind of a human being is quite remarkable. Equally remarkable (and disturbing) is what it reveals: a person trapped in a relentless cascade of violence, of death and destruction, of reductive myths and illusions. In contrast to typical diatribes about

TV and movies rotting children's brains, however, Baldwin does not blame the medium; it was the content of such media that mattered. These images and narratives said something about who we are as a people, as a country.

In this book, I have sought to demonstrate how profoundly engaged James Baldwin was in his final decade with contesting dominant narratives in mass media and popular culture. He did so through a variety of forms, some traditional, some not. In his final novel, *Just Above My Head*, he grappled with the meanings of fame, celebrity, and the crossover dream through the vehicle of black popular music; in his unpublished play, *The Welcome Table*, he explored the possibilities of love and intimacy amid the AIDS epidemic; in his final essays and articles, which were not coincidentally published in popular platforms such as *Playboy* magazine, he interrogated the meanings of masculinity, gender, and androgyny in the "hard body" blockbuster era and questioned the definitions of transgression and salvation amid the rise of televangelism, the Electric Church, and the religious Right; and in his final nonfiction book, *The Evidence of Things Not Seen*, he scrutinized the news media coverage of tragedies such as the Atlanta child murders, coverage that he believed exploited and perpetuated the tragedy, coverage that did not honestly confront and understand it. What connects these texts is their preoccupation with how media and culture relay stories—and meaning.

Baldwin's is a perspective that is lacking in the vast majority of accounts of the 1980s. He covers many of the same events but offers different evidence, different voices, different questions and ideas. He allows us, that is, to see the decade in fresh ways, while also seeing how connected that era is to the present. In his book, *Back to Our Future: How the 1980s Explain the World We Live in Now* (2011), journalist David Sirota argues for the importance of excavating and deconstructing the 1980s to understand the underpinnings of the world we live in today, whether regarding race, religion, gender, government, capitalism, or the military. Sirota describes the 1980s as not so much a historical moment as a language. "I don't remember the 1980s," writes Sirota, "as much as I speak it and think in it."[2] Indeed, never before in history had our identities, our understanding of the world, been as shaped by pop culture: TV shows and cultural crazes, commercials and cartoons, blockbuster movies and pop stars. Moreover, the 1980s saw an explosion of new media and technology: cable news, MTV, the VCR, the Walkman, the personal computer, video games. Such new technology and media were increasingly synergistic and controlled by a shrinking number of multinational corporations. "It was perfectly constructed," writes Sirota, "to reinforce narrow cultural memes, and in the eighties those were the ones emanating from an ultra-conservative Reagan Revolution, a growing Me Generation, a racist reaction to the civil rights movement, and a bitterly nationalistic backlash to the Vietnam disaster."[3]

While Sirota's account of the decade—and many others, including National Geographic's recent TV series *The 1980s: The Decade that Made Us* and CNN's *The Eighties*—rightfully recognizes its significance to the present, such treatments tend toward broad strokes and simplistic conclusions. For Sirota, all popular culture in the 1980s reinforces conservative Reaganist ideology. It all seems fun and harmless on the surface but under closer scrutiny contains more sinister messaging. Baldwin, however, saw the picture as more complex. Popular culture was not merely a capitalist tool intended to deceive, distract, and control people (though it certainly *could* do all these things and more); it was a battleground. Moreover, its messaging need not be consumed passively; we could speak back; we could—and *must*—create new forms, vocabularies, and stories.

Baldwin's contributions to media and cultural studies is just beginning to garner greater attention, as is his work in the 1980s. Yet as this book demonstrates, he holds up as one of the most daring and interesting critics of the late twentieth century, including of the Reagan era. It was not simply that he wrote *about* popular culture; it was that it changed the way *he* wrote. He recognized its influence on society and the individual, including himself; rather than dismiss it as ephemeral or nonserious, he actively grappled with and engaged with it. And, perhaps most important, he refused to accept its official narratives—or conventional interpretations of those narratives— whether from the Right or the Left. Long before interdisciplinarity and intersectionality became popular, or even were defined in cultural studies, he embraced them. "We are living in a world in which everybody and everything is interdependent," he said in 1986. "It is not white, this world. It is not black either. The future of this world depends on everybody in this room and that future depends on to what extent and by what means we liberate ourselves from a vocabulary which now cannot bear the weight of reality."[4]

That vocabulary, for Baldwin, encompassed new media, including visual media. Movies were as important as novels; television was as complex as a

human being. In the Information Age, this understanding of the relationship between media, technology, and identity is more important than ever.
We are surrounded by texts. We are barraged by competing narratives.
Our smartphones have become extensions of who we are. Social media
gives everyone with internet access a platform and a voice. In many ways,
the sheer volume, velocity, and capabilities are terrifying. Its power can
be manipulated in countless ways. But as Baldwin reminds us, the future
depends on what we make of it.

Chronological Bibliography

1979

WRITINGS

Just Above My Head. New York: Dial, 1979.
"Lorraine Hansberry, at the Summit." *Freedomways* 19 (1979): 269–72. Repr. in *James Baldwin: Collected Essays*.
"On Language, Race, and the Black Writer." *Los Angeles Times*, April 29, 1979. Repr. in *James Baldwin: The Cross of Redemption: Uncollected Writings*.
"Of the Sorrow Songs: The Cross of Redemption." *Edinburgh Review* 47 (August 1979). Repr. in *James Baldwin: The Cross of Redemption: Uncollected Writings*.
"If Black English Isn't a Language, Then Tell Me, What Is?" *New York Times*, July 29, 1979. Repr. in *James Baldwin: Collected Essays*.
"Open Letter to the Born Again." *The Nation*. September 29, 1979. Repr. in *James Baldwin: Collected Essays*.

INTERVIEWS

"James Baldwin: Looking Toward the Eighties." Interview by Kalama yu Salaam. *Black Collegian* 10 (1979). Repr. in *Conversations with James Baldwin*.
"James Baldwin: No Gain for Race Relations." Interview by Hollie I. West. *Miami Herald*, April 16, 1979. Repr. in *Conversations with James Baldwin*.

1980

WRITINGS

"Dark Days." *Esquire*, October 1980. Repr. in *James Baldwin: Collected Essays*.

"Notes on the House of Bondage." *The Nation*, November 1, 1980. Repr. in *James Baldwin: Collected Essays*.

"Black English: A Dishonest Argument." Wayne State University. February 1980. Repr. in *James Baldwin: The Cross of Redemption: Uncollected Writings*.

INTERVIEWS

"James Baldwin Finds New South Is a Myth." Interview by Leonard Ray Teel. *Atlanta Journal*, April 22, 1980. Repr. in *Conversations with James Baldwin*.

"James Baldwin: An Interview." Interview by Wolfgang Binder. *Revista/Review Interamericana* 10 (Fall 1980): 220–41. Repr. in *Conversations with James Baldwin*.

1981

WRITINGS

"The Evidence of Things Not Seen." *Playboy*, December 1981. Revised and expanded as *The Evidence of Things Not Seen* (1985).

INTERVIEWS

"In Dialogue to Define Aesthetics: James Baldwin and Chinua Achebe." *Black Scholar* 12 (March-April 1981): 72–79. Repr. in *Conversations with James Baldwin*.

1982

WRITINGS

I Heard It through the Grapevine. Directed by Dick Fontaine and Pat Hartley. Performed by James Baldwin and David Baldwin. Living Archives, 1982.

"A Letter to Prisoners." *Inside/Out* 3, no. 1 (Summer 1982).

1983

WRITINGS

"This Far and No Further." *Time Capsule* 7 (Summer/Fall 1983). Repr. in *James Baldwin: The Cross of Redemption: Uncollected Writings*.

1984

WRITINGS

"On Being White and Other Lies." *Essence*, April 1984. Repr. in *James Baldwin: The Cross of Redemption: Uncollected Writings*.

INTERVIEWS

"Revolutionary Hope: A Conversation between James Baldwin and Audre Lorde." *Essence*, December 1984.

"The Way Your Blood Beats." Interview by Richard Goldstein. *Village Voice*, June 26, 1984.

"The Art of Fiction LXXVII: James Baldwin." *Paris Review* 26 (Spring 1984). Repr. in *Conversations with James Baldwin*.

"James Baldwin: Reflections of a Maverick." Interview by Julius Lester. *New York Times Review of Books*, May 27, 1984. Repr. in *Conversations with James Baldwin*.

"James Baldwin Interview." Hampshire College Archives and Special Collections, May 1984.

"Blacks and Jews." University of Massachusetts at Amherst, February 28, 1984. Repr. in *James Baldwin: The Cross of Redemption: Uncollected Writings*.

1985

WRITINGS

The Price of the Ticket: Collected Non-Fiction. New York: St. Martin's, 1985.

Jimmy's Blues: Selected Poems. New York: St. Martin's, 1985.

The Evidence of Things Not Seen. New York: Holt, Rinehart, and Winston, 1985.

"Freaks and the American Ideal of Manhood." *Playboy*, January 1985. Repr. in *James Baldwin: Collected Essays*.

"The Fire This Time: Letter to the Bishop." *New Statesman*, August 23, 1985. Repr. in *James Baldwin: The Cross of Redemption: Uncollected Writings*.

"My Journey of Understanding." *TV Guide*, January 12–18, 1985.

INTERVIEWS

"An Interview with James Baldwin and Josephine Baker." Interview by Henry Louis Gates Jr. *Southern Review* 21 (Summer 1985): 594–602. Repr. in *Conversations with James Baldwin*.

1986

WRITINGS

"A World I Never Made." National Press Club, December 10, 1986.

INTERVIEWS

"An Interview with James Baldwin." Interview with David C. Estes. *New Orleans Review* 13 (Fall 1986). Repr. in *Conversations with James Baldwin*.

"An Interview with James Baldwin on Henry James." Interview with David Leeming. *Henry James Review* 8 (Fall 1986): 47–56.

1987

WRITINGS

"To Crush the Serpent." *Playboy*, June 1987. Repr. in *James Baldwin: The Cross of Redemption: Uncollected Writings*.

INTERVIEWS

"When a Pariah Becomes a Celebrity." Interview by Clayton O. Holloway. *Xavier Review* 7 (1987): 1–10.

"James Baldwin Interview." Interview by Mavis Nicholson. *Mavis on Four*, December 3, 1987.

"Architectural Digest Visits: James Baldwin." *Architectural Digest*, August 1987.

"Last Testament: An Interview with James Baldwin." Interview by Quincy Troupe. *Village Voice*, January 12, 1988. Repr. in *Conversations with James Baldwin*.

Notes

Introduction

1. According to biographer David Leeming, Baldwin knew that "people were wary of his own reputation as a homosexual, and he was disappointed that he had not been asked to participate [in the March on Washington] in any meaningful way" (Leeming, *James Baldwin*, 228). In his article, "Breaking into James Baldwin's House," Thomas Chatterton Williams notes that almost all the emerging criticism of Baldwin, "whether literary or political, explicitly ad hominem or euphemistic, was rooted in an intense and widespread aversion to Baldwin's sexuality and personal presentation." Williams reminds that even in the *Time* cover story, Baldwin is described as a "nervous, slight, almost fragile figure, filled with frets and fears . . . effeminate in manner." "He was [*Time* noted,] 'not, by any stretch of the imagination, a Negro leader.' King, for all his concern about the purpleness of the prose, would almost certainly have been aware that Baldwin was frequently mocked as 'Martin Luther Queen' in civil-rights circles." Despite such aversions and suspicions, however, Baldwin did participate in the March on Washington and joined in a nationally televised panel discussion, along with Harry Belafonte, Sidney Poitier, Joseph Mankiewicz, Charlton Heston, Marlon Brando, and moderator David Schoenburn to discuss the meaning of the March on Washington and race relations more broadly.

2. Als, "Enemy Within."

3. Scott, *James Baldwin's Later Fiction*, 16. Craig Werner notes that Baldwin's marginalization from the African American literary canon began at least as early as the 1980s and 1990s. In the introduction to James Baldwin in *The Norton Anthology of African American Literature* (1997), Henry Louis Gates Jr. and Nellie Y. McKay elaborate on criticisms of Baldwin's late career: "Many critics allege that, by the end

of his career, Baldwin was spouting rhetoric that compromised the moral persuasion and authority that had made his earlier work so powerful and compelling. Others charged that the line between his artistic preoccupations and his own personal and psychic life had become embarrassingly blurred. Still others observed that, in resorting to abstract sociological categories, Baldwin was flattening what had once been a richly complicated view of race and racialism in America and thus committing the same ideological excesses he had once condemned in Richard Wright" (1653). For a more comprehensive account of Baldwin's critical reception see, Miller, "Baldwin's Critical Reception," and Francis, *Critical Reception of James Baldwin.*

4. Anderson, "Trapped Inside James Baldwin."

5. Ibid.

6. Hall, "What Is This 'Black' in Black Popular Culture?," 105.

7. Arnold, *Culture and Anarchy*, 4.

8. Bloom, *Closing of the American Mind*, 81.

9. Baldwin, "Autobiographical Notes," 7.

10. Salam, "James Baldwin," 185.

11. Baldwin, "Mass Culture and the Creative Artist," 7.

12. Hall, "What Is This 'Black' in Black Popular Culture?," 104.

13. Ibid.

14. Ibid., 106.

15. Ibid., 107.

16. See, for example, Baldwin's essay on the 1954 musical film *Carmen Jones* in *Notes of a Native Son* (1955) or his 1959 article "On Catfish Row," about the Hollywood production of *Porgy and Bess* (1959). James Baldwin wrote and/or spoke about a range of major cultural figures and events in the late 1950s and early 1960s, from John Wayne to Martin Luther King Jr. In his early essays, however, Baldwin was mostly skeptical of mass culture—particularly those forms, like Hollywood, dominated by white perspectives. "What the mass culture really reflects," he writes in 1959, "is the American bewilderment in the face of the world we live in. . . . Movies are designed not to trouble, but to reassure; they do not reflect reality, they merely rearrange its elements into something we can bear" ("Mass Culture and the Creative Artist," 5–6). In his 1963 address, "A Talk to Teachers," similarly, he writes that "popular culture—as represented, for example, on television and in comic books and in movies—is based on fantasies created by very ill people, and [we] must be aware that these are fantasies that have nothing to do with reality" (678). Of course, implicit in Baldwin's critique was that popular culture had everything to do with reality—that indeed, those fantasies both reflected and perpetuated a reality Baldwin saw as destructive.

17. Baldwin, "Mass Culture and the Creative Artist," 7.

18. For more on *Nothing Personal*, see Miller, "Striking Addiction to Irreality."

19. Brustein, "Everybody Knows My Name."

20. Baldwin, "Nothing Personal," 692–93.

21. Williams, *Television*, 80.

22. Norman, "Reading a 'Closet Screenplay.'"

23. Leeming, *James Baldwin*, 297.

24. Ibid.

25. Baldwin's screenplay was ultimately published as a book in 1972, before being revived and adapted for Spike Lee's *Malcolm X* film in 1992. For more on how the screenplay was used for Lee's film, see Miller, "Lost and . . . Found?"

26. Brian Norman elaborates on Baldwin's blueprint for the film: "The 'closet screenplay' reads as a kaleidoscopic history of moving parts: fragments of Malcolm X circle among the same space with a mad jamming together of multiple temporalities, time loops, overdubs, and long parenthetical directorial commands. There is no saved Malcolm to calmly narrate flashbacks in a picaresque montage of the American self-made man that is as well choreographed as Lee's dance scene at the Roseland. Instead, occupying the narrator position to bring together a life story are snippets of dialogue from other scenes, other characters, announcers at political rallies, and, most importantly, Malcolm X's own orations, which serve as historical markers in the form of recorded speeches and other media footage. In his directorial notes, Baldwin describes this use of visual technology as 'remembered time'" ("Reading a 'Closet Screenplay,'" 105).

27. Baldwin, "The Price May Be Too High," 108.

28. Baldwin, *The Devil Finds Work*, 3.

29. Ibid., 9.

30. Ibid., 35.

31. *The Devil Finds Work* is one of many late-Baldwin works that has been reevaluated in recent years. In a 2014 article for *The Atlantic*, Noah Berlatsky describes it as "the most powerful piece of film criticism ever written." For more on Baldwin's work as film critic and theorist, see Cassandra Ellis's "The Black Boy Looks at the Silver Screen" in Miller, *Re-viewing James Baldwin*, and Ryan Jay Friedman's article, "'Enough Force to Shatter the Tale to Fragments': Ethics and Textual Analysis in James Baldwin's Film Theory." *ELH* 77, no. 2 (Summer 2010): 385–412.

32. Coombs, "Devil Finds Work."

33. Leeming, *James Baldwin*, 330.

34. Ibid., 333.

35. Cartwright, "'Sure, He Could Write."

36. Field, *All Those Strangers*, 7.

37. As Baldwin explained it: "After Martin [Luther King] was murdered, I had a great deal of trouble with that question—it took me a long time to believe again that writing really did anything. But the only way you can do it in the first place is as an act of faith. You don't put a nickel in a machine and something comes out. . . . The time of any artist—the time of any person—is brief. But that does not mean that he or she doesn't have an inheritance which one way or another he is compelled to pass down the line. So," he said with a shrug. "You work in the dark; you work in your time. The only real sin is despair . . . and you try to tell the truth" (qtd. in O'Reilly, "A Play This Time").

38. Cleaver, *Soul on Ice*, 100.

39. Elgrably and Plimpton, "Art of Fiction LXXVIII," 252.

40. Gates, "Fire Last Time."

41. Mailer, *Advertisements for Myself*, 471.

42. Leeming, *James Baldwin*, 304.

43. Troupe, "Last Testament," 282.

44. Baldwin, "The World I Never Made."

45. The term "intersectionality" was first introduced by Kimberlé Crenshaw in 1989 as a way to describe the ways in which "race and gender discrimination overlapped not only in the workplace but in other arenas of life." The term was further popularized by Patricia Hill Collins in the early 1990s; like Crenshaw, Collins saw discrimination as more than discrete categories, rather as overlapping forms of oppression, including race, gender, sexuality, class, and ethnicity. By the 2010s, the term appeared regularly, not only in academic contexts, but in popular discourse. For Crenshaw, the term was an attempt to "highlight the multiple avenues through which racial and gender oppression were experienced so that the problems would be easier to discuss and understand." See Crenshaw, "Demarginalizing the Intersection of Race and Sex: A Black Feminist Critique of Antidiscrimination Doctrine, Feminist Theory and Antiracist Politics," *University of Chicago Legal Forum* 140 (1989): 139–67; Collins, *Black Feminist Thought: Knowledge, Consciousness, and the Politics of Empowerment* (New York: Routledge, 1990, 2009).

46. Julius Lester, "James Baldwin—Reflections of a Maverick," *New York Times*, May 27, 1984.

47. Leeming, *James Baldwin*, 310.

48. Baldwin, "Dark Days," 798.

49. Ibid., 798.

50. Ibid., 798.

51. Salam, "James Baldwin," 185.

52. Mann, "Study Finds Gains."

53. As Atwater put it in an infamous 1981 recording: "You start out in 1954 by saying, 'Nigger, nigger, nigger.' By 1968 you can't say 'nigger'—that hurts you. Backfires. So you say stuff like forced busing, states' rights and all that stuff. You're getting so abstract now [that] you're talking about cutting taxes, and all these things you're talking about are totally economic things and a byproduct of them is [that] blacks get hurt worse than whites. And subconsciously maybe that is part of it. I'm not saying that. But I'm saying that if it is getting that abstract, and that coded, that we are doing away with the racial problem one way or the other. You follow me—because obviously sitting around saying, "We want to cut this," is much more abstract than even the busing thing, and a hell of a lot more abstract than 'Nigger, nigger'" (Perlstein, "Exclusive").

54. Baldwin, "Notes on the House of Bondage," 804.

55. Alexander, *New Jim Crow*, 6. As biographer David Leeming notes, imprisonment was an "important leitmotif in Baldwin's writing. In 1982 and 1983 he

wrote articles in support of prisoners for journals with which his old friend Marc Crawford, who was actively involved in exposing the abuses of the prison system, was associated. In two short articles, 'A Letter to Prisoners' and 'This Far and No Further,' he proposed that artists and prisoners have much in common, that both are inconveniences to the state, that both are 'free' in a way that a society which boasts of its freedom, even as it incarcerates huge percentages of its poor, cannot be. The state, Baldwin suggested, uses prisoners to create the illusion of safety in a society committed to economic gain for itself" (Leeming, *James Baldwin*, 359).

56. Alexander, *New Jim Crow*, 7.

57. Baldwin, *The Evidence of Things Not Seen*, 124.

58. Mann, "Study Finds Gains."

59. Alexander, *New Jim Crow*, 50–51.

60. Baldwin, *The Price of the Ticket*, xvii.

61. Baldwin, "Notes on the House of Bondage," 806.

62. Ibid., 806.

63. Desmond-Harris, "Racism is Real."

64. "CNN Exit Polls," http://www.cnn.com/election/results/exit-polls (accessed July 6, 2017).

65. Ryan, "This Was a Whitelash."

66. Baldwin, "Black English," 154.

67. Obama, "Remarks on Trayvon Martin."

68. Lee, "Baldwin's Complex Voice."

69. Ibid.

70. Williams, "Breaking into James Baldwin's House."

71. McBride, Introduction, 2.

72. Miller, Introduction, 7.

73. Other notable recent books on Baldwin include: *A Historical Guide to James Baldwin* (Oxford University Press, 2009) by Douglas Field; *James Baldwin and Toni Morrison: Comparative Critical and Theoretical Essays* (Palgrave, 2009), edited by Lovalerie King and Lynn Orilla Scott; and *The Critical Reception of James Baldwin, 1963–2010* (Camden House, 2014) by Consuela Francis.

74. Scholars and critics have paid particular attention to his involvement and engagement with film and music. See, for example, Ed Pavlic's presentation, "How Do You Get to Carnegie Hall? Music and Film in James Baldwin's Transnational Early 70s," at Union College in 2014, and the film series, "The Devil Finds Work: James Baldwin on Film," hosted by the Film Society of Lincoln Center and Columbia University School of the Arts in 2015. See also Miller's "Lost and . . . Found?" and "The Gangster in *The Devil Finds Work* as a Template for Reading the Parisian *Banlieues*" from the 2013 special issue of the *African American Review*.

75. Ta-Nehesi Coates (Twitter): "All of us are chasing Baldwin—even if we don't know it," January 25, 2015.

76. Baldwin, "Freaks and the American Ideal of Manhood," 815.

77. Baldwin, *The Welcome Table*.

78. Baldwin, "Open Letter to the Born Again," 784.

79. Elgrably and Plimpton, "Art of Fiction LXXVIII," 250.

80. Salam, "James Baldwin," 183.

81. Ibid.

82. Watkins, "Interview with James Baldwin."

Chapter 1. The Price of the Beat

1. Carter, "Primary Resources."

2. Ibid.

3. Carter, "*Playboy* Interview," 33.

4. Reagan, "Announcement for Presidential Candidacy."

5. Baldwin, *Just Above My Head*, 55.

6. Lester, "James Baldwin," 229.

7. Ibid., 231.

8. "I grew up with music, you know, much more than with any other language," Baldwin elaborated in a 1979 interview. "In a way the music I grew up with saved my life. Later in my life I met musicians, and it was a milieu I moved in much more than the literary milieu, because when I was young there wasn't any. So that I watched and learned from various musicians in the streets. When I was under age I was listening to the very beginning of what was not yet known as bebop. And I was involved in the church, because I was a preacher and the son of a preacher. And all of that has something to do with *Just Above My Head*, with an affirmation which is in that life and is expressed by that music, which I have not found in that intensity anywhere else. The book has something to do with the journey of a people from one place to another, a kind of diaspora which was unrecognized as yet, and in that journey what happened to them and what has happened to the world as a result of their journey and is still happening to the world. They brought themselves a long way out of bondage by means of the music, which *Just Above My Head* is at bottom about" (Binder interview, repr. in Standley and Pratt, *Conversations with James Baldwin*, 190–91).

9. Pavlic, "Jimmy's Songs," 163.

10. George, *Death of Rhythm and Blues*, 157.

11. Werner, *Change Is Gonna Come*, 211.

12. George, *Death of Rhythm and Blues*, 157.

13. Greenberg, "Where is Graceland?," 155.

14. Baldwin, "Of the Sorrow Songs," 146.

15. Ibid.

16. Ibid.

17. Dwyer, *Back to the Fifties*, 1.

18. Baldwin, *Just Above My Head*, 3.

19. Ibid.

20. Baldwin, "White Racism and Other Lies," 754.

21. Baldwin, "The Uses of the Blues," 78.
22. Baldwin, "The *Black Scholar* Interviews James Baldwin," 150–51.
23. Scott, *James Baldwin's Later Fiction*, 125.
24. Ibid., 126.
25. Baldwin, *Just Above My Head*, 13.
26. Ibid., 86.
27. Ibid.
28. Ibid., 13.
29. Ibid., 214.
30. Ibid.
31. Ibid.
32. Pavlic, *Who Can Afford to Improvise?*, 99.
33. Baldwin, *Just Above My Head*, 215.
34. Ibid.
35. Ibid., 216.
36. Ibid., 562.
37. Ibid.
38. Ibid., 250.
39. Ibid., 249.
40. Ibid., 575.
41. Ibid.
42. Ibid.
43. Ibid., 577.
44. Ibid., 249.
45. Ibid., 250.
46. Ibid., 28.
47. Ibid.
48. Ibid.
49. Ibid., 29.
50. Ibid., 6.
51. Ibid.
52. Ibid.
53. Ibid.
54. Ibid., 51.
55. Ibid., 312.
56. Ibid., 312.
57. Ibid., 79.
58. Ibid., 84.
59. Ibid., 84.
60. Ibid., 59.
61. Ibid., 560.
62. Ibid., 517.
63. Ibid.

64. Ibid., 128.

65. Ibid.

66. Ibid.

67. Ibid., 144.

68. Ibid.

69. Ibid., 507.

70. Ibid., 207–9.

71. Ibid., 209.

72. Werner, *Change Is Gonna Come*, 5.

73. Evans, *Ray Charles*, 161.

74. Baldwin, "The Uses of the Blues," 79.

75. George, *Death of Rhythm and Blues*, 147.

76. Baldwin, *Just Above My Head*, 300.

77. Ibid.

78. Ibid.

79. Ibid.

80. Ibid., 222.

81. Ibid., 557.

82. Ibid.

83. Ibid., 561.

84. Ibid., 567.

85. Ibid., 372–73.

86. Ibid., 373.

87. Early, *One Nation Under a Groove*, 105.

88. Baldwin, *Just Above My Head*, 92.

89. Ibid., 403.

90. Ibid., 454.

91. Ibid., 455.

92. Ibid.

93. Ibid., 23.

94. Ibid., 25.

95. Ibid., 24.

96. Lynn Orilla Scott notes several allusions to *The Wizard of Oz* in the final pages of *Just Above My Head*: "[T]he road, the driving rain, the country house, even the dream itself. In Hall's dream his home is a shelter for family and friends, a place where people come to get out of the driving rain. Inside the house they laugh and warm themselves by a fire Hall has built. But throughout the scene Hall is tormented by Arthur's question: 'Shall we tell them? What's up the road?' The novel concludes with Hall's response to Arthur followed by Hall's waking moment: 'No, they'll find out what's up the road, ain't nothing up the road but us, man, and then I wake up, and my pillow is wet with tears'" (Scott, *James Baldwin's Later Fiction*, 142). There is no wizard, that is, to offer salvation for the journeying characters. "Ain't nothing up the road but us" (*Just Above My Head*, 584).

97. Baldwin, *Just Above My Head*, 4–5.

98. Baldwin, "The Uses of the Blues," 152.

99. Baldwin, *Just Above My Head*, 500.

100. Baldwin, "Of the Sorrow Songs," 153.

101. Baldwin, "The Black Scholar Interviews James Baldwin," 152. In the same interview, Baldwin references lyrics from Stevie Wonder's song "Big Brother," from the artist's classic album, *Talking Book* (1972): "I ain't gotta do nothing to you; I ain't even gotta do nothing to you; you cause your own country to fall." Baldwin follows: "And that's what's happening. Now, the rest is up to us because we are responsible for each other and to each other. We are responsible to the future, and not to Chase Manhattan Bank" ("The *Black Scholar* Interviews James Baldwin," 152).

102. Baldwin, *Just Above My Head*, 419.

103. Ibid., 419–20.

104. Ibid., 419.

105. Ibid.

Chapter 2. Freaks in the Reagan Era

1. Fraterrigo, *Playboy*, 138.

2. Ibid., 207.

3. Ibid., 1.

4. Ibid., 141.

5. Gilbert, "Local Playwright."

6. According to Lowe, Baldwin wrote all his articles in longhand first, usually in bursts of four to five pages, and was always open to suggestions and criticism. After a few rounds of editing, he would type up his final draft and send it by mail (Gilbert, "Local Playwright").

7. Solomon-Godeau, "Male Trouble," 70.

8. Bly, *Iron John*, 2.

9. John Wayne represented arguably the most influential "ideal of manhood" in 1950s cinema. The 1980s saw numerous reincarnations of the John Wayne archetype: from Reagan's calculated imaging as rugged cowboy to Clint Eastwood's tough-guy posturing in films like *Sudden Impact* (1983).

10. Jeffords, *Hard Bodies*, 1.

11. Reagan, "Let Them Go Their Way."

12. For more on the connections between Ronald Reagan and the 1950s revival in the 1980s, see Troy, *Morning in America*; Dwyer, *Back to the Fifties*; and Sirota, *Back to Our Future*.

13. Morgado, "Ronald Reagan TV Ad."

14. Cobbina, "Blues for Mr. Baldwin," 258.

15. Baldwin, Introduction, *Notes of a Native Son*, xiii.

16. Baldwin, "Freaks and the American Ideal of Manhood," 814.

17. Ibid., 815.

18. Ibid.

19. Baldwin and Lorde, "Revolutionary Hope."

20. Ibid.

21. Ibid.

22. Baldwin, "Freaks and the American Ideal of Manhood," 814.

23. Ibid.

24. Goldstein, "Go the Way Your Blood Beats," 65.

25. Baldwin, "Freaks and the American Ideal of Manhood," 818.

26. Ibid., 815.

27. Ibid., 819.

28. Ibid.

29. Ibid.

30. Ibid.

31. Ibid.

32. Field, *All Those Strangers*, 61.

33. Baldwin, "Freaks and the American Ideal of Manhood," 823.

34. Ibid., 818.

35. Ibid., 823.

36. Ibid.

37. Ibid.

38. Ibid., 821.

39. Ibid., 822.

40. Ibid., 821.

41. Ibid., 819.

42. Goldstein, "Go the Way Your Blood Beats," 42–43.

43. Baldwin, "Freaks and the American Ideal of Manhood," 817.

44. Ibid., 827.

45. Baldwin, "Stranger in the Village," 129.

46. See Stephen Prince's *History of the American Cinema: A New Pot of Gold: Hollywood Under the Electric Rainbow, 1980–1989* (University of California Press, 2002) and *American Cinema of the 1980s: Themes and Variations* (Rutgers University Press, 2007).

47. Jeffords, *Hard Bodies*, 11.

48. Ibid., 15.

49. Ibid., 25.

50. In a series of memos, current Supreme Court Justice John Roberts, who was an aide to President Reagan at the time, actively discouraged Reagan from recognizing Michael Jackson at the White House. "Frankly," he wrote, "I find the obsequious attitude of some members of the White House staff toward Mr. Jackson's attendants, and the fawning posture they would have the President of the United States adopt, more than a little embarrassing. . . . It is also important to consider the precedent that would be set by such a letter. In today's *Post* there were already reports that some youngsters were turning away from Mr. Jackson in favor of a

newcomer who goes by the name 'Prince,' and is apparently planning a Washington concert. Will he receive a Presidential letter? . . . The Jackson tour, whatever stature it may have attained as a cultural phenomenon, is a massive commercial undertaking. The visit of the tour to Washington was not an eleemosynary gesture; it was a calculated commercial decision that does not warrant gratitude from our Nation's Chief Executive. Such a letter would also create a bad precedent, as other popular performers would either expect or demand similar treatment. Why, for example, was no letter sent to Mr. Bruce Springsteen, whose patriotic tour recently visited the area? . . . I recognize that I am something of a *vox clamans in terris* in this area, but enough is enough" (qtd. in Milbank, "Young Roberts to King of Pop").

51. Nancy Reagan reportedly confided to an aide about Jackson: "It's all so peculiar, really. A boy who looks just like a girl, who whispers when he speaks, wears a glove on one hand and sunglasses all the time. I just don't know what to make of it" (qtd. in Taraborrelli, *Michael Jackson*). Despite her bewilderment, she was said to be a big fan of the artist, even dropping by the set of his 1991 music video, *Black or White*.

52. Baldwin, "Freaks and the American Ideal of Manhood," 827.

53. Ibid.

54. Hall, "Cultural Identity and Diaspora," 393.

55. While a handful of black artists appeared on MTV before Michael Jackson and Prince—including older clips of legends like Jimi Hendrix, Tina Turner, Little Richard, and Bob Marley, as well as British New Wave acts like Musical Youth—they were much easier to justify than current American "black music" (R&B, disco, and soul) and made up a very small percentage of the network's overall programming until the spring of 1983.

56. While dance was not a feature of the hypermasculine action blockbuster, it became a huge part of 1980s cinema, in large part due to the influence of music videos. These films include *Fame* (1980), *Flashdance* (1983), *Footloose* (1984), *Breakin'* (1984), *Girls Just Want to Have Fun* (1985), *A Chorus Line* (1985), and *Dirty Dancing* (1987), among others.

57. Mercer, "Monster Metaphors," 40.

58. Reagan's infamous invocation of Springsteen occurred during a campaign stop in 1984 in Hammonton, New Jersey. "America's future," he said, "rests in a thousand dreams inside our hearts. It rests in the message of hope in the songs of a man so many young Americans admire: New Jersey's own Bruce Springsteen. And helping make those dreams come true is what this job of mine is all about." Many in the liberal media rushed to Springsteen's defense, arguing that President Reagan had missed the message of the song. In a September 21 concert in Pittsburgh, Pennsylvania, Springsteen himself responded to the controversy, saying: "The President was mentioning my name the other day, and I kinda got to wondering what his favorite album musta been. I don't think it was the *Nebraska* album. I don't think he's been listening to this one." Yet as Springsteen biographer Marc Dolan observes: "In the end, when you compared Springsteen's fall 1984 tour with Reagan's, no matter

how different their political visions were supposed to be, their rhetoric seemed a lot alike." *Bruce Springsteen and the Promise of Rock and Roll* (Norton, 2012).

59. Will, "Bruce Springsteen's U.S.A."

60. Garman, *Race of Singers*, 225.

61. "Last Word on Michael."

62. Greenburg, *Michael Jackson, Inc.*, 217; Greenburg, "Infographic."

63. Baldwin, "Freaks and the American Ideal of Manhood," 828. The full quote includes a final aside about "the bitter need to find a head on which to place the crown of Miss America," a reference to the forced resignation of the first black Miss America, Vanessa Williams, crowned in 1984. The backlash was immediate, from those angry about her race to those suspicious that she had distanced herself from her blackness. Later that year, Williams was pressured into relinquishing her crown when nude photos of her were leaked to *Penthouse* magazine. Following the incident, Williams went on to have a successful career as a singer, actress, and model. It took until 2015, however, before the CEO of the Miss America pageant issued a formal apology to Williams.

64. Troupe, "Pressure to Beat It."

65. Yuan, "Celebrity Freak," 368.

66. Fast, "Michael Jackson's Queer Musical Belongings," 282.

67. Vogel, "How Michael Jackson Made Bad."

68. Ralph Ellison once envisioned the "whole of American life as a drama acted out upon the body of a Negro giant, who, lying trussed up like Gulliver, forms the stage and scene upon which and within which the action unfolds" (*Shadow and Act* [New York: Knopf Doubleday, 2011], 27). Incidentally, Jackson provided a visual representation for this very scenario in his 1989 music video, *Leave Me Alone*.

69. "Last Word on Michael."

70. Ibid.

71. George, *Death of Rhythm and Blues*, 174.

72. Ibid.

73. See Wallace, "Michael Jackson."

74. Baldwin, "Freaks and the American Ideal of Manhood," 828.

75. Ibid., 816.

76. Ibid.

77. Hall, "Cultural Identity and Diaspora," 393.

78. Elgrably and Plimpton, "Art of Fiction LXXVIII," 252.

79. Baldwin, "Freaks and the American Ideal of Manhood," 828.

Chapter 3. The Welcome Table

1. Altman, "Rare Cancer Seen in 41 Homosexuals."

2. "Current Trends Update," 507.

3. Wallis, "AIDS."

4. World Health Organization, "Global Health Observatory Data: HIV/AIDS, http://www.who.int/gho/hiv/en.

5. As he put it in a 1981 speech to the New York Chapter of Black and White Men Together (BWMT-NY): "One has to reject, in toto, the implication that one is abnormal. That is a sociological and societal delusion that has no truth at all. I'm no more abnormal than General Douglas MacArthur."

6. Goldstein, "Go the Way Your Blood Beats," 44.

7. Ibid.

8. Ibid., 40.

9. Ibid.

10. While Baldwin accurately critiqued the racially stratified gay scenes in Greenwich Village and San Francisco, he did not acknowledge the vibrant, growing black and Latino gay communities that began to flourish in the 1970s, in concurrence with the emergence of the disco movement and dance clubs. Increasingly, such clubs became sites not only for pleasure and entertainment but also for community and activism. The 1970s also saw the emergence of prominent black lesbian activists and authors, including Barbara Smith and Audre Lorde. Founded and published in 1979, *Blacklight*, one of the first publications for African American gays and lesbians in the United States, signaled a new era of organization and openness for the black LGBTQ community.

11. Ibid., 43.

12. Bost, "At the Club," 2.

13. Tinney, "Baldwin Comes Out."

14. Goldstein, "Go the Way Your Blood Beats," 43.

15. Ibid.

16. Ibid., 45.

17. Thorsen, *James Baldwin*.

18. Jarbyus, "Thank You for Coming, James Baldwin."

19. Leeming, *James Baldwin*, 367.

20. Ed Pavlic, email message to author, September 15, 2016.

21. The manuscript I reference throughout this chapter is the 1987 draft held at the Houghton Library at Harvard University. All letters and related documents are from this collection (MS Am 3000: Baldwin, James, 1924–1987. The welcome table and other James Baldwin papers, circa 1961–1987. *Purchased with the Amy Lowell Trust and funds from the Hutchins Center for African and African American Research*) and another Baldwin collection held at the Houghton Library (MS Am 3027: Baldwin, James, 1924–1987. The welcome table and related James Baldwin papers, 1983–1990. *Purchased with the Susan A. E. Morse Fund, the Russel Crouse Fund for Twentieth Century Theatre, the Sidney J. Watts Fund, and the Thomas W. Streeter Fund and with the aid of the Hutchins Center for African & African American Research*).

22. James Baldwin, playbill, Houghton Library, Harvard University, 1990.

23. Landau, "HIV in the '80s."

24. Kramer, "1,112 and Counting."

25. Ibid.

26. Shilts, *And the Band Played On*, 245.

27. Selligman, "The AIDS Epidemic."

28. In her book *The Boundaries of Blackness: AIDS and the Breakdown of Black Politics* (Chicago: University of Chicago Press, 1999), Cathy J. Cohen notes that part of this neglect had to do with apathy within the black community. Her investigation explores a number of intersecting reasons "why, when faced with a disease that was threatening significant numbers of African Americans, traditional black leaders seemed to do nothing, or very little" (iv).

29. AIDS Action Council, "Policy Facts."

30. Shilts, *And the Band Played On*, 353.

31. White, "Reagan's AIDS Legacy."

32. Shilts, *And the Band Played On*, 578–79.

33. Ibid., 579.

34. Yarbrough, "Rock Hudson."

35. "President Reagan's AMFAR Speech," PBS *Frontline*, May 31, 1987.

36. Troy, *Morning in America*, 202.

37. Yarbrough, "Rock Hudson."

38. Ibid.

39. Haller, "Fighting for Life."

40. Ibid.

41. Ibid.

42. Ibid.

43. Landau, "HIV in the '80s."

44. Engel, *Epidemic*, 71.

45. Johnson, "Ryan White Dies."

46. Downing and Gillett, *Queer in Europe*, 64.

47. Landau, "HIV in the '80s."

48. Ibid.

49. While Baldwin shared some similarities with Foucault—both were famous, gay, expatriate authors renowned for their critiques of power and affiliated with France and America—there were also notable ways they thought differently about sex, intimacy, and love. Where Foucault reveled in role-playing, anonymity, and "limit experiences," Baldwin never felt comfortable with such approaches to relationships. "I don't want to sound distant or patronizing because I don't really feel that," he explained to Richard Goldstein in 1984. "I simply feel it's a world that has very little to do with me, with where I did my growing up. I was never at home in it. Even in my early years in the Village, what I saw of that world absolutely frightened me, bewildered me. I didn't understand the necessity of all the role playing. And in a way I still don't" (qtd. in Goldstein, "Go the Way Your Blood Beats," 59). Baldwin did, of course, recognize the fact that we all perform identity to some degree, and that "one can never really see into the heart, the mind, the soul of another" ("The Black Boy," 284). But for Baldwin, a fulfilling relationship nonetheless tried. It required taking off masks. Both wrote about sex as a sublime experience—yet where Foucault sought the thrill of "the overwhelming, the unspeakable, the creepy, the

stupefying, the ecstatic," Baldwin sought confession (a concept Foucault abhorred), reciprocity, the transcendence of union.

50. Miller, *Passion of Michel Foucault*, 21.

51. Kramer, "1,112 and Counting."

52. Shilts, *And the Band Played On*, 317.

53. Baldwin, "The Welcome Table," Houghton Library, Harvard University, 1985, 1.

54. Ibid., 17.

55. Ibid.

56. Ibid.

57. Ibid.

58. Ibid., 18.

59. Ibid.

60. Ibid.

61. Ibid.

62. Baldwin, *Giovanni's Room*, 5.

63. Goldstein, "Go the Way Your Blood Beats," 64.

64. Fiedler, *Love and Death in the American Novel*, 26.

65. Ibid. 24.

66. Goldstein, "Go the Way Your Blood Beats," 61.

67. According to biographer David Leeming and scholar Magdalena Zaborowska, early titles for the play included *The 121st Day of Sodom* and *Inventory*.

68. "Letter to Walter Dallas," Houghton Library, Harvard University, July 21, 1984.

69. Ibid.

70. The earlier draft was ninety-eight pages; the final draft was seventy-two pages.

71. Ibid.

72. Baldwin, "Architectural Digest Visits," 124.

73. Zaborowska, *James Baldwin's Turkish Decade*, 247.

74. Leeming, *James Baldwin*, 376.

75. Zaborowska, *James Baldwin's Turkish Decade*, 251.

76. Leeming, *James Baldwin*, 377.

77. Ibid.

78. Baldwin, "The Welcome Table," 5.

79. Ibid.

80. Ibid., 7.

81. Ibid., 9.

82. Ibid., 15.

83. Ibid., 23.

84. Ibid.

85. Ibid.

86. Ibid., 11.

87. Ibid., 33.

88. Ibid., 36.

89. Ibid., 42.

90. Ibid., 44.

91. Ibid., 52.

92. Ibid., 53.

93. Ibid.

94. Ibid., 54.

95. Ibid., 61.

96. Ibid., 19.

97. Ibid., 18.

98. Ibid., 19.

99. Ibid.

100. Ibid.

101. Ibid., 40.

102. Ibid., 41.

103. Ibid.

104. Ibid. The line, "The Lady's not for burning," refers to the 1948 play, *The Lady's Not for Burning*, by Christopher Fry.

105. Ibid.

106. Ibid.

107. Ibid.

108. Ibid., 45.

109. Ibid.

110. Ibid.

111. Ibid., 46–47.

112. Ibid., 47.

113. Ibid., 63.

114. Ibid.

115. Esslin, "Text and Subtext in Shavian Drama," 200.

116. James Baldwin, "Letter to Walter Dallas, July 4, 1987." Houghton Library, Harvard University.

117. Ibid.

118. Baldwin, "The Welcome Table," 17.

119. Troupe, "James Baldwin," 288.

120. Ibid. 288–89.

121. Baldwin, "The Welcome Table," 55.

122. Young, *James Baldwin's Understanding of God*, 184.

123. Baldwin, "The Welcome Table," 30.

124. Leeming, *James Baldwin*, 382.

125. Baldwin, "The Welcome Table," 50.

126. Ibid., 72.

127. Ibid.

128. Engel, *Epidemic*, 44–45.

129. Ibid. 45.

Chapter 4. "To Crush the Serpent"

1. Brooks, "From Edwards to Baldwin," 432.
2. Field, *All Those Strangers*, 82–86.
3. Ibid., 83.
4. Baldwin, *The Fire Next Time*, 308.
5. Ibid., 309–10.
6. Ibid., 314.
7. Douglas Field astutely notes that it is the music of the church, more than the church itself, that becomes Baldwin's preferred vehicle for "anti-institutional spirituality" (*All Those Strangers*, 95).
8. Baldwin, *The Fire Next Time*, 306.
9. Baldwin's connection to the black church remained characterized by paradox. See, for example, Christopher Hobson's essay, "Prophecy and Doubt in *Just Above My Head*," in which the author details how Baldwin sustains "both the possible falseness of prophetic hope and our continuing need for it, and to present the necessity for choice in a final dream that holds the key to the novel' s meaning." (*James Baldwin Review*, 1 (2015), 67).
10. Baldwin, "Open Letter to the Born Again," 784.
11. While the religious Right and Moral Majority have sometimes been used interchangeably, the former describes a coalition of like-minded, largely (but not exclusively) evangelical Christian groups focused on conservative political efforts, while the latter initially referred to a specific political action group founded in 1979 by Jerry Falwell. As time passed, however, the Moral Majority came to be identified more broadly with the same basic coalition and ideological concerns as the religious Right.
12. Baldwin, "To Crush the Serpent," 204.
13. Winner, "Reaganizing Religion," 181.
14. Richard Nixon, "Address to the Nation on the War in Vietnam," November 3, 1969, available at http://www.presidency.ucsb.edu/ws/?pid=2303.
15. "Born Again! The Evangelicals."
16. Baldwin, "Open Letter to the Born Again," 768–69.
17. Ibid., 769.
18. Carter, "*Playboy* Interview," 58.
19. Ibid., 33.
20. Miller, *Age of Evangelicalism*, 64.
21. Miller notes one simple but significant rhetorical transformation that began in the 1980s under the influence of the religious Right: "A commonplace in presidential discourse at the start of the twenty-first century, 'God bless America' appeared in a major presidential address precisely once before Reagan." (Ibid., 65). It is now, of course, an expected conclusion to many presidential speeches, conservative and liberal alike.
22. Sutton, *Jerry Falwell*, 1.
23. Williams, *God's Own Party*, 159.

24. In one show, Robertson spoke to a member of CBN's board of directors, Harald Bredesen, about the "anointing" of Ronald Reagan. Bredesen claimed that he had joined hands with Pat Boone, George Otis, and Ronald Reagan in prayer in 1970 when Reagan was governor of California, when Otis suddenly received a prophecy that God would make Reagan president if "he would walk in his ways" (Winner, "Reaganizing Religion," 188).

25. Robertson, "Action Plan for the 1980s," 119–20.

26. Ibid., 119–22.

27. Ibid., 122.

28. Winner, "Reaganizing Religion," 188.

29. Ibid., 184. Ironically, this seemingly apolitical sermon was a direct attack on Rev. Martin Luther King Jr. and civil rights efforts in Selma, Alabama. "If as much effort could be put into winning people to Jesus Christ across the land as is being exerted in the present civil rights movement," said Falwell, "America would be turned upside down for God" (Sutton, *Jerry Falwell*, 12).

30. Williams, *God's Own Party*, 177.

31. Sutton, *Jerry Falwell*, 12.

32. Wallace, "Segregation Now, Segregation Forever."

33. Banwart, "Jerry Falwell," 146.

34. Miller, *Age of Evangelicalism*, 63. Miller elaborates: "Falwell's influence may have been even greater on Reagan's re-election: November 1984, even more than November 1980, was Falwell's moment in the sun. Every national news network was on hand in Lynchburg to record his response to the election. A leading newsmagazine soon rated him the fourteenth most influential person in the nation (third in the private sector, behind businessman Lee Iacocca and newscaster Dan Rather)." (*Age of Evangelicalism*, 68).

35. Swatos, "Televangelism," 513.

36. "The Tech Boom," S1:E7, *The Eighties*, CNN (2016).

37. "Greed Is Good," S1:E4, *The Eighties*, CNN (2016).

38. Johnson, "Theme Park," par. 1.

39. Ibid.

40. Ibid.

41. "Greed Is Good," S1:E4, *The Eighties*, CNN (2016).

42. With increased media scrutiny surrounding the Bakkers' opulent lifestyle— which included gold-plated bathroom fixtures, Rolls-Royces, an air-conditioned dog house, and luxurious vacations—a federal investigation ensued about the Bakkers' financial affairs. Eventually, Jim Bakker was indicted on twenty-four charges, including fraud and conspiracy. He was convicted on all counts in 1988 and sentenced to forty-five years in prison, although he ended up serving just five years, due in part to a campaign led by his son, Jay, asking the parole board for leniency based on his father's rehabilitation. Meanwhile, Jerry Falwell, who had become a mortal enemy of Bakker's, took over PTL, including Heritage USA (See Ostling, "Of God and Greed").

43. See *Time*'s September 10, 2006, cover story, "Does God Want You to Be Rich?" for a detailed exploration of how the "electric church" and "prosperity gospel" evolved in the 2000s.

44. Baldwin, "Open Letter to the Born Again," 784.

45. Cannato, "Bright Lights, Doomed Cities."

46. Baldwin, *The Evidence of Things Not Seen*, 124.

47. *Wall Street*, directed by Oliver Stone (1987), 20th Century Fox, 2010, DVD.

48. Baldwin, "To Crush the Serpent," 199.

49. Ibid., 199.

50. "Mountains of blasphemous rhetoric have been written to deny or defend this fact," writes Baldwin ("To Crush the Serpent," 195).

51. Ibid., 196.

52. Baldwin, *The Fire Next Time*, 309.

53. Field, "James Baldwin's Religion," 86–89.

54. Baldwin, *The Fire Next Time*, 311.

55. Baldwin, "To Crush the Serpent," 196.

56. Ibid., 197.

57. Ibid.

58. Ibid., 198.

59. Johnson and Eskridge, "Legacy of Falwell's Bully Pulpit."

60. Baldwin, "To Crush the Serpent," 198.

61. Ibid., 199.

62. Young, *James Baldwin's Understanding of God*, 14. "The real architect of the Christian church," Baldwin asserted, "was not the disreputable, sun-baked Hebrew who gave it his name but the mercilessly fanatical and self-righteous St. Paul" (*The Fire Next Time*, 312).

63. Young, *James Baldwin's Understanding of God*, 14.

64. Werner, *Playing the Changes*, 223–35.

65. Richard Dyer, *White*, 14.

66. As Richard Dyer writes: "There are special anxieties surrounding the whiteness of white women vis-à-vis sexuality. As the literal bearers of children, and because they are held primarily responsible for their initial raising, women are the indispensable means by which the group—the race—is in every sense reproduced. . . . White women thus carry—or, in many narratives, betray—the hopes, achievements and character of the race" (*White*, 29).

67. Baldwin, "To Crush the Serpent," 200.

68. Simon, "GOP and Willie Horton."

69. Baldwin, "To Crush the Serpent," 199.

70. Ibid., 200.

71. Ibid.

72. Ibid.

73. Ibid., 201.

74. Ibid.

75. Ibid., 204.

76. Blake, "Marriage of Heaven and Hell."

77. Young, *James Baldwin's Understanding of God*, 14.

78. Baldwin, "To Crush the Serpent," 203.

79. Ibid., 203.

80. Field, *All Those Strangers*, 96.

81. Ibid., 98.

82. Ibid., 112.

83. Baldwin, "To Crush the Serpent," 202.

84. Foucault, *Order of Things*, 178–80.

85. Baldwin, "The Creative Process," 672.

86. Baldwin, "To Crush the Serpent," 204.

87. Lovett, "Evangelicals Back Donald Trump."

88. Baldwin, "To Crush the Serpent," 203–4.

89. Ibid., 204.

Chapter 5. Things Not Seen

1. Glawe, "Michael Brown's Hometown."

2. McLaughlin, "What We Know."

3. Irwin, Miller, and Sangot-Katz, "America's Racial Divide, Charted." While homicide rates are much higher among black men than black women (according to the Violence Policy Center, of the 6,309 black homicide victims, 5,452 [86 percent] were male, and 854 [14 percent] were female), violence against black women is nonetheless far too common and frequently overlooked. Indeed, black women are more likely to be the victims of domestic violence than any other demographic in America. In the Atlanta Terror, as Baldwin notes, the list of victims included two young girls (Angel Lanier and LaTonya Wilson), as well as twenty-seven young boys. Several other girls were killed in the city from 1979 to 1982; however, since their deaths were not perceived as conforming to the "pattern" of the other cases, they were almost entirely ignored.

4. As Teju Cole writes in the *New Yorker*, "The black body comes pre-judged, and as a result it is placed in needless jeopardy. To be black is to bear the brunt of selective enforcement of the law, and to inhabit a psychic unsteadiness in which there is no guarantee of personal safety. You are a black body first, before you are a kid walking down the street or a Harvard professor who has misplaced his keys" ("Black Body").

5. Goff, "Essence of Innocence."

6. Mai-Duc, "Cleveland Officer."

7. Leeming, *James Baldwin*, 361.

8. See, for example, Lawrie Balfour's book, *The Evidence of Things Not Said: James Baldwin and the Promise of American Democracy*, which grapples with many of *Evidence*'s themes, including the "race consciousness" Baldwin believed was necessary

to understand the complex web of institutions, ideologies, media narratives, and everyday encounters we experience as citizens in America. *Evidence*, however, is not one of Balfour's main sources. Perhaps the three most noteworthy analyses of *Evidence* have surfaced over the last decade. In his 2007 essay for *PMLA*, "Black Atlanta: An Ecosocial Approach to Narratives of the Atlanta Child Murders," Eric Gary Anderson examines violence and trauma in the context of "urban ecologies." Criminality and the South, he contends, are crucially intertwined in the American imaginary and necessary to understanding how the narratives of the Atlanta child murders were framed and understood.

9. Schur, "Unseen or Unspeakable?," 206.

10. Miller, *Criminal Power*, 155–56.

11. Baldwin, *The Evidence of Things Not Seen*, 10.

12. Baldwin, "Atlanta: The Evidence of Things Not Seen," 312.

13. Ibid.

14. See Ken Auletta's *Media Man: Ted Turner's Improbable Empire* (New York: Norton, 2005) and Hank Whittemore's *CNN: The Inside Story: How A Band of Mavericks Changed the Face of Television News* (New York: Little Brown, 1990) for more on the rise of CNN in the 1980s.

15. Troy, *Morning in America*, 86–87.

16. Baldwin, "Atlanta: The Evidence of Things Not Seen," 142.

17. Rosenberg, "When the Media Burned Atlanta."

18. In *The List*, former Atlanta police official Chet Dettlinger documents at least sixty-four additional unsolved Atlanta area killings that fit the criteria used to establish the pattern between the official twenty-eight. Seven murders that fit the parameters of "the list" occurred while Williams was in jail. An additional fifteen victims ages thirteen to twenty-eight were reported in Atlanta from 1982 to early 1983 (44).

19. Baldwin, *The Evidence of Things Not Seen*, 85.

20. Troy, *Morning in America*, 87–88.

21. Ibid., 87.

22. Rosenberg, "When the Media Burned Atlanta."

23. Harris, "Another Body Found."

24. Baldwin, "Atlanta: The Evidence of Things Not Seen," 141.

25. Ibid., 142.

26. Baldwin, *The Evidence of Things Not Seen*, 26.

27. Ibid., xv–xvi.

28. Ibid.

29. Dettlinger, *The List*, 46.

30. Baldwin, "Atlanta: The Evidence of Things Not Seen," 142.

31. Baldwin, *The Evidence of Things Not Seen*, 55.

32. Baldwin, "Atlanta: The Evidence of Things Not Seen," 308.

33. Ibid., 314.

34. Ibid., 316.

35. Although it is outside the scope of this chapter, a full article should be dedicated to differences between the two works and Baldwin's writing process on the four-year project.

36. Ibid., 142.

37. Baldwin, *The Evidence of Things Not Seen*, 79.

38. Schur, "Unseen or Unspeakable?," 206.

39. Alexander, *New Jim Crow*, 183.

40. Baldwin, "Atlanta: The Evidence of Things Not Seen," 142, 308.

41. Baldwin, "No Name in the Street," 396.

42. Baldwin, "Nobody Knows My Name," 203.

43. Ibid.

44. Ibid.

45. Baldwin, *The Evidence of Things Not Seen*, 57.

46. Ibid.

47. Ibid., 25.

48. Ibid., 26.

49. Baldwin, "Atlanta: The Evidence of Things Not Seen," 206.

50. Baldwin, *The Evidence of Things Not Seen*, 74.

51. Baldwin, "Atlanta: The Evidence of Things Not Seen," 142.

52. Ibid.

53. Baldwin, *The Evidence of Things Not Seen*, 49.

54. Ibid., xiv.

55. Ibid.

56. Ibid., 62–64.

57. Ibid., 49.

58. "Interview with Camille Bell."

59. Baldwin, *The Evidence of Things Not Seen*, 10.

60. Ibid., 11.

61. Ibid., xv.

62. Ibid., 11.

63. Notes Baldwin: "A people who can believe that Ethel and Julius Rosenberg coerced David Greenglass into stealing the secret of the Atomic Bomb from Los Alamos, thus allowing the Rosenbergs to sell this 'secret' to the Russians—and who sent them to the electric chair for this 'treason'—are poorly equipped to examine scientific evidence, or indeed, any evidence at all" (*The Evidence of Things Not Seen*, 98).

64. Ibid., 14.

65. Dettlinger, *The List*, 64.

66. Ibid., 48.

67. "Tapes Link KKK."

68. Ibid.

69. Curriden, "New Questions in Atlanta Murders."

70. Ibid.
71. Baldwin, *The Evidence of Things Not Seen*, 105.
72. Ibid., 112.
73. Ibid., 105.
74. Ibid., 15.
75. Ibid., 2.
76. Ibid., 72.
77. Flemming, "In Short: Nonfiction."
78. Baldwin, "Atlanta: The Evidence of Things Not Seen," 316.
79. Baldwin, *The Evidence of Things Not Seen*, 124.
80. Ibid., 122.
81. Ibid., 123.
82. Ibid., 88.
83. Ibid., 89.
84. Ibid., 123, 90.
85. Baldwin, "Atlanta: The Evidence of Things Not Seen," 312.

Epilogue

1. Baldwin, "The World I Never Made."
2. Sirota, *Back to Our Future*, xiii.
3. Ibid., xvii.
4. Baldwin, "The World I Never Made."

Bibliography

AIDS Action Council. "Policy Facts: Communities of Color and HIV/AIDS." January 2002.

Alexander, Michelle. *The New Jim Crow: Mass Incarceration in the Age of Colorblindness*. New York: New Press, 2010.

Als, Hilton. "The Enemy Within." *New Yorker*, February 16, 1998.

Altman, Lawrence K. "Rare Cancer Seen in 41 Homosexuals." *New York Times*, July 3, 1981.

Anderson, Eric Gary. "Black Atlanta: An Ecosocial Approach to Narratives of the Atlanta Child Murders." *PMLA* 122, no. 1 (January 2007): 194–209.

Anderson, Michael. "Trapped Inside James Baldwin." *New York Times*, March 29, 1998.

Arnold, Matthew. *Culture and Anarchy*. Oxford: Oxford University Press, 2009.

The Atlanta Child Murders. Dir. John Erman. YouTube. Abby Mann Productions, 1985.

Baldwin, James. "Architectural Digest Visits: James Baldwin." *Architectural Digest*, August 1987.

———. "The Art of Fiction: James Baldwin." In Standley and Pratt, *Conversations with James Baldwin*, 232–54.

———. "Atlanta: The Evidence of Things Not Seen." *Playboy*, December 1981.

———. "Autobiographical Notes." In Morrison, *Baldwin: Collected Essays*, 5–9.

———. "Black English: A Dishonest Argument." In Kenan, *Cross of Redemption*, 125–30.

———. "*The Black Scholar* Interviews James Baldwin." In Standley and Pratt, *Conversations with James Baldwin*, 142–58.

———. "The Creative Process." In Morrison, *Baldwin: Collected Essays*, 669–72.

———. "Dark Days." In Morrison, *Baldwin: Collected Essays*, 788–98.

———. *The Devil Finds Work*. New York: Vintage, 1976, 2011.

———. "Everybody's Protest Novel." In Morrison, *Baldwin: Collected Essays*, 11–18.

———. *The Evidence of Things Not Seen*. New York: Owl, 1995.

———. "The Fire Next Time." In Morrison, *Baldwin: Collected Essays*, 291–347.

———. "Freaks and the American Ideal of Manhood." In Morrison, *Baldwin: Collected Essays*, 814–29.

———. *Giovanni's Room*. New York: Delta, 1956, 2000.

———. "The House of Bondage." In Morrison, *Baldwin: Collected Essays*, 799–807.

———. "If Black English Isn't a Language, Then Tell Me, What Is?" In Morrison, *Baldwin: Collected Essays*, 780–83.

———. "James Baldwin, an Interview." In Standley and Pratt, *Conversations with James Baldwin*, 190–209.

———. "James Baldwin: Reflections of a Maverick." In Standley and Pratt, *Conversations with James Baldwin*, 222–231.

———. *Just Above My Head*. New York: Delta, 1978, 1979.

———. Letter to Walter Dallas, July 21, 1984. Houghton Library, Harvard University, Cambridge, Mass.

———. Letter to Walter Dallas, July 4, 1987. Houghton Library, Harvard University, Cambridge, Mass.

———. "Mass Culture and the Creative Artist: Some Personal Notes." In Kenan, *Cross of Redemption*, 3–7.

———. "Nobody Knows My Name: A Letter from the South." In Morrison, *Baldwin: Collected Essays*, 197–208.

———. "No Name in the Street." In Morrison, *Baldwin: Collected Essays*, 353–457.

———. "Nothing Personal." In Morrison, *Baldwin: Collected Essays*, 692–706.

———. "Of the Sorrow Songs: The Cross of Redemption." In Kenan, *Cross of Redemption*, 145–53.

———. "An Open Letter to Jimmy Carter." In Morrison, *Baldwin: Collected Essays*, 766–69.

———. "Open Letter to the Born Again." In Morrison, *Baldwin: Collected Essays*, 784–87.

———. Playbill (1990). Houghton Library, Harvard University, Cambridge, Mass.

———. Preface to *Notes of a Native Son*, by James Baldwin. New York: Beacon, 1955, 1984.

———. "Preservation of Innocence." In Morrison, *Baldwin: Collected Essays*, 594–601.

———. "The Price May Be Too High." *New York Times*, February 2, 1969.

———. "The Price of the Ticket." In Morrison, *Baldwin: Collected Essays*, 830–842.

———. *The Price of the Ticket: Collected Non-Fiction, 1948–1985*. New York: St. Martin's, 1985.

———. "Sonny's Blues." In *Going to Meet the Man*. New York: Vintage, 1948, 1995.

———. "Stranger in the Village." In Morrison, *Baldwin: Collected Essays*, 117–29.

———. "A Talk to Teachers." In Morrison, *Baldwin: Collected Essays*, 678–86.

———. "To Crush a Serpent." In Kenan, *Cross of Redemption*, 195–204.

———. "The Uses of the Blues," in Kenan, *Cross of Redemption*, 57–66.

———. *The Welcome Table* (1987). Houghton Library, Harvard University, Cambridge, Mass.

———. "White Racism and Other Lies." *Essence*, April 1984.

———. "White Racism or World Community?" In Morrison, *Baldwin: Collected Essays*, 749–56.

———. "The World I Never Made." National Press Club, C-SPAN, December 10, 1986. Available at http://www.cspan.org/video/?150875–1/world-never-made.

——— and Audre Lorde. "Revolutionary Hope: A Conversation Between James Baldwin and Audre Lorde." *Essence*, December 1984.

Balfour, Lawrie. *The Evidence of Things Not Said: James Baldwin and the Promise of American Democracy*. Ithaca, N.Y.: Cornell University Press, 2000.

Balmer, Randall. "Jimmy Carter's Evangelical Downfall: Reagan, Religion and the 1980 Presidential Election." *Salon*, May 25, 2014.

———. *Redeemer: The Life of Jimmy Carter*. New York: Basic, 2014.

Banwart, Doug. "Jerry Falwell, the Rise of the Moral Majority, and the 1980 Election." *Western Illinois Historical Review* 5 (Spring 2013): 133–57.

Blake, William. "The Marriage of Heaven and Hell" (1790). In *Blake's Poetry and Designs*, edited by Mary Lynn Johnson and John E. Grant, 66–82. New York: Norton, 2008.

Bloom, Allan. *The Closing of the American Mind*. New York: Simon and Schuster, 1987.

Bly, Robert. *Iron John: A Book About Men*. New York: Da Capo, 2004.

"Born Again! The Evangelicals." *Newsweek*, October 25, 1976.

Bost, Darius. "At the Club: Locating Early Black Gay AIDS Activism in Washington, D.C." *Occasion* 8 (Fall 2015).

Brooks, Joanna. "From Edwards to Baldwin: Heterodoxy, Discontinuity, and New Narratives of American Religious-Literary History." *Early American Literature*, 45, no. 2: 425–40.

Brustein, Robert. "Everybody Knows My Name." *New York Review of Books*, December 17, 1964.

Campbell, James. "Sorrow Wears and Uses Us." *New York Times*, September 8, 2010.

———. *Talking at the Gates: A Life of James Baldwin*. Berkeley: University of California Press, 2002.

Cannato, Vincent J. "Bright Lights, Doomed Cities: The Rise or Fall of New York City in the 1980s." In *Living in the Eighties*, edited by Gil Troy and Vincent J. Cannato, 70–84. Oxford: Oxford University Press, 2009.

Carenen, Caitlin. *The Fervent Embrace: Liberal Protestants, Evangelicals, and Israel*. New York: New York University, 2012.

Carson, Warren. "Manhood, Musicality, and Bonding in *Just Above My Head*." In Miller, *Re-viewing James Baldwin*, 215–32.

Carter, Jimmy. "*Playboy* Interview, 1976." In *Conversations with Carter*, edited by Don Richardson, 33–58. London: Rienner's, 1998.

———. "Primary Resources: Crisis of Confidence." PBS, *American Experience*, July 15, 1979.

Cartwright, Garth. "'Sure, He Could Write: But Is This Really the Father of Hip Hop?'" *Independent*, August 5, 2000.

Cleaver, Eldridge. *Soul on Ice*. New York: Delta, 1999.

Cobbina, Angela. "Blues for Mr. Baldwin." In Standley and Pratt, *Conversations with James Baldwin*. Jackson: University Press of Mississippi, 1989.

Cole, Teju. "Black Body: Rereading James Baldwin's 'Stranger in the Village.'" *New Yorker*, August 19, 2014.

Coombs, Orde. "The Devil Finds Work." *New York Times*, May 2, 1976.

Cowie, Jefferson R., and Lauren Boehm. "Dead Man's Town: Born in the U.S.A.,' Social History, and Working Class Identity." *American Quarterly* 58, no. 2 (2012): 353–78.

"Current Trends Update on Acquired Immune Deficiency Syndrome (AIDS)—United States." *Morbidity and Mortality Weekly Report 31*, no. 37 (September 24, 1982): 507. Available at https://www.cdc.gov/mmwr/preview/mmwrhtml/00001163.htm.

Curriden, Mark. "New Questions in Atlanta Murders: Did Prosecutors Withhold Evidence of Klan Involvement in Children's Deaths?" *ABA Journal* (May 1992): 36.

Desmond-Harris, Jenée. "Racism Is Real: Trump Helps Show It." *New York Times*, April 29, 2016.

Dettlinger, Chet. *The List*. Atlanta: Philmay, 1983.

Downing, Lisa, and Robert Gillett, ed. *Queer in Europe: Contemporary Case Studies*. New York: Routledge, 2016.

Dwyer, Michael. *Back to the Fifties: Nostalgia, Hollywood Film, and Popular Music of the Seventies and Eighties*. Oxford: Oxford University Press, 2015.

Dyer, Richard. *White*. New York: Routledge, 1997.

Early, Gerald. *One Nation under a Groove: Motown and American Culture*. Ann Arbor: University of Michigan Press, 1995, 2004.

Elgrably, Jordan, and George Plimpton. "The Art of Fiction LXXVIII: James Baldwin." In Standley and Pratt, *Conversations with James Baldwin*, 232–55.

Engel, Jonathan. *The Epidemic: A Global History of AIDS*. New York: Smithsonian Books, 2006.

Esslin, Martin. "Text and Subtext in Shavian Drama." In *1922: Shaw and the Last Hundred Years*, edited by Bernard F. Dukore, 199–208. University Park: Pennsylvania State University Press, 1994.

Evans, Mike. *Ray Charles: The Birth of Soul*. New York: Omnibus, 2005.

Fast, Susan. "Difference That Exceeded Understanding: Remembering Michael Jackson (1958–2009)." *Popular Music and Society* 33, no. 2 (May 2012): 259–66.

———. "Michael Jackson's Queer Musical Belongings." *Popular Music and Society* 35, no. 2 (May 2012): 281–300.

Fiedler, Leslie. *Love and Death in the American Novel*. McLean, Ill.: Dalkey, 1966.

Field, Douglas. *All Those Strangers: The Art and Lives of James Baldwin*. New York: Oxford University Press, 2015.

———. "Interview with David Linx." *African American Review*, 46, no. 4 (Winter 2013): 731–40.

Flemming, John. "In Short: Nonfiction." *New York Times*, November 24, 1985.

Foucault, Michel. *The Order of Things: An Archaeology of the Human Sciences*. New York, Vintage, 1994.

Francis, Consuela. *The Critical Reception of James Baldwin, 1963–2010*. Rochester, N.Y.: Camden House, 2014.

Fraterrigo, Elizabeth. *Playboy and the Making of the Good Life in Modern America*. New York: Oxford University Press, 2009.

Garman, Bryan K. *A Race of Singers: Whitman's Working-Class Hero from Guthrie to Springsteen*. Chapel Hill: University of North Carolina Press, 2000.

Gates, Henry Louis. "The Fire Last Time." *New Republic*, June 1, 1992.

George, Nelson. *The Death of Rhythm and Blues*. New York: Penguin, 1988.

Gil, Troy. *Morning in America: How Ronald Reagan Invented the 1980s*. Princeton, N.J.: Princeton University Press, 2005.

Gilbert, Steve. "Local Playwright Has Lived Fascinating, Diverse Life." *Sentinel Source*, October 12, 2014.

Glawe, Justin. "Michael Brown's Hometown Is under Occupation." *Daily Beast*, August 14, 2014.

Goff, Phillip A. "The Essence of Innocence: Consequences of Dehumanizing Black Children." *Journal of Personality and Social Psychology* 106, no. 4 (August 1, 2014): 526–45.

Goldstein, Richard. "'Go the Way Your Blood Beats': An Interview with James Baldwin." In *James Baldwin: The Legacy*, edited by Quincy Troupe, 57–74. New York: Melville, 2014.

Greenberg, Steve. "Where is Graceland? Pop Culture Through Music." In *Living in the Eighties*, edited by Gil Troy and Vincent J. Cannato, 152–66. Oxford: Oxford University Press, 2009.

Greenburg, Zack O'Malley. "Infographic: Michael Jackson's Multibillion Dollar Career Earnings, Listed Year by Year. Forbes, May 28, 2014. Available at https://www.forbes.com/sites/zackomalleygreenburg/2014/05/28/michael-jacksons-multibillion-dollar-career-earnings-listed-year-by-year/#317951233779.

———. *Michael Jackson, Inc.: The Rise, Fall, and Rebirth of a Billion-Dollar Empire*. New York: Atria, 2014.

Hall, Stuart. "Cultural Identity and Diaspora." In *Colonial Discourse and Postcolonial Theory*, edited by Patrick Williams and Laura Chrisman, 392–403. New York: Columbia University Press, 1994.

———. "What Is This 'Black' in Black Popular Culture?" *Social Justice* 20, no. 1–2 (1993): 104–11.

Haller, Scot. "Fighting for Life." *People*, September 23, 1985.

Hardy, Clarence E. *James Baldwin's God: Sex, God, and Crisis in Black Holiness Culture*. Knoxville: University of Tennessee Press, 2003.

Harris, Art. "Another Body Found in Atlanta River." *Washington Post*, April 1, 1981.

"Interview with Camille Bell." CBS News Special, February 27, 1982.

Irwin, Neil, Claire Cain Miller, and Margot Sangot-Katz. "America's Racial Divide, Charted." *New York Times*, August 19, 2014.

Jackson, Michael. "You Can't Win." By Charlie Smalls. CD. *Michael Jackson: The Ultimate Collection*. Sony, 2004.

Jarbyus. "Thank You for Coming, James Baldwin." *Daily Kos*, April 8, 2011.

Jeffords, Susan. *Hard Bodies: Hollywood Masculinity in the Reagan Era*. New Brunswick, N.J.: Rutgers University Press, 1994.

Johnson, Dirk. "Ryan White Dies of AIDS at 18: His Struggle Pierced Myths." *New York Times*, April 9, 1990.

Johnson, Emily. "A Theme Park, a Scandal, and the Faded Ruins of a Televangelism Empire." *Religion and Politics*, October 28, 2014.

Johnson, Hans, and William Eskridge. "The Legacy of Falwell's Bully Pulpit." *Washington Post*, May 19, 2007.

Kenan, Randall, ed. *The Cross of Redemption: Uncollected Writings*. By James Baldwin. New York: Vintage, 2010.

Kramer, Larry. "1,112 and Counting." *New York Native*, March 14–27, 1983.

Kun, Josh. "Life According to the Beat: James Baldwin, Bessie Smith, and the Perilous Sounds of Love." In *James Baldwin Now*, edited by Dwight A. McBride, 307–30. New York: New York University Press, 1999.

Landau, Elizabeth. "HIV in the '80s: 'People Didn't Want to Kiss You on the Cheek.'" CNN.com, May 25, 2011.

"The Last Word on Michael." *People*, December 30, 1984.

Lee, Felicia R. "Trying to Bring Baldwin's Complex Voice Back to the Classroom." *New York Times*, April 24, 2014.

Leeming, David. *James Baldwin: A Biography*. New York: Penguin, 1995.

Lester, Julius. "James Baldwin—Reflections of a Maverick." In Standley and Pratt, *Conversations with James Baldwin*, 222–31.

Lovett, Ian. "Evangelicals Back Donald Trump in Record Numbers, Despite Earlier Doubts." *Wall Street Journal*, November 9, 2016.

Mai-Duc, Christine. "Cleveland Officer Who Killed Tamir Rice Had Been Deemed Unfit for Duty." *Los Angeles Times*, December 3, 2014.

Mailer, Norman. *Advertisements for Myself*. Cambridge, Mass.: Harvard University Press, 1992.

Mann, Taynia. "Study Finds Gains for Black Middle Class." *Associated Press*, August 10, 1991.

McBride, Dwight A. Introduction to *James Baldwin Now*, by Dwight A. McBride, 1–9. New York: New York University Press, 1999.

McLaughlin, Elliot C. "What We Know about Michael Brown's Death." CNN.com. August 15, 2014.

McLuhan, Marshall. *Understanding Media: The Extensions of Man*. Cambridge, Mass.: MIT Press, 1994.

Mercer, Kobena. "Monster Metaphors." In *Welcome to the Jungle: New Positions in Black Cultural Studies*, by Kobena Mercer, 33–51. New York: Routledge, 1994.

Milbank, Robert. "Young Roberts to King of Pop: Request Denied." *Washington Post*, August 16, 2005.

Miller, D. Quentin. "Baldwin's Reception." In Scott, *James Baldwin's Later Fiction*, 2–19.

———. *A Criminal Power: James Baldwin and the Law*. Columbus: Ohio State University Press, 2012.

———. Introduction to *Re-viewing James Baldwin: Things Not Seen*, by D. Quentin Miller, 1–11. Philadelphia: Temple University Press, 2000.

———. "Lost and . . . Found? James Baldwin's Script and Spike Lee's Malcolm X." *African American Review* 46, no. 4 (Winter 2013): 671–85.

———. "Using the Blues: James Baldwin and Music." In *A Historical Guide to James Baldwin*, edited by Douglas Field, 83–110. New York: Oxford University Press, 2009.

Miller, James. *The Passion of Michel Foucault*. New York: Anchor, 1993.

Miller, Joshua. "'A Striking Addiction to Irreality': *Nothing Personal* and the Legacy of the Photo-Text Genre." In Miller, *Re-viewing James Baldwin*, 154–89.

Miller, Steven P. *The Age of Evangelicalism: America's Born-Again Years*. Oxford: Oxford University Press, 2014.

———. "The Evangelical Presidency: Reagan's Dangerous Love Affair with the Religious Right." *Salon*, May 18, 2014.

Morgado, Andre. "Ronald Reagan TV Ad: It's Morning in America Again." YouTube, November 12, 2006.

Morrison, Toni, ed. *Baldwin: Collected Essays*. New York: Library of America, 1998.

———. *Playing in the Dark: Whiteness and the Literary Imagination*. New York: Vintage, 1992.

Nash, Julie. "'A Terrifying Sacrament': James Baldwin's Use of Music in *Just Above My Head*." *MAWA Review* 7, no. 2 (1992): 107–11.

Norman, Brian. "Reading a 'Closet Screenplay': Hollywood, James Baldwin's Malcolms, and the Threat of Historical Irrelevance." *African American Review* 39, nos. 1–2 (Spring–Summer 2005): 103–18.

Obama, Barack. "Remarks by the President on Trayvon Martin." TheWhiteHouse.gov, July 23, 2013.

O'Reilly, David. "A Play This Time: The Fire Has Not Dimmed for James Baldwin, Whose 1950s Work 'The Amen Corner' Opens at the Annenberg Center Tomorrow Night." *Philadelphia Inquirer*, December 2, 1986.

Ostling, Richard N. "Of God and Greed." *Time*, June 24, 2001.

Page, Clarence. "Black Anger in Atlanta: James Baldwin Looks at 'Things Not Seen.'" *Chicago Tribune*, October 20, 1985.

Pavlic, Ed. "Jimmy's Songs: Listening Over James Baldwin's Shoulder." *James Baldwin Review* 2 (2016).

———. *Who Can Afford to Improvise? James Baldwin and Black Music, the Lyric and the Listener*. New York: Fordham University Press, 2015.

Perlstein, Rick. "Exclusive: Lee Atwater's Infamous 1981 Interview on the Southern Strategy." *Nation*, November 13, 2012.

Proctor, James. *Stuart Hall*. New York: Routledge, 2004.

Reagan, Ronald. "Let Them Go Their Way." Speech. 2nd Annual CPAC Convention, Washington, D.C. March 1, 1975.

———. "Ronald Reagan's Announcement for Presidential Candidacy." Ronald Reagan Library, November 13, 1979.

Robertson, Pat. "Action Plan for the 1980s." In Sutton, *Jerry Falwell*.

Rosenberg, Howard. "When the Media Burned Atlanta." *Los Angeles Times*, July 16, 2000.

Ryan, Josiah. "'This Was a Whitelash': Van Jones' Take on the Election Results." CNN.com, November 9, 2016.

Salam, Kalamu ya. "James Baldwin: Looking Towards the Eighties," in Standley and Pratt, *Conversations with James Baldwin*.

Schur, Richard. "Unseen or Unspeakable? Racial Evidence in Baldwin's and Morrison's Nonfiction." In *James Baldwin and Toni Morrison: Comparative Critical and Theoretical Essays*, edited by Lovalerie King and Lynn Orilla Scott, 205–22. New York: Palgrave Macmillan, 2006.

Scott, Lynn Orilla. *James Baldwin's Later Fiction: Witness to the Journey*. East Lansing: Michigan State University Press, 2002.

Selligman, Jean. "The AIDS Epidemic." *Newsweek*, April 18, 1983.

Shilts, Randy. *And the Band Played On: Politics, People, and the Epidemic*. New York: St. Martin's Griffin, 1987.

Simon, Roger. "The GOP and Willie Horton: Together Again." *Politico*, May 19, 2015.

Sirota, David. *Back to Our Future: How the 1980s Explains the World We Live in Now—Our Culture, Our Politics, Our Everything*. New York: Ballantine, 2011.

Solomon-Godeau, Abigail. "Male Trouble." In *Constructing Masculinity*, edited by Maurice Berger, Brian Wallis, and Simon Watson, 69–76. New York: Routledge, 1995.

Standley, Fred L., and Louis H. Pratt, eds. *Conversations with James Baldwin*. Jackson: University Press of Mississippi, 1989.

Sugarman, Josh. "Murder Rate for Black Americans Is Four Times the National Average." *Huffington Post*, August 1, 2014.

Sutton, Matthew Avery. *Jerry Falwell and the Rise of the Religious Right: A Brief History with Documents*. Boston: Beford/St. Martin's, 2013.

Swatos, William H. "Televangelism." *Encyclopedia of Religion and Society*, September 1, 2015.

"Tapes Link KKK to Atlanta Child Murders." *Associated Press*, August 6, 2005.

Taraborrelli, J. Randy. *Michael Jackson: The Magic and the Madness*. New York: Pan, 2004.

Thorsen, Karen, dir. *James Baldwin: The Price of the Ticket*. DVD. A Nobody Knows Production, Maysles Film. San Francisco: California Newsreel, 1989.

Tinney, James S. "Baldwin Comes Out." *Blacklight* 3, no. 5.

Troupe, Quincy. "James Baldwin, 1924–1987: A Tribute—The Last Interview." In Standley and Pratt, *Conversations with James Baldwin*, 287–92.

———. "Last Testament: An Interview with James Baldwin." In Standley and Pratt, *Conversations with James Baldwin*, 282.

———. "The Pressure to Beat It." *Spin*, June 1987.

Troy, Gil. *Morning in America: How Ronald Reagan Invented the 1980s*. Princeton, N.J.: Princeton University Press, 2006.

Vogel, Joseph. "How Michael Jackson Made Bad." *The Atlantic*, September 10, 2012.

Wallace, George. "Segregation Now, Segregation Forever." January 14, 1963. Available at http://www.blackpast.org/1963-george-wallace-segregation-now -segregation-forever.

Wallace, Michelle. "Michael Jackson, Black Modernisms and the Ecstasy of Communication." *Third Text* 3, no. 7 (1989).

Wallis, Claudia. "AIDS: A Growing Threat." *Time*, August 12, 1985.

Watkins, Mel. "Interview with James Baldwin." *New York Times Book Review*, September 23, 1979.

Werner, Craig. *A Change Is Gonna Come: Music, Race, and the Soul of America*. Ann Arbor: University of Michigan Press, 1998, 2006.

———. *Playing the Changes: From Afro-Modernism to the Jazz Impulse*. Urbana: University of Illinois Press, 1994.

White, Allen. "Reagan's AIDS Legacy/Silence Equals Death." *San Francisco Chronicle*, June 8, 2004.

Will, George F. "Bruce Springsteen's U.S.A." *Washington Post*, September 13, 1984.

Williams, Daniel K. *God's Own Party: The Making of the Christian Right*. New York: Oxford University Press, 2010.

Williams, Raymond. *Television: Technology and Cultural Form*. London: Routledge, 2004.

Williams, Thomas Chatterton. "Breaking into James Baldwin's House." *New Yorker*, October 28, 2015.

Winner, Lauren F. "Reaganizing Religion: Changing Political and Cultural Norms among Evangelicals in Ronald Reagan's America." In *Living in the Eighties*, edited by Gil Troy and Vincent J. Cannato. Oxford: Oxford University Press, 2009.

Wypijewski, JoAnn. "James Baldwin: A Guide in Dark Times." *The Nation*. January 21, 2015.

Yarbrough, Jeff. "Rock Hudson: On Camera and Off." *People*, August 12, 1985.

Young, Josiah Ulysses. *James Baldwin's Understanding of God: Overwhelming Desire and Joy*. New York: Palgrave Macmillan, 2014.

Yuan, David. "The Celebrity Freak: Michael Jackson's 'Grotesque Glory.'" In *Freakery: Cultural Spectacles of the Extraordinary Body*, edited by Rosemarie Garland Thomson, 368–84. New York: New York University Press, 1996.

Zaborowska, Magdalena. *James Baldwin's Turkish Decade: Erotics of Exile*. Durham, N.C.: Duke University Press, 2009.

Index

JOSEPH VOGEL is an assistant professor of English at Merrimack College. He is the author of *Man in the Music: The Creative Life and Work of Michael Jackson.*

The University of Illinois Press
is a founding member of the
Association of American University Presses.

———————————————————————

Composed in 10.25/14 Chaparral Pro
with Shree Devanagari 714 display
by Lisa Connery
at the University of Illinois Press
Manufactured by Sheridan Books, Inc.

University of Illinois Press
1325 South Oak Street
Champaign, IL 61820-6903
www.press.uillinois.edu